Remaking Beijing

Remaking Beijing

Tiananmen Square and the Creation of a Political Space

WU HUNG

THE UNIVERSITY OF CHICAGO PRESS

To Ningning and Lida

Published with the generous support of the Center for East Asian Studies, University of Chicago.

The University of Chicago Press, Chicago 60637
Reaktion Books Ltd, London EC1M 3JU

14 13 12 11 10 09 08 07 06 05   1 2 3 4 5

ISBN: 0-226-36078-4 (cloth)
ISBN: 0-226-36079-2 (paper)

Library of Congress Cataloging-in-Publication Data

Wu Hung, 1945–
     Remaking Beijing : Tiananmen square and the creation of a political space /
 Wu Hung.
          p. cm.
     Includes bibliographical references and index.
     ISBN 0-226-36078-4 (cloth : alk. paper) — ISBN 0-226-36079-2 (pbk. : alk. paper)
     1. Tian'an Men (Beijing, China) 2. Architecture and history—China—
 Beijing. 3. Architecture—Political aspects—China—Beijing. 4. Art and state—
 China—Beijing. 5. Beijing (China)—Buildings, structures, etc. I. Title.
     NA9072.B45T539 2005
     711'.55'0951156—dc22

                                                                    2004029737

Contents

Introduction

As soon as Beijing was made the capital of the People's Republic of China, this ancient city reached a fatal moment in its survival. Although Beijing had experienced numerous human and natural calamities during its 500-year history,[1] and although waves of modernization campaigns since the nineteenth century had altered some of its architectural features,[2] Beijing in 1949 still retained nearly all its traditional character and splendour. Layers of thick brick walls still concealed the yellow-roofed palaces, surrounded by a sea of grey courtyard houses built along narrow lanes. The city was still tranquilly flat. A few taller modern buildings here and there – none of them surpassing the seven-storey Peking Hotel on Chang'an Avenue – were fashionable anomalies. Cars and trams only ran through major streets. The remaining roads and side roads were dusty or muddy depending on the weather, better suited for rickshaws and mule carts to struggle through.[3]

How could this old city be transformed into the capital and a shining symbol of New China? This question was asked not only by Communist leaders but also by some Western-trained architects, who returned to their country to contribute their professional knowledge to her reconstruction.[4] The proponents of two different solutions were soon caught up in a heated debate.[5] Led by Liang Sicheng and Chen Zhanxiang (Charlie Chen), a group of conservation-minded architects envisioned building an administrative centre west of old Beijing, leaving the historical city intact. Other forces, however, including an unlikely coalition of left-wing Chinese architects, Soviet specialists and Western-trained urban planners of a modernist bent, argued that the capital could fully realize its symbolic potential only by locating the government in traditional Beijing. A crucial argument made by this second group was that, because the country's founding ceremony took place in Tiananmen Square, this locale should logically be the centre of new Beijing. Drawing on Moscow's experience, the proponents of this view also sought support from Marxist philosophy. Chen Gan (who later became the chief architect of Beijing's Municipal Institute of Urban Planning) thus went through Friedrich Engels's *Dialectics of Nature* and discovered a *raison d'être* for this argument in the significance of 'zero'. Engels writes:

[In analytical geometry:] Here zero is a definite point from which measurements are taken along a line, in one direction positively, in the other negatively. Here, therefore, the zero point has not only just as much significance as any point denoted by a positive or negative magnitude, but a much greater significance than all of them: it is the point on which they are all dependent, to which they are all related, and by which they are all determined . . . Wherever we come upon zero, it represents something very definite, and its practical application in geometry, mechanics, etc., proves that – *as limit* – it is more important than all the real magnitudes bounded by it.[6]

Applying this theory to Beijing's design, Chen Gan identified the throne hall in the imperial palace as the city's traditional zero point; all other architectural features were subordinate to this absolute centre, while reinforcing it. By relocating 'zero' to Tiananmen Square, the birthplace of the People's Republic, the city would acquire a new identity and a vantage point for its architectural restructuring. Beijing's centre of gravity would automatically shift southward, and the avenue running east–west through the square would become its new axis. 'Everything in the city will have to divorce itself from the old zero and align itself with the new zero. To be sure, at the very moment when the national flag rose in Tiananmen Square for the first time, history had determined that this locale should be the centre of the capital of New China, and had predicted Beijing's subsequent transformation and its rise in Asia.'[7]

The debate did not last long: less than a year after Liang Sicheng and Chen Zhanxiang made their conservation-orientated proposal (known as the Liang-Chen plan), Mao Zedong personally decided to locate the government in the old city.[8] Looking back at the debate, the failure of the Liang-Chen plan was inevitable because it contradicted the basic tenet of the Chinese Communist Party at that time, which emphasized revolution, not preservation. To Liang and Chen, it was all too plain that great pressure would be placed on the old city unless the administrative centre were set up outside, and that the destruction of historic Beijing was inevitable should it become the site of a growing number of modern buildings. But to Mao such concerns were irrelevant, because revolution meant destruction and transformation; it was only natural that Beijing should be remade when China was reborn.[9] In addition, as Wu Liangyong has noted, 'The Liang-Chen plan also lacked the grandeur expected at the time. The idea that the new republic should aspire to project an impressive image was repeatedly stated by politicians at all levels. At that point, only Tiananmen possessed the desired grandeur.'[10] Unable to satisfy this political need, the Liang-Chen plan was eventually criticized as 'an attempt to negate Tiananmen, the country's political centre cherished by the revolutionary people'.[11]

The consequence of Mao's decision cannot be exaggerated: all the subsequent destruction and construction of Beijing were fundamentally determined at this moment. As I will show at the end of this book, even today, when Beijing is developing into a global metropolis, all major urban projects have still to be based on this decision made 54 years ago. Some belated preservation efforts have been made, but they can never bring back traditional Beijing, now vanished forever. Again, Wu Liangyu, a long-time insider of Beijing's urban planning, looking back at this historical tragedy, remarked on its inevitability:

> Once the old city expansion plan was chosen, there was little chance for any alternative . . . Year after year, the old city centre was redeveloped to adapt to the needs of growth, and radial and ring roads were built. The more growth there was, the more expansion was needed. It is not unreasonable to say that most of Beijing's conservation and traffic management problems stem from the choice of this site.[12]

In short, Beijing's fate was sealed by locating the government in the old city, and this decision owed much to the symbolic gravity of Tiananmen Square. Many books have been written on Beijing's urban development and related debates.[13] This book will focus on the Square.

To become the centre of new Beijing and the People's Republic of China, Tiananmen Square itself had to be transformed from an insulated imperial quarter into an open space for political activity and visual representation.[14] I call this kind of public space a 'political space'. In various scholarly writings a public space is conceived either as a conceptual sphere of public discourse or as a physical place where public events take place.[15] I use the term 'political space' in both senses, as an architectonic embodiment of political ideology and as an architectural site activating political action and expression. Defined as such, an official political space such as Tiananmen Square inevitably lies within the dominant political system and helps to construct this system; but it also stimulates public debate and facilitates opposition. To individual participants in both official and unofficial events that have unfolded here, this space is connected with their personal experiences and aspirations, but it also frames such experiences and aspirations within broad historical movements.[16]

As I will recount in this book, Tiananmen Square began to acquire the significance of a public political space in the early twentieth century, when numerous political activities, including some of the most famous anti-government mass demonstrations, were held there. After 1949, however, the place was architecturally transformed into a dominant official space – a monumental complex that embodied the country's political ideology and consolidated its Communist leadership. It also became a major site of visual production and presentation. Some images displayed there – including painting, sculpture and mass parades – helped to articulate the notions of political authority and the people, as well as the relationship between the two. Other images and displays are concerned with time and space. Together with the architectural monuments in the Square, they have provided basic standards and references for constructing a 'revolutionary history of the people' and defining the country's political geography and temporality.

A crucial change occurred toward the end of the Cultural Revolution in the mid-1970s, since the government could no longer maintain its monopoly on the place. A spontaneous mass movement emerged in the Square in 1976, and was echoed thirteen years later by an even larger mass movement – the June Fourth pro-democratic demonstrations in 1989. Since then, the Square has remained a highly contested space. On the one hand, its official symbolism and visual culture have undergone subtle changes as new generations of Chinese leaders have tried to modify their images to suit the post-Cold War global environment. On the other hand, the place has continued to generate unofficial political expressions, including numerous experimental art projects, which, through appropriating official presentations and activating historical memories, have also made the Square a 'space of the avant garde'.

This brief outline of the Square's history suggests multiple issues and problems. Some of these are related to the Square's physical and contextual transformation: the destruction of its traditional framing; the construction of its new architectural and pictorial components; and its relationship with Beijing's changing cityscape. Other problems concern the Square's role as a primary site of public activity and expression: the various gatherings and demonstrations taking place there; the holiday spectacles created to punctuate a political calendar; the display of the revolutionary masses; the public perception of the leader; and the site-specific performances of unofficial artists. A third set of problems is related to issues of representation: the images of Tiananmen and Mao in official photographs and paintings, and various iconoclastic appropriations of these images by avant-garde artists. Bringing these issues into a single study, this book is not written for a particular academic field, but is located in a network of disciplines including art history, the history of architecture, modern Chinese history, urban studies, cultural studies and autobiography. In fact, one of my purposes in writing this book is to forge this interdisciplinary network.

My plan to discuss these issues in a book-length study emerged in 1991, two years after the June Fourth Movement ended in bloodshed. I did not finish the book until twelve years later, not because it had a lower priority than my other projects, but because it carried a personal significance and also posed a methodological challenge. While the plan was first conceived as a historical study of Tiananmen Square, it inevitably brought back memories connected to the place. By 1991 I had lived in the United States for more than a decade, during which time I received a doctoral degree and had begun to publish books and articles, mostly on ancient Chinese art. It seemed that in this process I had left my past behind: I had not returned to China in nine years, and in 1991 I was writing almost exclusively in English for a non-Chinese, academic readership. Leaving China at a time when historical scholarship there was equated to political statements, I enjoyed the freedom of detaching myself from my research subject: the only link between me and an ancient building or object was my research as an intellectual exercise. Although in theory I never believed that historical scholarship could be totally objective, I wrote in the third person as an uninvolved observer.

Writing on Tiananmen Square and Beijing naturally disrupted the harmony of this type of historical study. I grew up in Beijing and had frequent encounters with the Square throughout my childhood and into early adulthood. This personal relationship with the place began with a family outing in the early 1950s and deepened when I participated in a National Day celebration in the fourth grade. I marched in front of Tiananmen many times as a high school student, and later as a college student, and my feelings toward that monument changed together with my view of Mao and the Party. For seven years from 1972 I was on the staff of the Palace Museum in the Forbidden City, of which Tiananmen was the former front gate. From late March 1976 to early April I used to pass through this gate daily to join the anguished crowd in the Square mourning Premier Zhou Enlai, who, before his death in January, had become the people's only hope for rationality amidst the madness of the Cultural Revolution. There is no doubt that this experience is related to my research on the Square. But what is this relationship and how can my current research be linked to my past? Must a historian suppress personal memories (which are by definition subjective and trivial) to ensure a more objective, macroscopic historical reconstruction and interpretation? Can a historical narrative gain additional strength by incorporating personal memories? Can an author retain the dual positions of a historian and an autobiographer?

These questions led me to read a wide range of writings on history, memory and autobiography. Recognizing that my research and memories could never be kept completely separate,[17] in this book I have decided to tell a story about Tiananmen Square in two parallel narratives – a historical narrative and an autobiographical narrative: these have different focuses but an overlapping spatio-temporal scheme. The historical narrative investigates the Square as an external entity and observes its changing form and meaning. The construction of this narrative utilizes all sorts of evidence (archives, architectural plans, memoirs, photos, pictures and secondary scholarship) that can help me trace the Square's history. The autobiographical narrative (or 'self-narrative' as some psychologists call it)[18] recounts in the first person my encounters with the Square and reflects on my changing perception of the place. In this second narrative, fragmentary experiences are recalled and retold in a synchronic fashion as if I intended to relive them for a second time.

It is possible to describe the relationship between these two narratives as a simultaneous interpenetration of historical research and memory formation – two processes moving from opposite ends toward a shared mid-ground.[19] Such interpenetration is especially relevant to this book, because my historical reconstruction and personal recollections both focus on important political events and are closely related to collective memories associated with these events.[20] Indeed, many scholars, including the French sociologist Maurice Halbwachs and the Russian psychologist Lev Vygotsky, have questioned the idea that memory resides in the individual.[21] Halbwachs, in particular, asserts that all personal memories are formed and organized within collective contexts, because society always provides the framework for individual beliefs and behaviours, including their recollections of past events. This is especially true in a country like China, where the concept of privacy virtually did not exist in the years when I was growing up, and public and personal events were consistently

1 Zheng Lianjie, *Family History*, performance in Tiananmen Square, 1999.

intertwined. It is therefore not surprising that many of my memories are associated with a dominant official space such as Tiananmen Square. It also becomes understandable why many Chinese experimental artists have staged performances in the Square, relating their personal experiences with this place. Among these projects, Zheng Lianjie's *Family History* presents close conceptual parallels with this book and can help illuminate some of my goals.

Deceptively simple, this performance in 2000 consisted of little more than staging a tableau: holding up an enlarged black-and-white family photo, the artist and his nine-year-old son took another picture in Tiananmen Square (illus. 1).[22] The implications of the performance are rich and complex, however, largely due to Tiananmen's double role as the site of the performance and as the backdrop in the 'photo-within-a-photo'. Taken in 1957, the old family photo shows Zheng's parents and his five older brothers and sisters, posed before a painted Tiananmen backdrop in a photo studio. Born five years later, Zheng was not among them: he developed his own relationship with Tiananmen Square later, including participating in the June Fourth Movement in 1989. In spring 2000 his father had just passed away and his son was as old as his eldest brother in the photo. He dedicated the performance to his father as a tribute to the family's bygone generation: he displayed the photo in Tiananmen Square to indicate the shared political experiences of the family's members, including himself, and he conducted the performance with his son, who would carry the memory into the future.

In this performance, Tiananmen exists both as a subject and as the social context of Zheng's remembrance; the Square provides both past and present events with a single location. As indicated by its title, the performance is about the history of a family. But this micro-history is framed by a macro-history, both connected to Tiananmen Square. Similarly, in this book I represent the Square's history and my memories connected to the place in two interacting frames, constantly intersecting the historical account with short 'memory pieces' (which resemble Zheng Lianjie's 'photo-within-a-photo'). These memory pieces or autobiographical narratives have undoubtedly been influenced by my historical research, but they retain a personal perspective and complement the historical account told in the third person.[23] Perhaps most importantly, the juxtaposition of the two narratives generates tension. Refusing to be incorporated into the historical narrative, the autobiographical narratives instead remind readers of my specific experience, which must have influenced and even predetermined my historical reconstruction and interpretation.[24] The two narratives finally merge in the book's coda, which observes and analyses the transformation of Tiananmen Square and Beijing into the present millennium.

2 A worker
stopping
government
tanks on
Chang'an
Avenue on
4 June 1989.

3 May Fourth
Movement,
1919.

4 Victory March
of the Allied
Army in
Tiananmen
Square, 1900.

Tiananmen Square:
A Political History of Monuments

Fifteen years after 1989, we now view the June Fourth Movement in Tiananmen Square as history, and, as history, the event has been transformed into words – chronicles, memoirs, analyses – and images of three kinds. Recorded images are subjects of photo and TV journalism, edited and preserved for documenting that heated period of 50 days and nights (16 April–4 June 1989). A condensed image is a 'particular [that] represents the more general';[1] it is extracted from chronology to become a symbol: a single recorded image – a young man in a white shirt standing motionless before a row of slowly moving tanks (illus. 2). The precise time of the event is rarely remembered, and we still do not know the brave man's name. Printed in numerous books on modern China, however, this still scene transcends the rest and embodies them.

Then there is an enriched image – Tiananmen Square, a vast open ground centred on and defined by a series of monuments constructed over a period of some five hundred years. Many westerners learned its name only after June 1989, but to every Chinese, from a college freshman to the country's paramount leader, the Square has been the centre of political tension and attention throughout China's modern history. A series of mass movements there have become landmarks in this history: the demonstration on 4 May 1919 in protest against the Treaty of Versailles handing over Chinese lands to Japan (illus. 3); the patriotic march on 18 March 1926; the demonstration on 9 December 1935, which started the resistance movement against the Japanese invasion; the anti-autocratic movement during the Civil War on 20 May 1947; the mass memorial to the former prime minister Zhou Enlai on 5 April 1976; and finally the 1989 student uprising. Parallel to these grassroots movements runs another sequence of 'demonstrations' mobilized by the authorities to display power: the Victory March in 1900 by the Allied Army celebrating their occupation of Beijing (illus. 4);[2] General Zhang Xun's grand ritual in June 1917 to commemorate his restoration of the imperial order; the establishment of the puppet regime under Japanese patronage; the parade celebrating the recapture of Beijing by Republican troops; the founding of Communist China on 1 October 1949; and the elaborate National Day parade shortly after the People's Liberation Army blood-washed the Square in 1989. Since these two chains of events are intertwined in Tiananmen Square, everything there partakes of the fate of the state and of its one billion plus people.[3] Correspondingly, the Square partakes of every event and consequently changes its meaning. Its vast vista records nothing, and its monuments are too complex and diverse to express any particular idea. Like historical memory itself, the Square is renewed and enriched by ongoing events while at the same time encompassing them.

This chapter is about the Square in its entirety, an architectural site that provides a locus of coalescence for political expression, collective memory, identity and history. Recognized as such, the Square has been – and will continue to be – a prime visual means of political rhetoric in modern China to address the public and to constitute the public itself.

Tiananmen Square

In the early morning of 30 May 1989, Beijing's residents awoke to find a new statue, some seven metres high, in the Square (illus. 6). Representing a young woman holding a torch with both hands, it became the focus of worldwide attention for the next five days. I will return later to the political context and creative process of this short-lived statue; what I want to emphasize here is that its addition abruptly changed the Square's existing spatial structure and political significance. The statue raised the total number of monuments in the

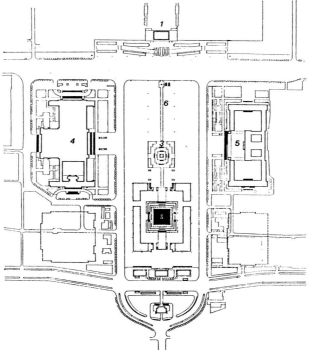

5 Plan of Tiananmen Square, showing the positions of six monuments from 30 May to 3 June 1989:
1. Tiananmen
2. Chairman Mao Memorial Hall
3. Monument to the People's Heroes
4. Great Hall of the People
5. Museum of Chinese History
6. Statue of *Goddess of Democracy*

6 Statue of the *Goddess of Democracy* in Tiananmen Square, 30 May – 3 June 1989.

Square to six and defined a new centre of gravity (illus. 5): along the central axis Tiananmen, or the Gate of Heavenly Peace, enclosed the Square to the north; above its closed and guarded central passage a giant portrait of Chairman Mao stared silently at the crowds below. Directly facing Mao's portrait was the new statue, the *Goddess of Democracy*, identified by the demonstrating students as their own symbol. Then there was the Monument to the People's Heroes, better known in the West as the Monument to the People's Martyrs, standing in the centre of the Square like a needle on an enormous sundial. South of the Monument was the Chairman Mao Memorial Hall – actually his mausoleum, which still holds his corpse in a glass case. Away from the central axis, two mammoth buildings – the Museum of Chinese History and the Great Hall of the People – flanked the Square to the east and west. One rarely finds such an assemblage of monuments of contradictory styles in such orderly formation. Their architectural disharmony and disciplined layout signify competition for political dominance, not cooperation to structure a common space.

7 Tiananmen
Square in 1949,
viewed from
Tiananmen's
balcony.

The war of monuments in the Square began in 1949. When Mao ascended Tiananmen and declared the founding of the People's Republic of China, ancient Tiananmen Square was slated to be reborn. Despite the enormous changes that had taken place in Beijing during the first half of the twentieth century, in 1949 Tiananmen Square still maintained the basic shape it had when first constructed in the fifteenth century, in the early Ming dynasty (1368–1644).[4] What Mao saw from Tiananmen's balcony was still a T-shaped enclosure guarded by three free-standing gates on its east, west and south sides; beyond the gates was the rest of the city – a flat vista of grey houses interrupted by some taller modern buildings (illus. 7).

We can easily find this T-shaped enclosure in old maps of Beijing (illus. 8). No name was assigned to this space, however; such an absence must mean that the enclosure was not conceived as a self-contained architectural unit. Indeed, although modern writers conventionally call this space 'historical Tiananmen Square', the name Tiananmen Square (Tiananmen guangchang) is itself a modern invention. Before the twentieth century, the T-shaped space in front of Tiananmen did not have an independent identity, but was recognized as a configuration of various architectural elements associated with two intersecting roads. The east–west road, the horizontal bar of the T, ran under Tiananmen and ended at the Left and Right Chang'an Gates. The vertical bar of the T linked Tiananmen to the gatehouse to the south, called either the Gate of the Great Ming or the Gate of the Great Qing, depending on the dynasty. Two rows of long timber houses, each consisting of 110 bays and known as the Thousand-step Porches, flanked this space and framed a north–south road that was a crucial section of the Imperial Passage, the north–south axis of traditional Beijing (illus. 9).[5]

Pre-modern Beijing encompassed a number of sub-cities: the Outer City, the Inner City, the Imperial City and the Forbidden City. Stretching from the

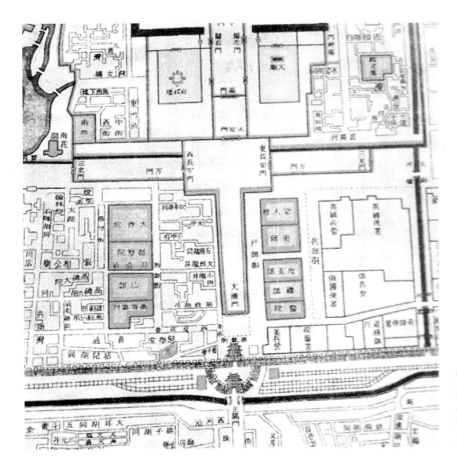

8 Tiananmen Square of the late Qing dynasty, as shown in a 1908 map of Beijing

Audience Hall inside the Forbidden City to Yongdingmen Gate on the southern walls of the Outer City, the axial Imperial Passage connected these four enclosures into a continuum (illus. 10). The section of this road in front of Tiananmen, in particular, symbolized the emperor's centrality, transcending any dualistic opposition.[6] Accordingly, the paired structures on either side of this path performed opposite but complementary roles to facilitate both auspicious and inauspicious civil rites. One major auspicious rite celebrated the selection of the country's top scholar-official. The governments of the Ming and Qing chose officials through an elaborate examination system, and issued the highest degree *jinshi* only after the court exam held every three years inside the Forbidden City.[7] Before taking this exam, examinees entered Left Chang'an Gate from the east. After the exam, the result was posted on yellow paper outside the gate. Left Chang'an Gate thus acquired the name of 'Dragon Gate', because, in Chinese folklore, when an ordinary carp jumps over such a gate it turns into a magical dragon.

In sharp contrast, the structures on the opposite, west, side were related to punishment and death; and Right Chang'an Gate gained the name 'Tiger Gate'

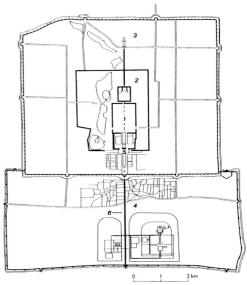

owing to the sense of danger it evoked. According to Imperial Law, twice a year a High Court was set up inside this gate to review death sentences. Every autumn, before the first frost fell, the accused in the capital would be brought there, through Right Chang'an Gate, to answer a simple question: 'Is your sentence just or unjust?' Most of the sentences were confirmed; according to one source, many prisoners had been tortured so severely that they could hardly speak.[8] Occasionally someone was lucky, and he would be received by his relatives waiting outside Right Chang'an Gate. A string of hawthorn would be hung around his neck, indicating that this person had at least one more year to live – until he entered the same gate again next autumn for his case to be reviewed once more.[9]

The directional symbolism of these rites and related architectural structures is based on ancient Chinese correlative cosmology, which teaches that the movement of the universe follows the ceaseless transformation of *yin* and *yang* forces and the five phases (wood, fire, metal, water and earth): life starts from the east (which corresponds to the element of wood, spring, rising *yang*, etc.) and ends in the west (which corresponds to the element of metal, autumn, rising *yin*, etc.).[10] By mimicking this cosmic programme, a human ruler could ensure the legitimacy of his rule.[11] The same principle also determined the locations of the various government departments, constructed either side of the

20

11 A plan of
Qing dynasty
Tiananmen
Square, showing
the government
departments on
either side of
the Square.

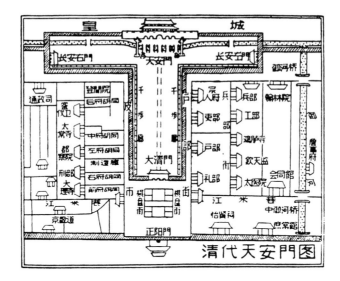

Imperial Passage behind the two Thousand-step Porches. During the Ming, the departments in the east group included, among others, the Prefecture of the Imperial Clan and the Ministries of Officialdom, Revenue, Manufacture, Rites and Medicine. Those in the west group included the headquarters of the Five Armies, Imperial Guard, Police and Justice. The Qing made only minor revisions to this arrangement (illus. 11).[12] A popular saying went: 'Those to the east govern our lives; those to the west govern our deaths.'[13]

Whether associated with east or west, the locations of these offices and the staging of rites in front of Tiananmen served to sustain the relationship between the ruler and the ruled. Standing at the top of the T and overlooking the space below, Tiananmen appeared as the head or the brain. Rays of the emperor's power and wisdom radiated through Tiananmen to every official institution and every corner of the empire. When we turn to modern Tiananmen Square, we find the same juxtaposition between the ruler and the ruled. But the T-shaped enclosure has been demolished and replaced by an immense open ground; new rulers emerged above Tiananmen to review mass parades below; and the parade, as a principal form of twentieth-century political ritual, came to embody the very notion of 'the people'.

Searching my memory, I realize that my earliest encounter with Tiananmen Square (not with Tiananmen, which I had seen a few years earlier) was already framed by a political event. It was 1955 and I was a fourth-grade student in a small rural elementary school outside Beijing. My father's 'work unit', the Research Institute of Economics, had just moved from central Beijing to a place in the western suburbs called Zhongguancun, where an entire City of Learning was being constructed, amid cornfields and local graveyards, to house China's Academy of Sciences, to which my father's institute belonged. My new school was in an abandoned Buddhist temple, with ruined but still colourful statues of arhats and heavenly kings lined up against the walls of the only classroom. The student body mixed local peasant boys and girls with professors' sons and daughters. From my peasant classmates I learned, among other things, how to catch crickets and raise them, and how to rank a cricket by carefully investigating the location of its nest. An extraordinary cricket, according to an unwritten canon in the school, always lived near an ancient tomb or shared its dwelling with a powerful 'companion animal', either a poisonous snake or an oversized toad.

During the September of that year, the school's principal made an important announcement at Monday assembly: three students from the school would be chosen to participate in the country's sixth anniversary celebration in Tiananmen Square on 1 October. At the following week's assembly it was disclosed that I was one of the three. My father was pleased with my newly gained distinction and personally took me to purchase the required paraphernalia, which included a pair of white sneakers and matching white socks. On 1 October I got up at 2 o'clock in the morning and took a seemingly endless journey to Tiananmen Square. Since public buses didn't run until dawn, a teacher took us by tricycle cart to the near-est train station at Qinghuayuan. After taking a train in darkness to Xizhimen, the north-west gate of Beijing's city walls, we continued by bus in early dawn towards our destination.

Strangely, this journey was almost the only thing I can remember clearly about that day (for the first time I realized the enormity of Beijing and experienced bodily the movement from border to centre); the rest of the day was filled with disorien-tating events prolonged by a purposeless exhaustion. After reaching the Square we were led to a certain place, and lined up in some sort of formation with hun-dreds or perhaps thousands of kids, all in white shirts. To my huge disappointment, we were told to remain there throughout the celebration: our role was not to take part in the parade – as I had mistakenly believed – but to wave paper flowers and shout slogans whenever we saw Chairman Mao emerging on Tiananmen's balcony. But this promise of seeing the Chairman soon proved impossible. Not only was I standing several hundred yards away from Tiananmen, but my view was completely blocked by the people in front of me and their waving flowers. Inevitably my shouts and waving became mechanical and limp, not triggered by sight but moved by a nameless collectivity of which I had become a part.

Until recently the concept of a 'square' (or *guangchang* in Chinese) was highly political in the People's Republic of China.[14] Every city, town or village had to have a square for public gatherings on important (thus political) occasions – holiday parades and pageants, announcements of the Party's instructions, and struggle rallies against enemies of the people. Public squares were con-structed with great enthusiasm from the 1950s to the '70s, when the govern-ment also mobilized endless political campaigns in pursuit of increasingly fanatical agendas. (By the same token, as I will mention later, the practice since the 1990s of turning part of public squares into lawns and parks signifies an effort to depoliticize urban space.)

Big or small, a square was conjoined with a platform built for the leaders (of a city, town or village) to review mass assemblies. A square thus became a legitimate place for people to meet their leaders (or vice versa), an indispensable joint between high and low, brain and body. As various squares became established in all administrative centres, they comprised a 'square system' corresponding to the hierarchy of the state – a parallel that unmistakably indicated a square's official function to shape a desirable public. Since 'enemy-class elements' (whose make-up changed from period to period) were generally excluded from these public meetings or were only present as targets of accusation, the masses' identity as 'the people' was proved by the square.[15]

Of all the platforms none has been more privileged then Tiananmen, the stand of the country's paramount leaders. Logically there had to be a square of equally unmatchable status for the public. Tiananmen has gained its meaning in the People's Republic of China by reinterpreting a traditional architectural structure, but the Square's significance derives primarily from its physical immensity.

Mao must have been troubled by what he saw from Tiananmen in 1949: even though the ground below was hurriedly expanded before the country's founding ceremony, still only some 70,000 people could parade through it. Shortly afterwards he ordered a new square to be built, a square 'big enough to hold an assembly of one billion'.[16] His words were explained by an official architect: 'The Chairman's mind, broad as the ocean, flies beyond the confines of the old walls and corridors and penetrates into the future. It is his vision that reveals the direction for constructing the new Square.'[17] Behind these bombastic words is a simple idea: only the biggest public, thus the largest square, could match the supreme power of the Chairman and Tiananmen.

Mao's ambition was never realized. (Despite every effort, the new Square completed in 1959 could hold only [!] 400,000 people and, rather ironically, it was only after the Chairman's death that it was further expanded to hold 600,000.) The problems involved in creating an open space of some 50 acres in the heart of Beijing, one of the most densely populated cities in the world, were more those of destruction than construction. New monuments around the Square, however massive in size, were achieved in short order: we are told that the Great Hall of the People and the Museum of Chinese History were completed within ten months between 1958 and 1959, and that the Chairman Mao Memorial Hall was finished within half a year in 1977. It took three decades, however, to destroy all the old structures surrounding the historical Tiananmen Square, including walls, gates, roads, steles, artificial rivers, bridges, sculptured wooden arches called *pailou*, and numerous administrative and residential buildings left from imperial times and foreign occupation. This Herculean destruction was again considered worthwhile: 'For the need of the new age, the old Square had to be reformed and replanned as soon as New China was founded.'[18]

As this statement makes crystal clear, the destruction of old buildings in front of Tiananmen did not just serve the practical purpose to make room for a large public square, but was considered a symbolic gesture to destroy the past. The Left and Right Chang'an Gates were torn down in 1952.[19] The

Thousand-step Porches had been demolished during the early Republican period, but the walls behind them still remained and kept the old T-shaped enclosure intact; these walls were destroyed in sections from 1955 to 1957. The small but important Zhonghua Gate (the former Gate of the Great Ming or the Great Qing) was levelled in 1958 to make room for the Monument to the People's Heroes. Thus, by the tenth anniversary of the People's Republic in 1959, the T-shaped enclosure before Tiananmen, along with its walls, gates and intersecting roads, had completely disappeared. In its place was an immense ground 500 metres east–west and 880 metres north–south, with a concrete floor measuring 440,000 square metres.

The Monument to the People's Heroes

Completed in 1958, the Monument to the People's Heroes rises 37.4 metres high at the centre of the Square, 440 metres south of Tiananmen (illus. 12). Topped with a small roof in the traditional Chinese palatial style, the granite obelisk resembles an infinitely enlarged stele, a common form of stone structure used in traditional China for commemorating the dead and for engraving authorized versions of the Confucian Classics. While the monument itself is built of some 170,000 stone blocks, a single-piece slab, 14. 4 metres long and weighing 60 tons, is inserted in the front side of the obelisk to bear a gilded inscription written by Mao in 1955: 'Eternal glory to the people's heroes'.[20] A longer text on the back, drafted by Mao in 1949, is shown in Zhou Enlai's calligraphy. The east and west sides of the obelisk are carved with relief images of 'red stars', flags, pines and cypresses – all identified as symbols of 'eternal revolutionary spirit'.

Directly under the vertical column is a double plinth. The upper plinth is decorated on all four sides with carvings of eight large wreathes of peonies, lotus and chrysanthemums – symbols of nobility, purity and perseverance. Ten white marble reliefs built into the lower plinth narrate the revolutionary history of the Chinese people since 1840. Each relief is 2 metres high; the 170 figures depicted are near life-size. None of these figures, however, is an identifiable personage. As the designers emphasized, the strength of these carvings derives from the figures' collective anonymity, not from their individual identity.[21]

Two flights of stairs on a double terrace lead visitors to these reliefs.[22] Both layers of the terrace are surrounded by white marble balustrades; and the floor plan of the lower one, which covers an area of more than 3,000 square metres, derives its shape from a crab-apple blossom. To the north, the monument faces Tiananmen over the open vista of Tiananmen Square; to the south, hundreds of large pine trees in 44 rows cover the area between the monument and the isolated Front Gate (Qianmen) surviving from old Beijing.[23]

The design process of the Monument started in 1949, but the stone structure was only unveiled a decade later. Considering its rather simple structural and technical requirements, as well as the amount of manpower that the regime could easily muster, the project took an unusually long period (as

24

already mentioned, other far more complex buildings in the Square were all
finished within a year). The problems involved were more those of theology
than technology. A few published reports on the project, though all following
official interpretation, allow us to glimpse some major debates regarding its
location, form and decoration, and enable us to speculate on the motivation
behind the final plan.[24]

The location of the Monument, as one finds it now in the Square, has
aroused the strongest criticism from art historians and architects all over the
world. Calling the granite giant a 'good sneeze' in 'a concert hall at just the
most exquisite and magical point of a musical phrase', the Australian art historian Simon Leys has expressed his outrage at its assault on the sublime architectural harmony of old Beijing ('the brutal silliness', 'the Maoist rape of the
ancient capital', a 'revolutionary-proletarian obscenity in the middle of the
sacred way', an 'insignificant granitic phallus receiv[ing] all its enormous
significance from the blasphemous stupidity of its location').[25] Mao and his
comrades, however, might be amused at his outrage, for Leys was denouncing
exactly the effect they were seeking. 'Someone thinks', we read in an official
document, 'that the view along [Beijing's] central axis . . . should not be
blocked. But through study we have recognized that the axis of the present
Square is no longer the past Imperial Path. The importance of the Monument
will be most effectively accentuated by this central position.'[26]

This passage, written by a chief designer of the Monument in 1978, is misleading, however, on two accounts: it seems to suggest, first, that the location
was determined by him and his professional colleagues, and, secondly, that
this decision came after the new Tiananmen Square was completed. An exam-

ination of historical evidence discloses the falseness of both impressions: the location of the Monument was decided by the Party leadership long before the expansion of the Square and even before the establishment of the People's Republic of China. As soon as Mao's army took over Beijing in March 1949, a special consultative committee was organized under the Party's leadership to design a commemorative monument for the future regime. The first question delivered to the committee was about the monument's location. Different opinions were offered: some members of the committee suggested placing the monument east of Tiananmen or west of Beijing; others proposed to build it atop an ancient structure such as Duanmen behind Tiananmen. The last plan was simply (and perhaps rightly) called 'absurd' by Mao. Taking the matter into his own hands, Mao's chief assistant Zhou Enlai 'worked hard on the issue. He took special trips to Tiananmen's tower, from where he contemplated the square and studied the relationship between Tiananmen and the [future] Monument in terms of their distance and relative proportion. He finally arrived at the decision to build the Monument on the axis between Tiananmen and Zhonghua Gate.'[27] This plan was passed unanimously in the First Plenary Session of the Chinese People's Political Consultative Conference on 30 September 1949, the day before the new Republic's founding ceremony. At the same meeting Mao also wrote an inscription for the Monument (which was later engraved on the back). Coming out of the conference hall, all the chief officials of the government, who had received their posts at the same meeting, went directly to a spot south of Tiananmen, where Mao took a shovel and laid the Monument's foundation stone (illus. 13).[28]

The actual planning and construction of the Monument started in 1952. A leadership group called the Committee for Constructing the Monument to the People's Heroes was established. The head of the committee was Peng Zhen, then Beijing's mayor and a crucial member on the Central Committee of the Chinese Communist Party. Three vice-directors included the architect Liang Sicheng, the sculptor Liu Kaiqu, and Xue Zizheng, the Secretary-in-Chief of the Beijing municipal government. Under them, two special divisions took charge of the Monument's design and construction, respectively. It would be misleading for two reasons, however, to think that the Monument was actually designed by these professionals. First, in order to practise Mao's doctrine that 'the people, and the people alone, are the motive forces of world history', the committee had to solicit designs of the Monument from the 'revolutionary masses'. Second, the decision about almost every detail of this Monument had to be made eventually by political leaders, not by architects and artists.

When Mao laid down the Monument's foundation stone in 1949, he only decided the structure's location in the Square, not its orientation. Should the Monument face south, according to a classical rule in Chinese city planning? In such a position, however, it would become one of many south-facing buildings punctuating the central axis of Beijing. This plan, agreed upon by all members of the planning committee, was changed at the last minute before the central slab (for Mao's inscription) was inserted into the obelisk. An

13 Mao laying down the foundation stone of the Monument to the People's Heroes, 1949.

instruction came down from the top: the Monument should face north. It was Peng Zhen who made this decision with Mao's and Zhou's consensus.

This change was made for good reasons, given the new ideological context. Once turned around to face north, the Monument became a direct counterpart of Tiananmen. These two juxtaposing structures then embraced an open space – Tiananmen Square – in the middle. But more profoundly, the new scheme signified an intention to group all architectural elements in the Square into a self-contained unit independent from the rest of Beijing. Once this unit was formed, a new perspective and a new hierarchical structure of the city emerged: the Square became the meeting point of the four directions and thus the heart of the capital and the whole country. The same scheme also meant that all architectural forms in the Square had to be planned according to their internal coherence. They provided one another with standards and reference points in form, proportion, orientation and distance. The Monument had to be viewed from Tiananmen; Tiananmen had to be approached from the Square; and the Square only became real when it was enclosed by Tiananmen and the Monument (and later also by the Great Hall of the People and the Museum of Chinese History to the east and west). In drawing a figure a child first paints a head and then adds arms and legs; in new Beijing the Tiananmen complex has determined the rest of the city.

But a central question still remains: what exactly *is* the Monument? We can pursue the answer in two different ways. First, the Monument embodies some fundamental values of the Party insisted upon by the authorities throughout the planning process. Second, these values were also realized negatively through the screening, rejection and criticism of competing approaches. These two parallel processes, which had already become clear in deciding the Monument's site and orientation, continued to control the planning. A third debate centred on its form. Some architects, blind to the Party's needs, kept proposing their own naïve plans. They designed gate-like low buildings with a heavy roof and open passageways (illus. 14b); the idea was still to harmonize the Monument with the traditional city of Beijing. These plans were severely criticized as attempts to 'restore ancient ways'; the Monument, according to the official approach, should be a solid high-rise, a form that could 'best represent the lofty spirit and unsurpassable achievements of the people's heroes'.[29] In the next stage of selection, therefore, only vertical shapes were considered (illus. 14e–l). Two types of plans were again eliminated. The first kind, derived from Stalinesque prototypes that place heroic figure(s) on top of a stone base (illus. 14k–l), was rejected on the grounds that such three-dimensional statues would unavoidably overshadow Mao's inscription, which could only be engraved on the base under the figure's feet. The second type of design, made by those who tried hardest to follow the Party's line, translated Mao's words literally into images. Once Mao had stood above Tiananmen and said that he hoped one day to see hundreds of chimneys (symbols of China's industrialization and modernization) from there. In a hurry, some designers drew diagrams showing a 'monument' consisting of three chimney-like high rises (illus. 14m). Even the Party could not accept such a plan.

After the low terraces, Classical building styles and anthropomorphic images had all been eliminated, the designers' minds were now focused: the Monument had to be a vertical form suitable for Mao's inscription (illus. 14i–j). In other words, they finally realized that what they should look for was not a monument but a 'monumental medium' for the Chairman's writing; the ancient stele then became a logical solution. Such a process ran throughout the designing of the Monument and was repeated on different levels at different stages. Even when the stele form was agreed upon, new debates started all over again about details: should the Monument be hollow inside so that visitors could climb onto it? Should its terrace be a platform for reviewing mass assemblies? Should its base be turned into an exhibition hall of Chinese revolutionary history? Again these plans were rejected one by one: 'To permit people to enter the Monument would harm its dignity; to combine the Monument with a museum would confuse its purpose; to design it as a platform would contradict the primary status of Tiananmen.'[30] We must realize that such a process, no matter how lengthy and tedious, was considered necessary because through it the designers themselves could be educated and reformed. The inevitable outcome was a correct and unanimous understanding of Mao's inscription written on 30 September 1949 (illus. 15b):

Eternal glory to the people's heroes who laid down their lives in the people's War of Liberation and the people's revolution in the past three years.
Eternal glory to the people's heroes who laid down their lives in the people's War of Liberation and the people's revolution in the past thirty years.
Eternal glory to the people's heroes who from 1840 laid down their lives in the many struggles against internal and external enemies for national independence and the freedom and well-being of the people.

To those unfamiliar with Maoist rhetoric, this passage may seem redundant to the point of meaninglessness. But to Chinese who have been schooled in the Confucian tradition, a sacred text always implies secret codes. Mao's riddle has three key words: the dates 'three years . . .', 'thirty years . . .' and 'from 1840'. The last two dates, in Mao's historiography, periodize China's modern history into two phases: 'the democratic revolution of the old type' from 1840 to the 1920s, and the 'democratic revolution of the new type' since the 1920s (it differs from the previous type in being under Communist Party leadership). The first date refers to civil war against Chiang Kai-shek from 1946 to 1949, which ended with the establishment of the People's Republic of China.

The inscription has other key words that do not periodize history but link separated historical phases into a continuum. The monotonous phrase 'Eternal glory to the people's heroes who laid down their lives in the people's War of Liberation and the people's revolution' is repeated over and over to signify a universal theme running through China's modern history. Still, the inscription contains yet a third secret code in its narrative structure: the 'revolutionary history' is told in flashback. It is, therefore, a retrospective reconstruction of the past from a present vantage point – it is Mao's vision of history.

15 a and b
Inscriptions on the
Monument to the
People's Heroes:
above Mao's hand-
writing for the
inscription on
the front side
right Mao's inscrip-
tion in Zhou Enlai's
handwriting for
the back.

人民英雄紀念碑

三年以來在人民解放戰爭和人民革命中犧牲的人民英雄們永垂不朽

三十年以來在人民解放戰爭和人民革命中犧牲的人民英雄們永垂不朽

由此上溯到一千八百四十年從那時起為了反對內外敵人爭取民族獨立和人民自由幸福在歷

次鬥爭中犧牲的人民英雄們永垂不朽

一九四九年九月三十日

中國人民政治協商會議第一屆全体會議建立

The ten reliefs on the lower plinth of the Monument constitute a pictorial representation of the revolutionary history by mimicking these codes. (In fact, unless one deciphers these codes it is impossible to comprehend these marble pictures.) The subjects of the reliefs were not selected by artists, but were proposed by a special Historiography Committee headed by Fan Wenlan, the leading historian of the Party's history during the 1950s. After 'a careful investigation of the history of the Chinese revolution', they came up with nine crucial events as possible subjects for the relief carvings. Mao personally reviewed the proposal and changed three events. The final selection of the eight historical events was made by the Central Committee of the Chinese Communist Party at several meetings chaired by Mao himself.[31]

Viewed as an independent historical narrative, the eight reliefs follow a linear pattern, proceeding from the east side of the Monument to the south, west and north sides. (The beginning of the sequence in the east implies the movement of the sun – a chief metaphor for the Party and the Chairman.) This chronological progression, however, is reversed in the actual architectural setting, because the scene on the front side of the Monument is the last episode of the historical narrative; the placement of this scene thus forces a visitor to read the other carvings in flashback. Moreover, the two scenes on the front and back of the Monument are much larger, and form a north-south pair to divide the rest of the carvings into two groups to the east and west. It seems that in structuring the carvings the designers were forced to employ two contradictory principles, one sequential and one symmetrical. Although each principle provided something useful for the Party's theologians, their competition disrupts a logical reading of the scenes.

The carving on the front of the Monument (illus. 16a), entitled *Crossing the Yangzi River* (1949), documents Mao's final victory over the Kuomintang. Two smaller reliefs, *Supporting the Front* and *Welcoming the People's Liberation Army*, flank this principal carving just as in ancient art donors surround a king or a god. These three scenes, which form a large composition and stand for the three-year War of People's Liberation from 1946 to 1949, leads the spectator to trace the previous chapters of 'revolutionary history'. The sculptured frieze on the three other sides of the plinth is divided into two equal parts. The two reliefs on the east side and the first one on the south side depict the three most important events during 'the democratic revolution of the old type': *Burning Opium* in Canton (1840), which initiated modern Chinese history (illus. 16b); the *Jintian Uprising*, which began the Taiping Rebellion (1851) (illus. 16c); and the *Wuchang Uprising*, which ended China's dynastic history (1911) (16d). To the west are three other scenes that stand collectively for 'the democratic revolution of the new type': the anti-colonial march on 30 May 1925 (illus. 16f), the birth of the Communist military force in 1927 (illus. 16g), and the guerrilla war against the Japanese invasion during the Second World War (illus. 16h). A scene connecting these two subsequences in the middle of the south side represents the *May Fourth Movement* (1918) (illus. 16e); its position corresponds to its historical status as 'the turning point from the democratic revolution of the old type to the democratic revolution of the new type'.[32]

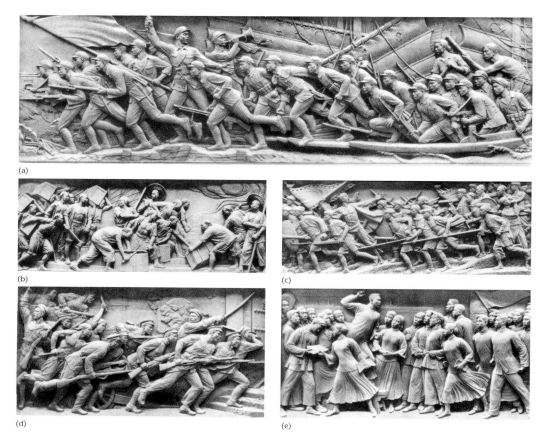

(a)

(b)

(c)

(d)

(e)

16 Eight main relief carvings on the Monument to the People's Heroes:
a. *Crossing the Yangzi River*
b. *Burning Opium*
c. *Jiantian Uprising*
d. *Wuchang Uprising*
e. *May Fourth Movement*

While Mao's vision of history is presented by selected flashbacks, the historical 'continuum' expresses itself in the repetition of forms. Some sculptors first thought to portray historical figures, showing leaders and participants for each event. But this plan was soon ruled out because the Monument, and hence its carvings, were supposed to stand for a collective body of people. Instead of drawing portraits, therefore, the artists' major task became to cast a single idealized archetype, which was then repeated and multiplied, and whose manifestations were combined into ten compositions. The result is surreal: a single actor appears both synchronically and diachronically 170 times across ten acts of a lengthy drama. No matter how busy he is, however, his face remains expressionless and his gesture(s) and movement(s) highly disciplined. The monotony of the reliefs perfectly echoes Mao's mantra-like inscription.

This historical investigation leads us back to our original question: what exactly is the Monument? It seems that, although the structure was not unveiled until 1958, it was *established* the day before 1 October 1949, when Mao laid its foundation stone south of Tiananmen and when his inscription was approved by the Political Consultative Conference. All later decisions were already implied, and the final form of the Monument grew from this seed. Our question can be thus rephrased: why did the Monument have to precede the People's Republic, and why did it have to be located before Tiananmen? What is the relationship between the timing and the placement?

The precise timing signifies an attempt to insert a punctuation mark in the flow of history, separating the past from the present; at that very moment the previous chapters of history were frozen into a permanent form (an 'implied' monument, the existence of which was attested to by its foundation stone and inscription). The possibility of summarizing the past – of fixing and affirming it

f. *May Thirtieth Movement* g. *Nanchang Uprising*, and h. *Guerrilla Warfare against the Japanese Invasion.*

(f)

(g)

(h)

33

– further indicates a present-minded vantage point that, in this case, was attributed to the victorious people who were to build this monument to their collective predecessors.

But what constitutes the people's past? In traditional historiography the past encompasses (at least theoretically) all previous happenings, whereas in Maoist historiography the past is explicitly dualistic: one past is heroic and virtuous, the other decadent and evil. The former is the 'revolutionary history of the people'; the latter is China's 24 dynasties (of Slave Society and Feudal Society) and Semi-Feudal and Semi-Colonial Society that characterized the Republican period. Before the triumph of the people in 1949 only the second history could be and had been documented, but now it was time to forge a new history.

This new history was necessary because it would legitimate and corroborate the establishment of the People's Republic. It was a 'revolutionary calendar' that served to 'provide an a priori frame of reference for all possible memory'.[33] In fact, logically speaking nothing but the past can assume the role as witness of the present. For both Mao Zedong and Zhou Enlai, however, the issue was far more practical and visual. Neither had much knowledge of city planning. What they did have was a point of view: the Monument had to be measured according to the presence of Tiananmen, where the Chairman would soon announce the birth of the People's Republic. While the Monument would embody the past of 'the revolutionary history', the opposing Tiananmen would stand for the present and future of that same history. The timing and placement of the Monument, therefore, meant that when Mao ascended Tiananmen on 1 October the Monument was already 'there', as a witness and legislator. It was understood that all the mortal beings gathered in the Square would die: the Monument would eventually become the *only* witness and legislator of the event.

The Monument is dedicated to the deceased heroes, but these heroes remain impersonal and conceptual. The monotonous inscriptions and relief carvings do not bear people's living memories, and no individual veteran of revolutionary wars dedicated a wreath to the Monument in memory of his dead comrades-in-arms. If the Monument has any commemorative value, the subject of commemoration is the founding of New China. Its reliefs and inscriptions were copied in textbooks to be memorized and to inspire awe. In fact, the Monument was not intended to be connected with any individual except Mao. The inscriptions and reliefs, as we have learned, all manifest his interpretative paradigms. When he stood above Tiananmen he faced his own words in his own calligraphy, and when he was not there his huge portrait stared down at them. The opposition of Tiananmen and the Monument thus stemmed from Mao's own bifurcation: as he had created both the past and the present of the people's history, he stood for both past and present, the people and history.

For more than 25 years this official ideology dominated the construction and interpretation of the Square. All new structures were added to confirm it. The Great Hall of the People and the Museum of Chinese History were hurriedly built before the regime's tenth anniversary, during the period of the Great Leap

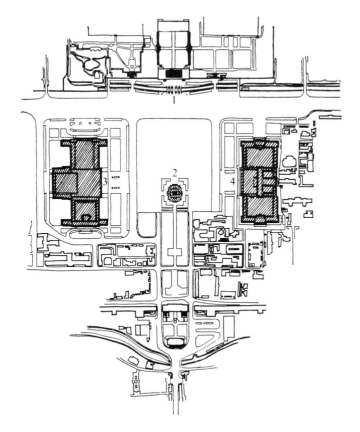

17 Tiananmen
Square in 1959:
1. Tiananmen
2. Monument to
the People's
Heroes
3. Great Hall of
The People
4. Museum of
Chinese History

Forward, which, according to Mao's prediction, would finally realize communism in China. While these two new monuments continued to periodize 'revolutionary history', they opposed each other along the Square's east–west axis and formed a second pair of juxtapositions between past and present (illus. 17). This diagram shows the symbolic structure of the Square in 1959:

PRESENT
(Tiananmen)

PRESENT   PUBLIC   PAST
(Great Hall of the People)   (Tiananmen Square)   (Monument to the
                                                      People's Heroes)

PAST
(Museum of Chinese History)

The strict and static scheme of this monumental complex externalized Mao's vision of revolution, history and people on a spatial plane. The Square was surrounded and defined by the monuments, as were the public gatherings surrounded and defined by the past and present assigned to them. It seemed that once this structure was fixed and affirmed it would last for all time, and indeed it remained unchallenged even during the most chaotic period of the Cultural Revolution (1966–76). But in 1976 the situation began to change.

This change may be understood as the re-emergence of a repressed past. As mentioned earlier, during the Ming and Qing dynasties the space in front of Tiananmen did not only offer a place for auspicious celebrations, but was also associated with capital punishment: twice a year death sentences were reviewed here and the alleged criminals were brought here for their final trial. This second rite was abolished after the fall of the Qing; the new rulers of the People's Republic further updated the auspicious ceremonies with mass parades. For more than two decades they seemed to have succeeded. The endless pageants in the Square presented a disguised reality of a contented people cheering at their leaders. But then, in 1976, everything suddenly changed: the Chairman died; Tiananmen was empty; the heated Cultural Revolution had turned into a nightmare; the Gang of Four was about to seize power. From all directions people came to the Square, of their own will and to express their own will. When they tried to speak out and prove they were 'the people', they were arrested and beaten.

Suddenly the colourful puppet shows ended; the Square once again became associated with outlaws, the accused and death. Suddenly the submerged dark side of the Square jumped back out. The age-old memory of Tiananmen Square as a place of public abuse and humiliation was refreshed, challenging the official myth surrounding it. In retrospect we realize that the antagonism between the ruler and the ruled had been always there, in the very opposition between a public ground and a privileged platform, and that it will continue to exist as long as the regime is unable to identify this opposition.

From 5 April to 4 June

My boyhood fascination with Tiananmen Square had completely vanished by the beginning of the Cultural Revolution, replaced by a mixture of fear and silent resistance. I was not in the Square on 18 August 1966, when a mass assembly of Red Guards inaugurated the Cultural Revolution. Three friends and I gathered in my room at my parents' house (where we used to meet regularly to enjoy classical music and discuss Western art and literature), listening with growing panic to the live broadcast of the event. Punctuated by thunderous cheers from 500,000 Red Guards, Mao and his hand-picked successor Lin Biao charged these ecstatic young men and women to destroy all enemies of the people on earth. I was then a third-year college student and had little experience in political matters, but at that moment I realized my inevitable fate: given all my 'defects', including my bourgeois family background (my parents were 'bourgeois intellectuals' and had both studied in the United States before the revolution), my passion for Western art, literature and philosophy, and my circle of friends who shared these interests, I was on the opposite side to the people and would be destroyed by the spreading red terror.

I was fortunate to survive imprisonment and numerous criticism sessions over the next four years. As the revolutionary fever gradually subsided, I was allowed to return to Beijing in 1972 and was given a job in the Palace Museum located inside the Forbidden City, albeit still carrying the label of a 'reformed counter-revolutionary'. People with this identity were considered untrustworthy and found themselves forever under the watchful eyes of the Party secretary. But, little by little, my scholarship on ancient bronzes and stone inscriptions was recognized, and my daily duties changed from cleaning exhibition halls to researching the museum's antiquity collections. Until 1978, however, I was not allowed to publish my research findings; my dubious political status was brought into question whenever a new campaign of class struggle was mobilized to expose hidden enemies of the state.

Because the museum didn't have enough regular housing for its staff, I was given a corner of an ancient compound inside the Forbidden City as my dormitory. One of thirteen courtyards on the eastern border of the Palace town (conventionally known as the Thirteen Rows), the compound was sandwiched between two tall walls of the Forbidden City and originally housed part of the imperial drama troupe. In the early 1970s it was unoccupied and in a state of semi-ruin. The courtyard was overgrown with tall weeds; people said they saw foxes running between exposed beams and lintels. I was among the earliest residents of the compound and lived there until 1980. During those eight years more and more staff members of the museum with their families moved into this and adjacent courtyards, and the place even began to feel like a neighbourhood. But when the heavy gates of the Forbidden City swung shut every evening, the Thirteen Rows was cut off from the rest of Beijing; and we as its residents could neither reach the outside world nor be reached by it.

Living inside the Forbidden City meant living behind Tiananmen, the front gate of the City. But such close physical proximity never inspired in me the kind of intimacy people often develop with a famous building in their neighbourhood. It rarely occurred to me, for example, that Tiananmen was architecturally connected to the place where I was living and working. Rather, this 'gate' had divorced the Forbidden City to become the antithesis of its former body. While the Forbidden City (as well as people like me who safeguarded its ancient buildings and antiquity collections) was associated with a dusty past, Tiananmen symbolized the revolutionary present and belonged to the Square outside.

This situation briefly changed, however, during 1976. Between 23 March and 4 April more than 100,000 Beijing residents went to the Square to mourn for Premier Zhou Enlai. I was one of them. To us – ordinary Chinese who had suffered much in a decade of madness during the Cultural Revolution – Zhou had become our only hope for rationality. Now he was dead; we wailed for him and for ourselves. It was then that Tiananmen resumed its role as the front gate of the Forbidden City: everyday I bicycled through it to visit the Square and share my anguish there with thousands of people whom I had never met before. Like them, I placed white paper flowers on the pine trees surrounding the Monument to the People's Heroes, and composed poems lamenting the tragedy that had befallen the Chinese people. Unknowingly I was in the midst of a mass movement that finally ended in bloodshed. Afterwards, the gate of Tiananmen was closed and no member of the Palace Museum was permitted to go through it to the Square. The Party secretary in the museum organized study sessions to track down those who had participated in

The 1976 mass mourning for Zhou Enlai (later known as the April Fifth Movement) was the first public demonstration in post-1949 Beijing.[34] When people went to Tiananmen Square they did not randomly fill this vast ground. Instead they gathered around the Monument to the People's Heroes and turned this monument, which had been part of the regime's political rhetoric, into their own symbol.

In January Zhou Enlai died. The Gang of Four, led by Mao's wife Jiang Qing, planned to push the bloody 'class-struggle' to a new limit. As part of this plan, they condemned Zhou as the 'biggest Confucian' (a negative term in their language for political conservatives) and prohibited people from mourning him. All the anxiety, frustration, disillusion and anguish that had troubled Beijing residents for more than a decade merged into a shared feeling of grief, and from this a grassroots movement began to take shape. 'When Premier Zhou died', one mourner said,

> many people were weeping – in the streets, on the buses. A mournful silence reigned [in the city]. It was uplifting, really uplifting. There was a sense of relief. In the past, for so long in China, there had been no occasion when you could feel your feelings uplifted . . . But with Zhou's death, you came to real- ize when other people were weeping that your grief was their grief, too. We were isolated before, but then people became close.[35]

On 23 March a single wreath of white paper, the traditional symbol of mourning, was placed at the foot of the Monument. The two ribbons streaming from the wreath bore an inscription in commemoration of Zhou Enlai. For the first time in its history the Monument was associated with the memory of an individual. Further dedications and gatherings were forbidden, but the prohibi- tion only brought more wreaths, mourners, and finally the protest on 4 April, the day of the Qingming Festival (the traditional day for holding memorial serv- ices to the dead). One hundred thousand people came this day and the next, on their bicycles and with their children. The assembly had no organizer and no plan; if there was a single factor that attracted people to the Square, it was not Tiananmen, but the Monument. By this time, white wreaths had been covered by red flags and slogans, and weeping had been replaced by songs, the beating of drums, the celebratory popping of firecrackers and poems:

> China is no longer the China of before
> Its people are no longer wrapped in ignorance
> Gone for good is the feudal society of the First Emperor.[36]

Then, on the night of 5 April, the bulbous lights around the Square suddenly flashed on the Monument and the demonstrators surrounding it. Some 10,000

18 Tiananmen Square in 1977, viewed from the south.

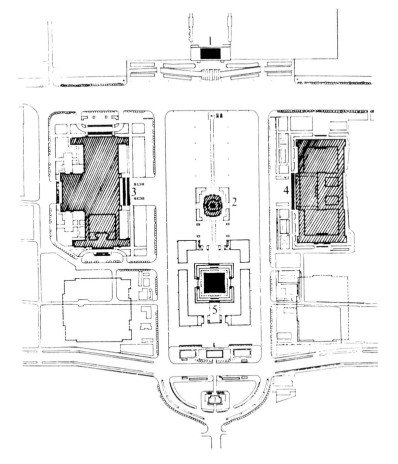

19 Plan of Tiananmen Square in 1977: 1 Tiananmen 2 Monument to the People's Heroes 3 Great Hall of the People 4 Museum of Chinese History 5 Chairman Mao Memorial Hall.

armed police, soldiers and 'worker-militiamen' rushed into the Square. Some demonstrators tried to explain; they were beaten to the ground and taken away. Before dawn the stains of blood on the Monument were carefully cleansed (although some were missed). The meaning of the Monument, however, was never the same. This historical fabrication had come to life, and its empty inscription – 'Eternal glory to the people's heroes' – had gained real meaning. It was now a living monument that wove people's recollections of their struggle and death into a whole. Surrounding it, a new public emerged.

Both the Square and the Monument are ironies because in a changing political discourse their intact physical forms (like repeated visual 'quotations') destroy their previously established meanings. The Chairman Mao Memorial Hall, which was unveiled in 1977 at a ceremony to mark the anniversary of the Chairman's death, is again an irony, but it took no time to become one: by adding this monument to the Square, its patrons had unconsciously undermined the symbolic system they had established and tried to perpetuate (illus. 18–19).

I will discuss this new monument – its design, political purposes and 'exhibition' function – in Chapter Three. Here it is enough to say that its addition in 1977, quite unexpectedly, acknowledged the achievement of the mass movement the previous year. The Memorial Hall changed the map of the Square as it took over the Monument's original role to become the counterpart of Tiananmen. The opposition and connection between the past and present of 'revolutionary history' were then most graphically expressed by this new juxtaposition: while the living Mao's image was still hung on Tiananmen's façade, his embalmed corpse dwelt in the Mausoleum (see illus. 97). Thus we find a new scheme of the Square:

PRESENT
(Tiananmen)

PRESENT	PUBLIC	PAST
(Great Hall of the People)	(the Square centred on the Monument)	(Museum of Chinese History)

PAST
(Chairman Mao Memorial Hall)

One fact immediately becomes recognizable when we compare this structure with the old one (see the diagram on p. 35): the Monument no longer defined the southern limit of the Square but stood in the middle of the public space (which had now been expanded to hold an assembly of 600,000 instead of 400,000). The Monument was now isolated, encircled and cut off in every direction by one of the four structures. Since ordinary people were restricted from entering these buildings in 1977,[37] the Monument became the only place in the Square that they could visit freely, and they went there with their recollections of the recent demonstration and its tragic ending. In

20 A stone stele
in a traditional
graveyard.

fact, after the 1976 demonstration and the 1977 addition of Mao's Memorial
Hall, the Monument had become superfluous to official symbolism but
indispensable for a growing dissident public. It was as if the Party had been
controlled by some invisible force to establish a monument for this public
or to yield a monument to it. Its glorious past was now symbolized by Mao's
corpse,[38] leaving the Monument to the living.

In an important article, Pierre Nora classifies monuments into two types
called 'dominant and dominated *lieux de mémoire* (sites of memory)':

> The first, spectacular and triumphant, and, generally, imposed – either by
> a national authority or by an established interest, but always from above –
> characteristically have the coldness and solemnity of official ceremonies.
> One attends them rather than visits them. The second are places of refuge,
> sanctuaries of spontaneous devotion and silent pilgrimage, where one
> finds the living heart of memory.[39]

The case of the Monument to the People's Heroes allows us to see that a single
monument can be either type, depending on what kind of memory is associated with it and what kind of activity is related to it. This structure was built
as a 'dominant' monument, but over time it has become a 'dominated' monument – dominated by other 'dominant' monuments surrounding it.[40]

Once the Monument was imbued with new memories, it was reinterpreted. In official documents the Monument derived its shape from ancient steles recording important political events or authorizing standard versions of the Classics, but in an ordinary person's eyes it began to look like a tablet that would be built in a family graveyard (illus. 20). Just as they might visit and revisit a family graveyard to honour their dead kin, so people visited and revisited the Monument to refresh their memories of previous struggles and sacrifices. The Monument gradually became *the* place for protests.[41] A feeling of kinship linked it to the protesters: someone they knew had died there and, like them, the Monument was also isolated and imprisoned. Gathering around the Monument they could feel hostile eyes secretly watching them from all sides, and armed soldiers about to rush out from the Gate, the Great Hall and the Mausoleum to punish them.[42]

The 1989 student movement (later known as the June Fourth Movement) began as a repetition of the April Fifth Movement in 1976.[43] On 15 April Hu Yaobang died; like Zhou Enlai he was believed to be an open-minded leader and a supporter of the people, and again, like Zhou Enlai, he had been criticized by the Party before his death. But unlike 1976, by 1989 a disillusioned public had gradually formed, and the Monument had assumed a new identity. The 1976 protest occurred a hundred days after Zhou's death, but only a few hours after Hu's death wreaths and white flowers had already appeared before the obelisk. What we find here is an intimate connection between 'memory' and 'event'. Memory, though invisible and hidden, bridges separated events into a continuous process. The memory of the 1976 movement resurfaced and was revitalized during the first few days of the 1989 demonstration. But soon new demands were raised, gathering new momentum. In the same way this movement will again provide future demonstrations with a new point of departure.[44]

Similar processes also operate within a single mass movement and interweave it into a whole. During a political explosion events are often not determined by conscious plans or explicit logic; they seem to occur individually without much premonition. The *Goddess of Democracy*, for example, appeared suddenly in the Square as several pieces shipped there on tricycle carts.[45] The crowd watched with amazement as a statue 10 metres tall took shape, and they began to respond to it. The event was spontaneous: the 'Goddess' was unheard of before. Still, there are clues enabling her origins to be traced in previous events and images in the movement.

An important change in the 1989 demonstration took place four days after Hu Yaobang's death.[46] On 19 April a portrait of Hu made by students from the Central Academy of Fine Arts, the top art school in the country, was carried to the Monument. Placed above the plinth, it directly opposed Mao's portrait on Tiananmen (illus. 21). Under the new image representatives of different colleges gave memorial speeches. Around 6 p.m., a man climbed onto the plinth and introduced himself as a veteran of the 1976 demonstration. He told his audience that the movement should not stop at commemorating the dead. More importantly, he suggested, people should speak openly about the future. The crowd

welcomed his appeal, and his lecture, on the subject of democracy, initiated a long series. Among those who followed him, a student read a poem entitled 'A Stele': 'Like a stele that remains silently under wind and rain, you – my country-men – have been only taught to know how to submit meekly to oppression.'

The rapid development of the movement during the following days proved that the poem could only refer to the past. From 22 April scattered activities were consolidated into an organized political protest. 'Freedom' became the most frequent catch-word.[47] In response to the government's announcement to 'clear' the Square, more then 200,000 people poured in and occupied the Square, establishing their headquarters beside the Monument (illus. 22).[48] Martial law was declared on 20 May, but the number of people in the Square increased to more than one million; a giant white banner appeared on the Monument, bearing the four-character inscription: 'Long Live the People'. On 23 May three young men from Mao Zedong's birthplace defaced the Chairman's portrait on Tiananmen (illus. 23). On 25 May a replica of the Statue of Liberty was paraded through the streets of Shanghai and was set in front of City Hall (illus. 24). On 30 May, after three days of preparation, students of the Central Academy of Fine Arts erected the statue of the *Goddess of Democracy* in the Square before Mao's portrait (see illus. 6).

Although these events seemed to have no direct connection, they signified consecutive stages in a pursuit for a visual symbol of the new public. This image-making movement began by portraying a new, public hero (Hu Yaobang) in protest against the old, official hero (Mao Zedong). This act implied further developments of the movement in two directions: the first was to forge a more general symbol and the second was iconoclasm. The *Statue of Liberty* was a ready-made general symbol, since she externalized the protesters' shared demand for freedom. As this foreign image was replicated (as were the English words 'democ-racy' and 'freedom' on numerous banners and flags), the iconoclastic tendency was vented in a physical defacement of Mao's portrait. The appearance of the *Goddess of Democracy* represented the final stage of the process: a borrowed sym-bol was modified into an indigenous image. No matter how much the *Goddess*

22 Demonstrators in Tiananmen Square, 22 May 1989.

23 Mao's portrait splashed with paint, 23 May 1989.

owed her form and concept to the *Statue of Liberty* or other existing monuments, it was not a copy. According to Hsingyuan Tsao, who closely observed and recorded the making of the *Goddess of Democracy*, the Federation of Beijing University Students first suggested that the sculpture be a replica of the *Statue of Liberty*, like the one that had been made by Shanghai students a few days earlier. But a Chinese image – a strong, young woman – was preferred instead.[49] With very limited time at their disposal, the artists – a group of undergraduate students in the Central Academy – transformed an existing studio practice work (of a man grasping a pole with two raised hands) into the *Goddess*, and made the 10 metre-high statue from styrofoam plaster in three days.[50]

But the question arises: why didn't people stick to the Monument as their symbol? Probably because even the Monument to the People's heroes was still a borrowed monument. It seems that the movement had reached such a heated stage that political messages could no longer be implied: these messages had to be shouted out loud so people could be heard. The giant memorial stele could no longer convey such messages. In fact, there had been an attempt to transform it into a more vivid and forceful icon: white flowers buried its plinths, Hu's portrait was placed there, and a banner inscribed 'Long Live the People' covered Mao's 'Eternal Glory to the People's Heroes'. A new symbolic form was demanded, a human figure for the living rather than a gravestone for the dead – and here was the *Goddess of Democracy*, a young female who stood bravely against Mao to challenge the whole bureaucratic and ideological system.[51] Soaring above the cheering demonstrators, she was immediately understood by everyone in the Square: 'She symbolizes what we want', explained a young worker. Then, stabbing his chest, 'she stands for me'.[52] In the statue's unveiling ceremony on 30 May, a young girl read a statement (signed by the eight art academies that had sponsored the project) that contained these sentences:

> Today, here in the People's Square, the people's goddess stands tall and announces to the whole world: a consciousness of democracy has awakened among the Chinese people! The new era has begun! From this piece of ancient earth grows the tree of democracy and freedom, putting forth gorgeous flowers and a bountiful harvest of fruit![53]

The message was received by the authorities and the matter was dealt with as a great emergency. For next two days *People's Daily*, the Party's official newspaper, denounced the statue; the evidence, however, was still the old Tiananmen myth:

> Someone erected a statue of the 'Goddess of Democracy' without authorization in dignified Tiananmen Square and this evoked various comments among the people. According to people's common sense, the erection of any monument in Tiananmen Square must first be approved by the government and must be based on a relevant government decree.
> In the Square the Tiananmen rostrum, the national flag pole, the Monument to the People's Heroes, the Chairman Mao Memorial Hall, the Museum of Chinese History and the Great Hall of the People are all built in good order and the layout is serious and solemn. The Square is a site to hold grand ceremonies and major state activities and is an important place for domestic and foreign tourists to visit with reverence. It is the heart of the People's Republic and is the focus of the world's attention.
> All citizens have the duty to cherish and protect Tiananmen Square. This is equal to cherishing and protecting our motherland and to cherishing and protecting our own rights. The Square is sacred. No one has the power to add any permanent memorial or to remove anything from the Square. Such things must not be allowed to happen in China![54]

Three days after this article was published the *Goddess* was destroyed: 'A tank like a roaring crazy beast ran over the students' tents. It then drove full speed ahead towards the statue of the *Goddess of Democracy*. With a loud crash the *Goddess* fell on the ground into fragments. She was dead, lying together with those murdered youths.'[55]

When the student demonstrations burst out in Tiananmen Square in 1989, I had been an immigrant in America for almost ten years, during which time I finished my graduate studies at Harvard and started to teach art history there. Just a year earlier my wife Judy and I had bought an 80-year-old house in Somerville, a working-class town next to Cambridge. We spent a whole year renovating the place, including turning its garbage-filled tiny backyard into a dream garden (which eventually won a local garden competition). Life was peaceful and harmonious; it seemed that I was finally able to escape the nightmarish memories of the Cultural Revolution and to pursue a new life with a built-in sense of security. China had become increasingly distant and only associated with the past. I had not returned there since 1981, because my parents were worried that I would be unable to leave again and refused such a visit. So after Judy and I were married in 1987 she went alone to Beijing to meet her in-laws.

With the student demonstrations unfolding in Tiananmen Square, my forgotten past was resurrected and reconnected with China's present. Day and night, Judy and I watched the TV broadcasts of the event. A large group of Western journalists had gathered in Beijing to cover a summit between Deng Xiaoping and Gorbachev, but found themselves unexpectedly witnessing a spontaneous social uprising. We were exhilarated by the students' demands for democracy, and enraged by the threats of the hard-line leaders to punish the demonstrators. When martial law was declared, a familiar feeling of anger and helplessness filled me, as if time had returned to 5 April 1976, the day of the suppression of the mass mourning for Zhou Enlai. This feeling turned into sharp pain when I heard about the massacre in the Square, and saw photos of the killing – another brutal war that the government had waged against its own people.

But there was one thing missing for me: fear. Although my memories of the April Fifth Movement made me an imaginary participant in the June Fourth Movement, I was not in the Square in 1989 to share the students' fear of being arrested or killed, of leaving their loved ones forever, of losing their own lives. I had known such fear but had left it behind. Then I realized – with a sense of humiliation and defeat – that I was and could only be a distant spectator of the demonstrations, that the June Fourth Movement was and would remain a 'reality' delivered to me by television and newspapers, and that between me and the Square in 1989 were, and would always be, words and images that both link and separate us.

25 A government tank destroying the *Goddess of Democracy*, 3 June 1989.

Among the photos of the massacre I saw was a series of pictures showing the destruction of the *Goddess of Democracy*. Like a living person, she was knocked down and gradually fell to the ground (illus. 25). These images reminded me of an earlier report: one of the sculptors of the *Goddess* said they had made the statue as large as they could so the government would not be able simply to remove it: 'If they decide to do this they'll have to smash her into pieces, thereby exposing their anti-democratic faces.'[56] I remembered that some leaders of the demonstration had predicted the massacre and suggested retreat, but the majority of students answered that only their blood could provoke the Chinese people and inspire further struggle.

I recalled also a 'performance' conducted in an unofficial exhibition (called *China/Avant-Garde*) held in Beijing a few months before the student demonstration: a young artist and her boyfriend shot at her own installation, which comprised two mannequins – a young man and a young woman – making calls (to each other?) in two separate telephone booths (illus. 26). The work was damaged and the artist and her boyfriend were arrested. Another work

26 Tang Song and Xiao Lu, *Dialogue*, installation/performance in the *China/Avant-garde* exhibition, National Art Gallery, Beijing, 5 February 1989.

27 Wei Guangqing and others, *Suicide Project No. 1*, photograph of a performance in the *China/Avant-garde* exhibition, National Art Gallery, Beijing, February 1989.

in the same exhibition, created by a group of Nanjing artists led by Wei Guangqing, was a series of photographs recording a performance entitled *Suicide Project No. 1* (illus. 27): a wounded man swathed in white bandages is lying across railroad tracks, waiting for a train to run him over.

None of these incidents seemed coincidental. Together they indicate an attempt to carry out a kind of 'planned' suicide. This attempt emerged either from absolute disillusion or from desperation, so that suicide had become one's only means to influence the future. The statue of the *Goddess of Democracy* was a monument that was *intended* to be destroyed, because its monumentality would derive from such self-sacrifice. In this way, this statue separated itself from those permanent 'revolutionary monuments' whose photo images fill a textbook. These permanent monuments are consequences of revolutions – like the Monument to the People's Heroes, built to mystify a glorious past – but not revolutions themselves. The very concept of 'permanence' seems so alien to the idea of revolution, which, after all, means to rebel against supposed 'permanence'. The construction of such monuments, therefore, announces the end of revolution and the beginning of a 'permanent' order. The statue of the *Goddess of Democracy* was different because what it intended to invoke were not memories of the past but memories of itself; and, to leave such memories to the future, it was prepared to be destroyed.

In this way, the *Goddess of Democracy* became a 'martyr'. But unlike those murdered demonstrators, her image could be replicated and through replication she could be reborn. Many replicas of the *Goddess* have been built around the world. In Hong Kong's Victoria Park, replicas of the *Goddess* and the Monument to the People's Heroes were placed face to face (illus. 28). A single traditional symbol – the Chinese character for memorial – replaced Mao's inscription on the Monument, while the living stood together with the *Goddess* and paid their silent homage to the dead.

The war of monuments continued in Tiananmen Square after the June Fourth Movement. Even though the *Goddess of Democracy* was destroyed, her vanished image continued to haunt the triumphant regime. For the victory

march commemorating the fortieth anniversary of the regime on 1 October
1989, another statue representing the unity of worker, farmer, soldier and intellectual was built in front of Tiananmen (illus. 29). The figures were submissive:
their eyes and hands were no longer raised; and expressionlessly they held a
steel rod or grain, a gun or a book, to signify their assigned duties. The political
map of the Square thus changed again: this new symbol of 'the people' was
placed right below Mao's restored portrait, in the shadow of Tiananmen. Like
an abandoned battlefield, the vast and deserted Square was left behind. A sense
of tightened security was achieved, but at the price of retreating to a smaller
enclosure. This new statue was, in fact, a weak and forced response to the
democratic movement. Most tellingly, it was constructed on the very spot
where the *Goddess* had once stood. No other act could reveal better the
regime's intention of repression and its fear, and the subject of this fear was
again the memory of the *Goddess of Democracy*.

50

TWO

Face of Authority: Tiananmen and Mao's Tiananmen Portrait

As in many other languages, the Chinese word for 'face' (*mian*) has as its root definition the front side of the human head. From here the word has acquired three additional meanings.[1] First, still referring to the human face, it can mean 'likeness'. A face therefore need not be a real part of human anatomy, but can be a fabricated image, a portrait that registers a person's 'physiognomic likeness'.[2] When such an artificial image is positioned as 'the front side of the head', it becomes a mask – a painted or sculptured face that is worn by a person to enhance or alter his or her appearance. Used in this way, a *mian* is a representation as well as a means of performance and disguise. A similar relationship can be found between a face-image and anything that bears it, even if the bearer is not a human subject. The appearance of the bearer is altered and its meaning changed, since it now has the potential of being conceived as a surrogate body.

This then leads to the second meaning of *mian*: extended to non-figural forms, this word is employed to describe architecture and objects. Most frequently it refers to a single plane of a three-dimensional form, usually the front, which serves a specific function and displays a particular design. A *mian* can be the elevated façade of a building or the flat cover of a book; the image and inscription it displays signify the nature and content of its body – the building or book itself. According to Roman Jakobson's well-known distinction, therefore, this representational 'face' is a metonymic device: while it remains an integral part of the body, its special shape and design separate it from the body and enable it to represent or substitute for the body.[3] But in some cases, due to historical changes or a deliberate design, an architectural front may become a free-standing structure. Its specific form and decoration still associate it with the notion of a 'face', but it is a bodiless face with an expanded symbolism. One such example is the famous church of São Paulo in Macao, whose surviving façade now stands alone to symbolize the city and its colonial past (illus. 30). Another example is a typical 'shop front' (*dian mian*) in traditional Chinese architecture (illus. 31). Designed as an ornate archway with a row of protruding poles, it was also erected independently in front of an entire commercial district.[4] Using Jakobson's formula again, we can say that the role of such a 'bodiless' façade has shifted from metonymic to metaphoric: without an attached body its meaning no longer depends on the principles of

30 The façade
of São Paulo
Cathedral,
Macao.

31 A typical
shop front in
traditional
Beijing.

contiguity and alignment, but is based on similarity and substitution. A free-standing 'front' can thus have a large architectural complex – city or country – as its 'metaphorical body'.

Third, used as a transitive verb, *mian* no longer pertains to a self-contained feature of a human or architectural form, but instead signifies a position or context. Typically the verb helps to construct two kinds of statements. The first, in which a person or building 'faces' a particular direction, defines the orientation of the person or the building in an implicit spatial system; the significance of the orientation is embedded in the symbolism of this spatial system in a given culture, religion or cosmology. The second kind of statement, in which a person or building 'faces' another person or building (or a group of people and buildings), specifies the juxtaposition or encounter of the two parties involved. Both statements were used by ancient Chinese philosophers to define rulership and the relationship between the ruler and the ruled. The phrase 'facing south to rule' (*nan mian er zhi*) refers to the formal position of an emperor (as well as the throne and the throne hall) and implies the propriety of his governance. In other examples an emperor is described as facing his subjects in the south, ensuing that 'all people are in harmony and the whole world is at peace'.[5]

These three implications of *mian* – namely, a 'face' as a portrait or mask, as an architectural façade, and as a signifier of spatial systems and relationships – enable us to understand the most illustrious 'face' of all in the People's Republic of China. This is the giant portrait of *Mao Zedong* hanging on the front wall of Tiananmen or, more correctly, the combination of the portrait and Tiananmen. One a figurative face and the other an architectural one, the two together constitute an image that has become the authoritative symbol of the state. This Chapter analyses this composite image. My discussion starts from Tiananmen, which, in addition to being an architectural 'front', supplied the portrait with a context, location and body.

Every Chinese of my generation remembers this song from childhood:

> I Love Beijing's Tiananmen,
> The place where the sun rises.
> Our great leader Mao Zedong
> Guides us as we march forward!

Owing more to its cheerful melody than to its unimaginative lyrics, this song became one of the most beloved children's songs in the country. While its lyrics were memorized by boys and girls even in kindergarten, we learned early that Tiananmen was the seat of the Great Leader and immersed in Mao's sun-like brightness. In fact, for some years I actually believed that Mao lived in Tiananman. At that time apparently I didn't understand the difference between metaphor and literal description, so whenever I drew Tiananmen I also circled it with radiating lines, a pattern of sunlight that I thought was a standard feature of the monument.

It was therefore a huge disappointment when I saw Tiananmen for the first
time (at least in my memory) with my own eyes. I was then in the first or second
grade. My parents took my sister and me for a family Sunday outing. Departing
early from our home in the northern part of the city, we first visited Beihai Park
and Coal Hill, and then travelled southward through the Forbidden City. It must
have been well past noon when we finally finished viewing the numerous halls
and courtyards of former emperors and their concubines. Starved and exhausted,
I was on the verge of a tantrum, when my mother encouraged me to walk a little
longer because Tiananmen was right ahead of us. My first encounter with
Tiananmen was therefore from the 'back', and I was confused because the building, approached from the rear, was virtually indistinguishable from the many halls
and gate-towers I had just visited that morning. But my biggest shock that day
came when I realized that we could actually walk through Tiananmen like any normal
gate. It was only after I emerged on the other side and turned around that I saw
Tiananmen looking as it did in my picture books. But somehow I felt cheated
because no book had told me anything about the place behind Tiananmen and the
passageway that went through it.

Many things have happened since my initial encounter with Tiananmen. My
faith in this primary monument of New China was challenged, restored and
destroyed at various stages of my life. When I went into third grade, for
example, I was convinced that the happiest child in China was the plump boy
featured in posters everywhere, who had presented flowers to Chairman Mao
on Tiananmen one National Day celebration. During the Great Leap Forward
campaign, I was in junior high school and paraded in front of Tiananmen with
great enthusiasm and pride. A few years later, when the Cultural Revolution
started, Tiananmen became to me a source of anxiety: it still retained its power
over me, but a power that threatened to destroy my existence. I was not freed
from this repressive power even after I emigrated to America: watching

students killed in front of Tiananmen on 4 June 1989, I felt as if I were there,
struggling under its shadow.

Only after a trip to Beijing in 1994 was I finally liberated from Tiananmen's
spell – a revelation that arrived when the building no longer held back its (unimpressive) secret. Astonished, I found that this former stand of Chairman Mao had
been turned into a tourist attraction, selling tickets to anyone who was willing to
spend 15 yuan (about us $4 at the time) to assume Mao's gaze (illus. 32). I bought a
ticket and toured the building. Inside the tower above the gate was an enormous
hall that had been transformed into an oversized living-room (illus. 33). The air
was stuffy and the decoration gaudy. Rosewood chairs and matching furniture
were patterned with ornate openwork dragons. Strangely, after so many years,
I was still surprised to find that the leaders of New China would adopt imperial
tradition by having their own 'dragon thrones' made. The chairs were arranged in

34 Tiananmen
tie clip, souvenir
sold on site.

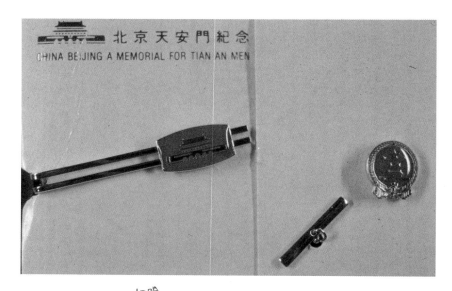

large semicircles. Partitioning the circles were free-standing screens painted
with colourful images of auspicious flowers and birds. Again, as works of art they
could be ranked only among the worst examples of court products.

Souvenirs were sold in the hall, so tourists could return home with a bona
fide Tiananmen tie clip or a Tiananmen brooch (illus. 34). On the balcony outside
the hall, some tourists were imitating Mao, waving toward the empty Square
below. I found myself following them, as if in doing so I could refresh my
memories about this place from Mao's vantage point, as if I could see myself
in the Square from his eyes and imagine what he would think.

Tiananmen

When Mao ascended Tiananmen on 1 October 1949 and declared the birth of
the People's Republic of China, he also concluded the long transformation of
the building he stood on. This transformation coincided with China's coming
into the modern age. Before 1911, when China was ruled by an emperor in the
Forbidden City, Tiananmen was an integral element of a large system of imperial architecture.[6] It gradually broke loose from this system during the first half
of the twentieth century. After 1949 it finally became a self-contained political
symbol – an embodiment of the Communist regime and its leadership. It also
became firmly associated with Mao, serving as a rostrum for him to review the
parades of millions of people. Since Mao's death in 1976, his portrait has continued to occupy Tiananmen's façade, overlooking Tiananmen Square and his
mausoleum to the south.

Originally built during the Ming and reconstructed during the Qing,[7]
Tiananmen was, as its name indicates, a *men* or 'gate'. More specifically, it was
one of a series of magnificent 'gate towers' located on Beijing's north–south

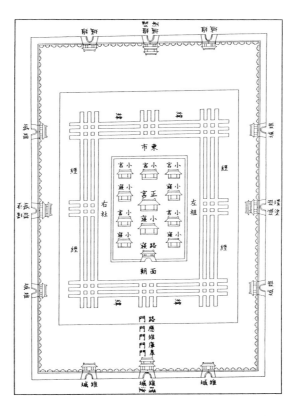

35 A schematic plan of the Zhou dynasty capital.

axis as the formal entrances to the series of four walled sub-cities (see illus. 10).[8] Each of these gate towers had a wooden-structured building standing on a tall brick base connected with the city walls; tunnel-like passageways underneath the tower led to the enclosed space. Tiananmen's traditional function and symbolism were thus realized in a larger architectural complex known as Beijing,[9] particularly in connection with the city walls and other gates. Indeed, gates and walls were principal features of a capital in traditional China because they both shaped a city and made it meaningful. The walls created repeated enclosures, one nesting inside another; the gates allowed a processional path to penetrate the walls and thus to link the broken spaces into a continuum.

Without much difficulty we can trace this design back to antiquity; a description in a 2,500-year-old ritual canon shows a very similar pattern (illus. 35).[10] The difference between imperial Beijing and its remote ancestor was not its structure but its infinite horizontal expansion: walls and gates were added and the central axis was elongated. Although such an unbroken tradition in city planning may be admirable, one wonders why a culture would so insistently reject any fundamental change. In particular, what did these gates and walls mean and why did they become an imperial obsession?

The ultimate explanation for this obsession was perhaps the political tenet that power could be maintained only by keeping it secret. (What was displayed, then, was the 'concealment' of power.) The walls were layers of barriers that repeatedly separated 'inner' from 'outer';[11] the gates led to (but refused to show) something deep inside the labyrinth of rectangles. The walls were 15 metres thick; a passageway resembled a dark, tomb-like tunnel. When the gates slowly swung open during a grand audience, ministers and noblemen would fall on their knees in awe before passing through them towards the emperor's throne. Outsiders remained outside; otherwise they would gain access to secrecy and power.

The 'thing' concealed behind the walls and gates was the emperor – the embodiment of the imperial order – who could maintain his power because he was invisible from the outside and because he, and only he, saw everything outside from his private space:

> The Way of the ruler lies in what cannot be seen, its function in what cannot be known. Be empty, still and idle, and from your place of darkness observe the defects of others. See but do not appear to see; listen but do not seem to listen; know but do not let it be known that you know . . . Hide your tracks, conceal your sources, so that your subordinates cannot trace the springs of your action. Discard wisdom, forswear ability, so that your subordinates cannot guess what you are about. Stick to your objective and examine the results to see how they match; take hold of the handles of government carefully and grip them tightly. Destroy all hope, smash all intention of wresting them from you, allow no man to covet them.[12]

This ancient political philosophy was so powerfully manifested in the design of imperial Beijing that even an early twentieth-century visitor could not help being bewildered by it when walking through its walls and gates:

> He passed through one blank wall and beneath one brooding gate-house after another, to find beyond it only a featureless avenue leading to yet another wall and gate. Reality was softening into a dream. His mind, so long attentive to a distant goal somewhere ahead in this labyrinth of straight lines, so long expecting a climax that never seemed to come.[13]

As an integral element of the architectural programme of traditional Beijing, Tiananmen was most intimately connected with the Imperial City, for which it served as the front gate.[14] While the Forbidden City at the heart of Beijing was the personal domain of the Son of Heaven, the Imperial City protected the Forbidden City and contained imperial parks, armouries and residences of royal relatives, ministers and powerful eunuchs. With thick walls and guarded gates, these two sub-cities in central Beijing blocked off more than two-thirds of the east–west traffic routes within the Inner City. An ordinary Beijinger had to make a considerable effort to travel between the east and west parts of the city, either circling around Di'anmen, the Gate of Earthly Peace that marked the north end of the Imperial City, or taking a detour behind Qianmen, the grand Front Gate located south of Tiananmen.[15] If one

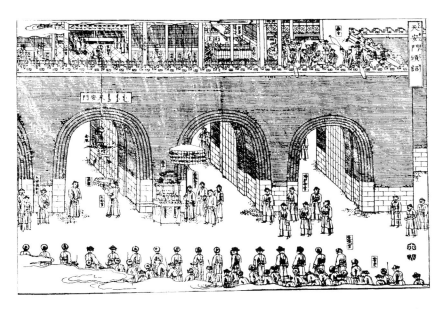

took this second route one could glance at Tiananmen's yellow roof. But the Gate of Heavenly Peace was sealed deep inside the T-shaped enclosure of the traditional Tiananmen Square and beyond an outsider's reach.

In the old days the central gate of Tiananmen was used only when the emperor left the Forbidden City to offer sacrifices to Heaven and Earth, to lead a military expedition, or to take a grand tour to inspect the provinces (see illus. 124). But Tiananmen defined a symbolic threshold even when it was not used as a royal passageway. On such occasions the building facilitated symbolic communication between the emperor and his subjects. The grandest of all ceremonies held on Tiananmen during the Ming and Qing was the issuing of imperial edicts when a new emperor was enthroned or a royal heir was born. The Minister of Rites would receive the edict from the throne hall. Placed on a 'cloud tray' under an imperial yellow umbrella, the edict would be carried in a portable 'dragon pavilion' onto Tiananmen's tower; officials and selected commoners would kneel down facing the emperor deep inside the Forbidden City. After an imperial envoy read the edict aloud on Tiananmen's balcony, and after the officials and selected commoners kowtowed nine times in response, the imperial document would be put in the mouth of a gilded wooden phoenix, which was lowered by a rope to another 'cloud tray' below (illus. 36). Again it would be put in a 'dragon pavilion', carried along the Imperial Passage to the gate at the south end of the T-shaped traditional Tiananmen Square. Once crossing this gate the edict would enter the public sphere (see illus. 11). After reaching the Ministry of Rites behind the eastern Thousand-step Porch, it would be copied and sent around the country.[16]

What we find in this ornate ritual performance is how the pre-modern Tiananmen Square worked.[17] Rather than forming a static pair, Tiananmen and the space below – hence the ruler and his subjects – communicated with each other through symbols. Neither the ruler nor his subjects were present: they were represented, the former by an elaborate set of ritual paraphernalia and the latter by chosen representatives. While any trace of individuality was obliterated in this performance (even the representatives had to kneel with their faces to the ground), the monolithic power of the imperial authority was enhanced. By the same token, the ritual also highlighted the identity and symbolism of the place where it unfolded: as the 'front' of the Imperial City, Tiananmen both concealed and exhibited the imperial power.

Tiananmen became accessible to the general public after China entered the modern era. The last imperial edict to come down from the gate-tower, issued by Empress Dowager Longyu on 12 February 1912, announced the abdication of the last Qing emperor. Two years later the Left and Right Chang'an Gates were permanently opened. As a direct consequence, the sealed space in front of Tiananmen was connected to the city at large and integrated into a modern avenue. Beijing's residents could now travel east–west by crossing this space, and they could also scrutinize the famous (but dilapidated) gate with their own eyes.

Other changes around Tiananmen also contributed to the gradual isolation of the gate-tower from its original architectural and symbolic context. First, the demolition of the walls of the Imperial City (that is, the city for which Tiananmen served as the main entrance) started in 1917 and continued throughout the next decades.[18] As this sub-city gradually disappeared from Beijing's map, Tiananmen's old identity as a 'city gate' was also abolished. (The north gate of the Imperial City, Di'anmen, was levelled to the ground in 1954 after a prolonged debate. With its demolition the architectural counterpart of Tiananmen, as well as the structural balance underlying the design of the Imperial City, also vanished.)

Second, in old Beijing, Tiananmen was flanked by two important imperial structures: the Imperial Ancestral Temple (Taimiao) to the east and the State Altar (Shejitan) to the west. These two ritual structures lost their function after the fall of the Qing, and were consequently transformed into public spaces. In 1914 the State Altar was renamed Zhongyang Gongyuan or Central Park to become the first public park in Beijing.[19] The conversion of the Ancestral Temple into another park, Heping Gongyuan or Peace Park, took place fifteen years later, in 1929.

Finally, after the fall of the Qing, the front section of the Forbidden City, which contained the three throne halls, became the property of the republican government and was opened to the public in 1914. The entire Forbidden City (except for Tiananmen) was transformed into the Palace Museum in 1925, soon after the Qing court finally moved out (the last emperor of the Qing had been allowed to stay on in the rear section of the Forbidden City after he abdicated the throne).[20] The museum used the north gate of the Forbidden City (called Shenwumen or the Divine Martial Gate) as its formal entrance (illus. 37); the visitors thus entered the former imperial place through its 'back door'.[21]

During the two decades from 1911 to 1929, therefore, all imperial structures surrounding Tiananmen were turned into public spaces of various functions. But Tiananmen did not belong to any of these spaces – neither to the museum

behind it nor to the parks next to it. Rather, it grew into the centre of a public space of a different order. Soon after the area before Tiananmen was opened to the public, it became a prime site for political gatherings and demonstrations, mostly organized by liberal and left-wing intellectuals from Beijing's colleges, in response to national and international controversies.[22] This was a crucial moment in China's modern history: the founding of the Republic in 1911 did not bring peace, order or unity to China. Instead, the early republican years were plagued by monarchist plots, warlordism and intensified foreign imperialism. Committed to reviving their strife-ridden country, these intellectuals – both professors and their students – launched a series of campaigns to transform China into an independent modern nation. While accepting Western science, political systems and culture as the foundation of a new social order, they were also fiercely patriotic; the demonstrations they organized in front of Tiananmen were more often than not stimulated by strong nationalistic sentiments.

The most famous of these demonstrations – the one that started the May Fourth Movement in 1919 – was triggered after the First World War by the verdict of the Versailles Peace Conference concerning Shandong.[23] Although China contributed to the Allies' victory, the Western nations that controlled the conference handed over Germany's rights in this Chinese province to Japan. Participants in the May Fourth demonstration in Tiananmen Square recalled that they had come to this place less than six months earlier, on 17 November 1918, to celebrate the winning of the war, and that leading intellectuals like Cai Yuanpei and Chen Duxiu all gave impassioned speeches on the victory of Western democracy over German despotism. But now, enraged by what they saw as a Western betrayal, some 5,000 students again went to Tiananmen to protest against foreign imperialism and demand justice. Endorsed by people throughout the nation, their action put pressure on the Chinese delegation at Versailles to reject the peace treaty (see illus. 3).

The May Fourth demonstration marked the beginning of a new era in Chinese political history, in which public opinion and mass demonstrations emerged as powerful forces in influencing national and international politics.

The event also marked the appearance of a new kind of public space in China, which acquired its identity and significance from the public demonstrations and political opinions manifested there. As such demonstrations increased in size and power throughout the early twentieth century, the significance of Tiananmen as a representative of such 'political space' was heightened. Six years after the May Fourth demonstration, on 10 June 1925, a much larger demonstration took place in Tiananmen Square to protest about a massacre of twelve protesters by Shanghai police under the command of British officers (known as the 'May Thirtieth Massacre' in modern Chinese history).[24] The Beijing demonstrators constructed five temporary platforms before Tiananmen; from there representatives of 157 mass organizations – not only students but also industrial workers, farmers and shopkeepers – addressed a large audience about the grave danger faced by China and its people (illus. 38). The demonstration reached its climax when the assembly passed a series of demands, including boycotting British and Japanese goods, abolishing all unequal treaties with Britain and Japan, and regaining all British and Japanese concessions in Chinese cities.

Generally speaking, in the first half of the twentieth century political demonstrations in Tiananmen Square were concentrated in four periods: 1918–19, 1925–6, 1935–6 and 1946–8.[25] The May Fourth demonstration in 1919 and the June Tenth demonstration in 1925 were the central events of the first two periods. The nationalistic sentiment that permeated these earlier political expressions found an even sharper focus after the Japanese invasion of China began and Manchuria became a Japanese colony in 1931. Two years later Japanese armies occupied Tongzhou, a strategic town outside Beijing. In 1935 Japan started a new campaign to take over the whole of north China. Some high officials in the Republican government proposed 'yielding' Beijing and other northern cities to the invaders. Sensing a national calamity approaching, 200,000 students and Beijing residents gathered in front of Tiananmen on 9 December 1935, where they staged a large rally against Japanese aggression and the government's policy of non-resistance. Viewed by the authorities as a

38 Demonstration in Tiananmen Square, 10 June 1925.

39 Demonstrators in Tiananmen Square during the Anti-war, Anti-hunger Movement, 20 May 1947.

Communist movement, however, the demonstration was suppressed and ended in bloodshed. Seven months later Japanese troops entered Beijing.

Japan's surrender in 1945 was immediately followed by civil war. China and its people continued to suffer. Students returned to Tiananmen; the target of their demonstrations was now the Republican government. The largest of these demonstrations was the 'Anti-war, Anti-hunger' movement in May 1947. Mobilized by left-wing student organizations, the movement started at various university campuses and culminated in a large demonstration in front of Tiananmen (illus. 39). Ignoring the government's warning, 7,000 students from different schools marched along Chang'an Avenue on 20 May, shouting slogans and distributing anti-government leaflets. They raised their voices when passing Tiananmen, now with an enormous portrait of Chiang Kai-shek installed on its balcony (see illus. 50). According to one memoir of the event, facing Chiang's portrait students shouted out 'Down with dictators! Down with autocracy!' They also sang a song that attacked Chiang for exploiting students, enslaving people, destroying Chinese culture and obstructing post-war peace. The song's title was repeated in each of its stanzas: 'You, You, You – You Scoundrel!'[26] Chiang's portrait on Tiananmen gave the 'you' an instant identity.

Exemplified by these crucial events, the numerous mass demonstrations held in Tiananmen Square in the first half of the twentieth century had a strong nationalist and anti-government orientation. This orientation brought largely spontaneous public activities under the general rubric of the 'democratic revolution of the new type' promoted by the Chinese Communist Party.[27] 'Only the Communist Party can save China!': this simple declaration by Mao motivated a whole generation of young students to join the revolution, and also appealed to a growing public who had become increasingly disillusioned with Republican rule. We can thus understand why so many people went to Tiananmen to celebrate 'the people's victory' after the Communist troops took Beijing in February 1949, and why 6,000 students voluntarily cleaned Tiananmen Square before the inauguration ceremony of the

63

40 Mao
announcing the
establishment
of the People's
Republic of China
on Tiananmen,
1 October 1949.

People's Republic. When thousands of commoners and soldiers gathered under Tiananmen on 1 October 1949, many of them truly believed Mao's words: 'Chinese people have finally stood up!' To them, his appearance in person on this former imperial building must have finally symbolized the beginning of a new era: it meant that the hidden ruling power had finally emerged and submitted itself to them (illus. 40). No other gesture could more effectively prove the newness of the Communist leadership and no other act could more convincingly seal the title of People's Republic.

Tiananmen's meaning was once again renewed; and its new significance as the chief symbol of the People's Republic was strengthened by physically altering this ancient building and its environment. Whereas Tiananmen lost its old identity as a 'city gate' once the Imperial City was demolished, another major architectural project in Beijing – the creation and expansion of an east–west road in front of Tiananmen – made it an independent monument. Called Chang'an Avenue, this road had grown into a modern avenue even before 1949: the first tram in Beijing was installed there in 1924, and new building materials had been used to pave and re-pave it (illus. 41).[28] The road was then conceptualized as the city's main traffic route in the late 1930s, and was extended all the way to the east and west suburbs.[29] The most dramatic development of this avenue, however, took place after the establishment of the People's Republic. In 1949 Chang'an Avenue was 15 metres wide. A year later its width was doubled – an achievement made possible by demolishing historical land-marks, including brick gates and wooden archways across the road, and by moving two groups of stone sculptures (a pair of *huabiao* columns and a pair of lions) 6 metres toward Tiananmen.[30] This two-fold process of destroying/altering old structures and expanding/creating the avenue continued during

the following years: the Left and Right Chang'an Gates were demolished in 1952; Chang'an Avenue was widened to between 32 and 50 metres in 1955; and the section before Tiananmen was further expanded to 80 metres wide before the tenth anniversary of the People's Republic in 1959 (illus. 42). The road also reached the remarkable length of 40 kilometres that year, far beyond the confines of the city of Beijing. Burying the old north–south imperial passageway underneath, it provided Beijing with a new east–west axis. Mass parades and traffic now proceeded under Tiananmen's shadow, not through its gate.

Repeated remodelling and redecoration of Tiananmen, all intended to enhance its significance as a 'living' monument, also changed the appearance of this ancient building. Two huge slogans, written in red characters against a white background, were permanently added to its façade before the inauguration of the People's Republic. The one to the left reads 'Long Live the People's

41 A street car running along Chang'an Avenue, 1950.

42 Chang'an Avenue after the expansion of 1959.

65

Republic of China'; the other reads 'Long Live the Central Government of the People' (which was later changed to 'Long Live the Union of People in the World'). The building was then itself remodelled. It is a little-known fact that Tiananmen was completely rebuilt in 1969 and 1970 according to a new design. The wooden tower above the brick nostrum was dismantled and restructured. The *dougong* brackets under the eaves were enlarged to enhance their sculptural appeal, resulting in the monument's height being increased by almost a metre. The roofline was also altered to accentuate 'a more elegant curve'.[31] Further adorned with red lanterns and contour lights, Tiananmen was indeed no longer a vintage building left from the past, but 'a shining, brand new monument with unmatched dignity and significance'.[32]

On a more conceptual level, Tiananmen became a certified symbol of the new regime. It was chosen as the focal image of the country's insignia, under five gold stars that symbolized the leadership of the Communist Party and the unity of the revolutionary people (illus. 43).[33] The official explanation of this design, issued by the new government in June 1950, claims that: 'Tiananmen symbolizes . . . New China, which was born here.'[34] In this design and its interpretation, therefore, Tiananmen was finally divorced from any architectural context to become an *emblem* – an image that has 'a direct verbal definition well known by all members of a group, class or culture.'[35] As an emblem, Tiananmen's frontal, schematic image is replicated on the country's banknotes

43 Mao announcing the final design of the emblem of the People's Republic of China, 1949.

and coins and on the front pages of all government documents. The insignia also hangs under the eaves of the real Tiananmen to epitomize its newly gained monumentality (illus. 44).

To be sure, this new monumentality of Tiananmen is not entirely irrelevant to its traditional identity as an architectural 'front': it still constitutes a *mian* or 'face', albeit in a different sense. With its ties to traditional Beijing severed and its connection to Communist ideology firmly established, this building has now acquired a 'metaphoric body', sanctioned after 1949 as the People's

Republic of China. This particular body-face relationship also helped to cement Mao's symbolic status for the regime: when a huge portrait of Mao was installed on Tiananmen on 1 October 1949 as a permanent feature of the building, Mao also came to embody the People's Republic of China. Since then, Tiananmen as an architectural 'front' has acquired a figurative face; together they constitute a monument commanding Tiananmen Square to the south.

Mao's Tiananmen Portrait

To understand this image we need to return to the early twentieth century, when a new type of public portrait for political leaders appeared in China. Before this moment, the concept of a *public* political portrait simply did not exist, since it was not a Chinese habit to exhibit the image of an emperor or official on public occasions or on public commodities, such as coins. Two kinds of imperial portraits were made during the Ming and Qing dynasties. Called 'pictures of amusement' (*xing le tu*) and 'imperial visages' (*yü rong*), respectively, each served a separate purpose and had a different pictorial style. A 'picture of amusement' was made for an emperor's private viewing and often situates the emperor in an informal or fictional environment: he is playing a musical instrument or enjoying the hunt; he is disguised as a Taoist monk, an ordinary labourer, or even a foreigner. In contrast, an 'imperial visage' had an official status and ceremonial function.[36] Works of this type uniformly employ a pictorial style that rejects any depiction of physical environment, bodily movement or facial expression. Some of the imperial visages convey a greater sense of personality, others reveal a strong impact of European 'naturalistic' modelling techniques, but none of them violates the basic codes of the genre: as a formal portrait, a 'visage' picture must present a ruler in a perfect frontal view against an empty background. The identity of the sitter is largely revealed by his costume covered with embroidered dragons, the primary symbol of the Son of Heaven.

To a modern viewer such imperial visages may not seem so distant from portraits of modern political leaders in terms of pictorial style, but they had radically different uses. The main purpose of an imperial visage, and hence the main reason for its creation, was to display it in ancestral halls in the imperial palace. A 'visage' portrait in such a sacred place stood as a substitute for a deceased emperor to receive ritual offerings (illus. 45).[37] A row of visages also constituted a pictorial chronicle, in which each image represented the reign of a ruler and hence a segment of China's dynastic history. Since neither an ancestral hall nor the portraits were accessible to the general public, the ancestral rituals and the pictorial history remained the private affair of the ruling family.

Changes became noticeable even before the Qing perished. Influenced by the Western practice of displaying portraits of political leaders in public spaces and on important ceremonial occasions, the last two Qing emperors, Guangxu and Xuantong, adopted a new attitude toward their own images, and began to publicize these images instead of concealing them. Photographic portraits of

imperial members were also reproduced through commercial outlets.[38] Even the notorious Empress Dowager Cixi presented her portraits to foreign monarchs and at world expositions (illus. 46);[39] each image, however, was accompanied by an imperial edict, with instructions that the portrait must be transported *en face* in specially designed vehicles, because the Empress Dowager should never take the inferior posture of looking backward.[40] Such taboos were abandoned by the new generation of Chinese leaders in the post-imperial era, whose images became a constant feature of newspapers, pictorials, postcards and cigarette cards – commercial mass media that constituted a new print culture (illus. 47). But such portable, printed images could never replace a framed public portrait. Whether an oil painting or enlarged photograph, a framed portrait belonged to a specific public space and helped to define the specificity of the space. So here we return to Tiananmen, which gradually merged with the face of China's paramount leader over the two decades from the 1920s to the 1940s.

Not coincidentally, this 'merger' started with Sun Yat-sen, commonly recognized as the father of modern China. Sun died in March 1925 in Beijing. The funeral was held in Central Park – the former State Altar next to Tiananmen.[41] Several hundred thousand people attended the memorial service and accompanied the hearse along Chang'an Avenue. In the open hearse was a large portrait of Sun; the deceased national hero was represented by his 'face image' on this and subsequent public ceremonies (illus. 48).[42] The first portrait installed on Tiananmen was also that of Sun, as documented by a photograph in *Shi bao* (*The Times*) on 23 March 1929, with a caption that reads: 'The newly painted Dr Sun's portrait' on Tiananmen (illus. 49).[43] Showing Sun's frontal image, the portrait was hung above the central gate and flanked by written slogans. All these conventions were later inherited by Mao's Tiananmen portrait.

After the Republican army recaptured Beijing at the end of the Sino-Japanese war, a portrait of Chiang Kai-shek appeared on Tiananmen on

46 A portrait
of *Empress
Dowager Cixi*,
painted by
Hubert Vos
in 1905.

3 December 1945 (illus. 50).[44] Both the size and location of the image signified the new leader's ambition: no longer hanging on the wall, this enormous painting stood above Tiananmen's balcony, with its upper edge almost reaching the roof of the gate-tower. From this commanding point Chiang looked down with a stern expression. As mentioned earlier, this portrait immediately became a focus of political tension. While glorifying China's current leadership, it also provided anti-government demonstrators with a target.

Chiang's portrait was replaced by Mao's when the Republican government was overthrown. The public responded to the change with enthusiasm at the

袁世凱

黎元洪

張作霖

杜錫珪

盧永祥

趙恆惕

曹錕

靳雲鵬

47 Political leaders
during the
Republican period.

48 Funeral train
taking Sun Yat-
sen's body to
his mausoleum
in Nanjing,
1929.

49 Sun Yat-sen's portrait
on Tiananmen, 1929.

time, but the substitution of images, when viewed retrospectively, signified
only the changing of leaders, not a new concept of leadership. Significantly,
when Mao's portrait first appeared on Tiananmen, it stood above Tiananmen's
balcony, just like Chiang's portrait before it (illus. 52).[45] This event took place
on 12 February 1949, ten days after the Communist army took over Beijing:
200,000 people reportedly gathered in front of Tiananmen to celebrate
Beijing's liberation.[46] Although Mao was absent (he arrived in Beijing six
weeks later, on 25 March), his larger-than-life image commanded the mass
gathering. It is likely that the organizer of the event, a committee representing
Beijing's students and residents, selected one of Mao's popular images and
commissioned some art students to enlarge it in an oil painting. Eight
months later, a different portrait was installed on Tiananmen for the country's
founding ceremony (illus. 53). Mao clearly approved the image, based on a
photograph taken by Zheng Jingkang in Yan'an and bearing the legend
'Celebrating the birth of the People's Republic of China', in Mao's handwriting
(see illus. 55).

This portrait (a huge image of Mao, 6 × 4.6 metres wide, hung at the exact
centre of Tiananmen's front wall) sealed Mao's relationship with the monu-

51 Stamps
issued in celeb-
ration of the
establishment of
the People's
Republic of
China, 1949.

72

ment. Other images created at the time similarly paired Mao and Tiananmen. A series of stamps that commemorated the founding of the People's Republic, for example, illustrate Tiananman in the foreground. Mao's portrait on the building is barely recognizable, so the designer blew it up into a giant head looming over the gate (illus. 51). Also from this time, a peculiar pictorial convention was invented to highlight the portrait's 'transcendent' status, so that many pictures represented the portrait as perfectly rectangular, even when Tiananmen itself was painted from a diagonal angle (illus. 54). The message is clear: as the 'absolute' image of the Chairman, the portrait must not subject itself to any 'distortion' of natural laws or human perception.

Mao's portrait has remained on the same spot for more than fifty years. It stayed even after Mao died and his 'mistakes' were openly discussed. The rationale for the immortality of the portrait, as I will discuss later in this Chapter, is that it had become a primary symbol of the nation and the Party. On the other hand, as important as it is, this portrait was surrounded by a strange silence: until recently there was little, if any, published report and discussion about its creation and variations, and the painters' names were kept largely unknown even in artistic circles. Information about this portrait became available only in 1998 and 1999, when a large body of historical data concerning the early years of the People's Republic was published before the fiftieth anniversary of the country. With some conflicting details, various accounts identify at least five painters, who between them painted some 50 to

52 Mao's first portrait on Tiananmen, 13 February 1949.

53 Mao's portrait hung on Tiananmen on 1 October (National Day) 1949.

60 'Tiananmen portraits' of Mao. (Damage from sunlight and the elements required that the portrait be renewed every year, usually before National Day on 1 October. Sometimes new portraits are also installed before International Labour Day on 1 May.) We are also able to track at least five different versions of the portrait and to link them in a chronological sequence.[47] The result of this investigation shows that, while the subject and placement of the portrait have remained unaltered, its representation and meaning have been subject to constant transformation. This process demonstrates how a public image of a national leader functions in a changing political environment, and reveals

subtle but important negotiation about the concept of authority in Chinese politics.

The 1949 portrait was painted by Zhou Lingzhao, a well-known artist and professor from the National Art Academy (Guoli Yizhuan). As mentioned earlier, this image was based on a popular photograph of Mao, taken by Zheng Jingkang at the Communist base Yan'an several years earlier.[48] Zheng's photograph shows Mao wearing an 'octagonal cap' and a coarse woollen jacket (illus. 55). The image is shot from a low angle, so that Mao appears to be raising his head and looking far off into the distance, beyond any onlooker. Zhou's painting did not completely copy the photograph, however: according to one report, he first painted Mao's collar loose as shown in the photograph, but was asked to depict the collar buttoned tight to make the image more appropriate for the solemn occasion.[49] Still, the painting shows traces of informality and a distinctive artistic style. In the portrait, Mao's cap leans to one side and the brim is crooked. The broad brushwork and strong contrast of light and shadow indicate the painting style favoured by this particular artist.

55 Mao in Yan'an, photo by Zheng Jingkang, with Mao's handwriting: 'Celebrating the birth of the People's Republic of China. Mao Zedong, 3 October 1949'.

This portrait was soon replaced: Hu Qiaomu, then the head of the News Bureau in the Central Government, invited his old acquaintance Xin Mang to create another portrait of Mao to hang on Tiananmen. Unlike Zhou Lingzhao, who had worked in Shanghai before 1949, Xin had joined the revolution long before 1949 and was a teacher in the Lu Xun Art Academy in Yan'an. Upon Xin's recommendation, several other Yan'an artists, including Zuo Hui and Zhang Songhe, joined him to take on the assignment. They selected a different photograph as their model, in which Mao was uncapped and attired in a more formal manner. As with the first portrait, however, the image is taken from a low angle and Mao looks upward (illus. 56). The three-quarters view of the Great Leader further prevents any possible eye contact between him and the viewer. For this reason the portrait was criticized by the 'revolutionary people' after it appeared on Tiananmen in 1950 on International Labour Day: 'With his eyes turned upward the Chairman seems to disregard the masses.'[50] Accordingly Xin Mang and his colleagues came up with a third Tiananmen portrait of Mao, based on yet another photograph. This time Mao no longer raises his head, but still turns his face slightly to one side and seems to avoid the viewer's gaze (illus. 57). This portrait was replaced again in 1952; the new portrait was created by Zhang Zhenshi of the Central Academy of Art and Crafts, who was destined to paint the same image for the next ten years.

Although never mentioned in any political or art-historical document, the 1952 substitution marked an important stage in Mao's portrait on Tiananmen. The period before this was one of experimentation: both the Party leaders and the artists were still unsure what would be the best way to represent Mao in this sacred place. As a result, different compositions were tried and dismissed in quick succession. The 1952 portrait concluded this experimentation by setting up a number of conventions, which would be followed by all versions of the portrait in the following years. Compositionally, in this new version Mao's posture is perfectly frontal, and he stares straight into the viewer's eyes (illus. 58). I have

58 National Day celebration in Tiananmen Square, 1 October, 1952.

77

termed this design an iconic, 'open' composition, whose meaning relies not only on the image itself but also on a hypothetical viewing subject outside the picture.[51] In this case, Mao's gaze acknowledges a 'revolutionary people' before him, even when he faces only an empty Tiananmen Square.

Compared to the 1949 portrait, the 1952 version had a much enhanced impersonal style, which was then shared by all later versions of the Tiananmen portrait. In these works, traces of brushwork are painstakingly concealed, and the shadow on Mao's smooth face is much reduced. The pictures are nearly two-dimensional and resemble carefully edited studio photographs – but studio photographs enlarged a hundred times and translated into oil. This impersonal, monotonous style contributed to a feeling of 'invisibility' about these images: although the importance of the Tiananmen portrait is well known and people pose for photos in front of it every day, no one seems to look at it with real interest. Related to this phenomenon is the invisibility of the artist – another precedent established by the 1952 version. Starting with Zhang Zhenshi, who painted this version, making the Tiananmen portrait was no longer considered a creative endeavour, but an act of image-making that should deliberately reject any creative impulse and individuality. The model for the portrait was also no longer selected by a painter; instead his duties were reduced to rendering a chosen photograph into an oil painting and to copying this painting year after year.[52] The Party stopped assigning these duties to well-known artists, but instead created a special profession of Tiananmen portrait painter, who would stay on to paint the portrait for many years, often until retirement. Zhang Zhenshi, the first of these, worked at this post for more than ten years, from 1952 to 1963.[53] He was followed by two professional artists from the Beijing Art Company. One of them, Wang Guodong, served from 1964 to 1976. His job was inherited by his student Ge Xiaoguang.[54] Ge, then just 18 years old, has been painting the portrait for the past 23 years.[55]

When the worship of Mao reached its zenith during the Cultural Revolution, every factory, school or institute had to place a statue or large portrait of Mao to revere at its entrance. My own school – the Central Academy of Fine Arts – suddenly became very popular: its teachers and students were constantly invited to help create such images, and they also provided revolutionary workers and peasants with training sessions to learn how to paint Mao's 'standard portrait'.[56]

But I was not among these teachers and students: I had been singled out as a 'counter-revolutionary student' in the spring of 1968, when the Cultural Revolution was about to enter its third year and when Jiang Qing mobilized a new campaign to uncover enemies hidden even among college students. Along with a sizable group of my friends and classmates, I was suspected of being a member of a counter-revolutionary ring having an illicit relationship with foreign spies. We were arrested by competing organizations of Red Guards, interrogated, beaten up and kept in solitary confinement for several months. A public accusation meeting was held that autumn to conclude my case: my suspected crime had been

confirmed and I was formally identified as an enemy of the people. Afterwards I was no longer subject to solitary confinement, but was still kept in an enclosed quarter in the school under 24-hour surveillance. With me were Dong Shabei and Wan Qingli, two other members of the alleged counter-revolutionary ring.

To reform our bourgeois ideology we were ordered to help make lithographic reproductions of Mao, Lin Biao, Jiang Qing and other Cultural Revolution leaders. Created by the Red Guards in the school, these portraits had become enormously popular in Beijing and were in constant demand (illus. 59). Our work was largely physical, mainly polishing lithograph slabs under running water. Occasionally we were ordered to print the images. But we would rather avoid such honour, even though the job was certainly more interesting, because any slip in making Mao's image could get us into great trouble. Stories abounded: a painter was jailed, for instance, when people found a white line had surfaced in a Chairman Mao portrait he had made, splitting the Great Leader's face into two. It was futile for him to explain that this was caused by a simple technical imperfection: the canvas was made of two pieces of fabric; the paint had fallen off at the joint and exposed the background.

The Cultural Revolution entered another phase in spring 1979. Colleges and universities throughout the country were taken over by Workers' Mao Zedong Thought Propaganda Teams, sent by Revolutionary Committees from different cities and provinces. Under the new leadership, the factions of Red Guards in our school were disbanded and united into a single front of revolutionary teachers

59 Cultural Revolution poster, by Shen Yaoyi, 1968, woodblock print.

and students. 'Ox demons and snake spirits' (terms used during the Cultural Revolution for class enemies of all descriptions) previously held in custody by these separate factions were also brought together into a single camp.

There were more than a hundred of us 'ox demons and snake spirits' in the Central Academy of Fine Arts – and I was the youngest. In fact, there were only three students; the others were mostly art professors. My roommates included Wu Zuoren, Dong Xiwen, Ai Zhongxin, Xu Xingzhi, Li Keran and Li Kuchan, all among the most illustrious names in modern Chinese art history. But now they were mere shadows of their former selves. No one dared to talk about art except to praise Mao's portraits and propaganda pictures in official magazines.

The camp was divided into four groups, each occupying a classroom of the school's former Sculpture Department. In our room, about a dozen bunk beds were lined up against three of the walls; the fourth wall displayed a 'standard portrait' of Mao, surrounded by numerous sunflowers made of gold paper against a red background. The portrait was a printed version: not even the best artists in the country, as 'ox demons and snake spirits', were allowed to depict the Great Leader. They could use their talent only to design and make the sunflowers, the symbol of loyalty and devotion. Every day, camp life started and ended with demonstrations of such devotion. Standing in front of Mao's portrait and waving the Little Red Book, we chanted in unison: 'We respectfully wish our Great Leader ten thousand years with no bounty, ten thousand years with no bounty, ten thousand years with no bounty!'

After this ceremony we sang revolutionary songs, often those inspired by Mao's poems. Then it was time for us to confess our crimes and mistakes to the Chairman, to report to him what we had learned from studying his writing and in what way we could better express our loyalty to him. When Jiang Qing hailed the oil painting *Chairman Mao on his Way to Anyuan* as a 'revolutionary masterpiece', we hung a copy on the wall and took turns commenting on its 'profound spirituality' and 'perfect artistry'. Some people's voices trembled and others had tears in their eyes. It was difficult to think all this emotion could be faking. Perhaps while praising that mediocre painting, they were actually thinking about their own lives and uncertain future.

Largely because of their anonymous 'artisan' status, none of the professional Tiananmen portrait painters was persecuted during the Cultural Revolution. As Seth Faison of the *New York Times* begins his report on his 1999 interview with Wang Guodong: 'Until recently . . . the circumstances surrounding the nation's most prominent painting were considered off-limits to the curious.'[57] In particular, Wang 'was ordered not to talk about his job, because anything to do with Mao or his image was so politically sensitive'. While Wang had pangs of pride when he rode through Tiananmen on his bicycle and glanced up to find his work on the majestic gate-tower, few of his acquaintances knew that he had been painting the portrait for a whole decade.[58] It is curious why information about this portrait had to be so tightly controlled. One can, of course, find the reason, as Faison has done, in the Party's penchant for secrecy. But the silence sur-

rounding the portrait has a more particular effect of dismissing the authorship of the image. The anonymity of the painters means the autonomy of the painting: it no longer seems a work created by a particular human hand, but an image that is always there and changes on its own. People passing Tiananmen rarely think about who painted the portrait or notice its changes. But the image has indeed been changing: the middle-aged Chairman in the 1952 portrait became in the 1963 version an older man with a faint smile on his lips, which again became an even older man in the 1967 version, whose mask-like face shows no sign of emotion or thought (illus. 60). With the authorship of these different versions erased, the changes in the Tiananmen portrait and the ageing of its subject are collapsed into a single, natural process. The portrait appears to age on its own, and the image seems both autonomous and automatous.

This leads us to consider an important question: What is the relationship between the portrait and Mao, or between a public image of a political leader and the leader himself? More specifically, in what sense does the portrait represent Mao, and in what way are the changes in the portrait related to that of its subject? The relationship between Mao and the Tiananmen portrait, I propose, can be conceptualized as consisting of four operations: magnifying, substituting, masking and detachment. Magnifying means enlarging a subject's appearance when the subject himself is present, thereby increasing the significance and 'aura' of the subject, causing him to be held in greater esteem and respect. The Tiananmen portrait exercised this role typically when Mao ascended Tiananmen to review a National Day parade. During such a grand ritual, Tiananmen Square was covered with 300,000 or 400,000, or even

500,000 'revolutionary masses'. Few in this human ocean could make out Mao's tiny silhouette in the distance. Yet they cried out with joy and excitement, because the Chairman was there, and was looking at them (see illus. 72). Unconsciously, they perceived Mao and the portrait together: Mao's human body was magnified by his enormous portrait and merged with the portrait. In contrast, substituting means replacing Mao with the portrait, which stood for the absent Chairman most of the year. With Mao's giant image posted on its front wall, Tiananmen was 'occupied' even when no mass parade was taking place and the Chairman was not on the rostrum. This significance of the portrait is most acutely felt when it is temporarily removed from Tiananmen for replacement or repair: the gate-tower suddenly becomes naked and 'faceless', and the Square suddenly loses its focus.

As explained at the beginning of this Chapter, to mask means to enhance or alter a person's appearance with a fabricated face; masking thus implies both disguise and performance. The Tiananmen portrait is a mask, whether it magnifies or substitutes for Mao, because in both cases the image is highly idealized and never overlaps with the real Chairman in age or looks. For one thing, the portrait is always younger than its subject: a standard version of the portrait is normally used for many years without change, even though during these years Mao has aged considerably or even died. Although each version is based on a photograph, the photographic model is already heavily edited and the portrait further idealizes it. Each version stresses certain character traits. For example, it is reported that Wang Guodong 'made a special effort to emphasize Chairman Mao's benevolence and kindness, while at the same time he brought out other dimensions in the Chairman's character, such as his sharpness, resourcefulness and penetrating intelligence.'[59] Ge Xiaoguang, on the other hand, reportedly said that he had 'done his best to represent the broad mind and deep thoughts of Chairman Mao through carefully depicting his gaze. To him, Mao's gaze serves to unite a leader with the people and to link the past with the present and future.'[60]

Ge's words reveal an important function of the Tiananmen portrait as a mask. By magnifying Mao's face or replacing Mao with a face-image, this portrait effectively emphasizes the power of his gaze. I have mentioned that, starting from 1953, Mao has been depicted as staring directly into the onlooker's eyes. Since then, his gaze has dominated Tiananmen Square and the population it symbolizes. This effect was consciously sought after by the painters of this portrait. Again citing Ge Xiaoguang:

This image is very different from any indoor painting in its method of representation and visual effect . . . It should be equally ideal when viewed from front or sideways, and equally powerful when viewed from any spot in Tiananmen Square, whether from the Golden Water Moat, the national flag pole, or from the Monument to the People's Heroes.[61]

Finally, detachment means the portrait's eventual separation from its figural subject to acquire a broader signification. A three-step process of detach-

Chinese text in image: 伟大的领袖和导师毛泽东主席追悼大会 / 中华人民共和国万岁 / 世界人民大团结万岁

61 Mao's mass
funeral in
Tiananmen
Square on
18 September
1976.

ment took place after Mao's death. First, a memorial ceremony was held in Tiananmen Square on 18 September 1976 (illus. 61). Tiananmen's balcony was left empty and sealed off with a black banner. All the Party leaders stood below the gate-tower on a temporary platform. The ceremony reached its climax when the leaders, as well as 500,000 'revolutionary masses' behind them, faced Tiananman and the Tiananmen portrait – no longer a coloured oil painting but an enormous black-and-white image made for the occasion – in silent tribute. The portrait was later changed back to a coloured version, but it had gone through a 'funeral' and resurfaced as a resurrected image.

Second, the Chairman Mao Memorial Hall was unveiled in 1977 at the anniversary of the Chairman's death; the corpse of the Great Leader was displayed inside it for public viewing (see illus. 97). Located at the south end of Tiananmen Square, this mammoth building formed a direct counterpart to Tiananmen. The opposition between the two structures, as well as the counterrelationship between Mao's preserved corpse and his portrait as a living person, expressed graphically the separation between the past and the present. The idea is that, although Mao is dead, his Tiananmen portrait will continue to represent the country and Communist leadership. This expanded signification of the portrait was finalized by Deng Xiaoping in 1980, the third step in renewing the image's meaning. Punished by Mao during the Cultural Revolution, Deng's return to the leadership in 1977 brought about a re-evaluation of Mao and the political movement Mao started. The 'Mao cult' was criticized in the following years; the huge statues and portraits of the Great Leader in many schools and factories were destroyed or removed in the early 1980s. As a signal of this trend, the two large Mao images above the main entrances of the Great Hall of the People in Tiananmen Square came down on 30 July 1980.

When the Italian reporter Oriana Fallaci interviewed Deng Xiaoping in August that year she immediately focused on the fate of the Tiananmen portrait: would it be kept or removed? Deng's answer was that, although the other 'excessive images' of Mao had to go, this particular image would stay. In his words, 'We will forever hang Chairman Mao's portrait on Tiananmen as a symbol of the People's Republic, and will forever commemorate him as the founder of our Party and country.'[62] With this statement, the new symbolism of the portrait was sanctioned as part of 'Deng Xiaoping thought': representing Mao as if he were still alive, this portrait now stands for an eternal present of the Party and the country, while Mao's physical body in the Memorial Hall serves as a reminder of an imperfect past leader.

Displaying the People: National Day Parades and Exhibition Architecture

The people, and the people alone, are the motive forces of world history.[1]
Mao Zedong

To display is to unfold to view an organized body of signs: images, words, objects, buildings and people. These signs are not necessarily ready-made and collected; they are often fashioned and assembled for a display, especially when this display serves to showcase a self-fulfilling political ideology. Although still a representation, such a display has less to do with describing and depicting the phenomenal world; its challenge is instead to turn political ideology inside out, revealing through concrete means what is supposed to be most essential to it – the source of political power and legitimacy, the structure of political institutions and geographies, and the short- and long-term objectives of a regime. Exactly for this reason, this type of display has a primary but unspoken agenda in forging a symbolic language, which manifests abstract notions and principles as visual spectacle, and translates ideas and theories into shared experience.

This Chapter explores the content and logic of this symbolic language of display in the People's Republic of China, which achieves its most authoritative and grandiose expression in Tiananmen Square. To be sure, what are exhibited here are not alien cultures or aesthetic objects, but 'the people', an imaginary collective sanctioned in the country's constitution as the source of power, the cornerstone of the state, the foundation of society and the creator of history. Various kinds of displays are staged in the Square to expound the rich potential of this political concept through every possible method; and indeed the invention and enrichment of these methods has constituted a large portion of the Square's history. It is here that the people's history is narrated in exhibitions and inscriptions, the people's heroes are revered through monuments and memorials, and the Great Hall of the People symbolizes the unity of the country's 34 provinces and regions (including the 'renegade province' of Taiwan). A ritual calendar further allows the people to manifest itself in bodily form before its leaders on a regular basis; these rites thus symbolically transfer power from the people to the leadership.[2]

The two sections in this Chapter focus on two major forms of visual display in the Square: holiday parades of the masses; and a collection of 'exhibition architecture' including the Great Hall of the People, the Museum of

Chinese History and the Chairman Mao Memorial Hall. These two forms loosely correspond to Michel Foucault's classification of heterotopias.[3] According to him, the modern museum arises from 'the idea of constituting a place of all times that is itself outside of time and inaccessible to its ravages', as opposed to other heterotopias that are linked to time 'in its most fleeting, transitory, precarious aspect, to time in the mode of festival'.[4] There is a crucial difference between my case and Foucault's, however: while Foucault studies a nineteenth-century European culture that defined Man as a universal subject, the notion of universal humanity is firmly rejected in Tiananmen Square. In Mao's political theory, the People's Republic of China distinguishes itself from a 'bourgeois republic' in being 'a state of the people's democratic dictatorship', in which democracy is extended only to the people, while dictatorship is applied to those excluded from the ranks of the people.[5] The content of the people would change from time to time; but its leadership must remain steadfast, as the Chinese Constitution declares: 'The Communist Party of China is the core of the leadership of the whole Chinese people.'[6] As we will see, these ideas have provided a theoretical framework for designing and perceiving all sorts of exhibitions and visual displays in Tiananmen Square.

Holiday parades and exhibition architecture are discussed here in conjunction also because they are both involved in 'showing and telling', which Tony Bennett defines as a practice 'of exhibiting artifacts and/or persons in a manner calculated to embody and communicate specific cultural meanings and values.'[7] Important to the central thesis of this Chapter, the subject and object of the 'showing and telling' in the Square are supposed to be the same. On the one hand, the people – its past, present and future – is the content of the displays (which, in fact, construct the people by transforming an abstract concept into images, performances and narratives). On the other hand, the people also constitute the primary audience of the displays (as visitors to the monuments, viewers of the exhibitions and onlookers at the holiday parades). It is again Foucault who has most succinctly characterized such an 'empirico-transcendental' subjectivity 'as an object of knowledge and as a subject that knows: enslaved sovereign, observed spectator.'[8]

This Chapter, therefore, approaches display not just in terms of the content and manner of exhibitions and parades, but also as methods and processes of communication and identity-formation. The monuments, exhibitions and holiday celebrations in the Square are displays as well as self-displays, and 'serve both to inscribe the bodies of individual citizens and to inscribe the state as a political body'.[9] While this is true for all exhibitions and parades in China that 'represent the people', the Square stands for the whole nation – a significance that has given rise to the most ostentatious and extravagant displays and self-displays in the People's Republic of China.

The National Day Parade

I cannot remember how many times I marched in the National Day parades in Tiananmen Square, at least six or seven after my first encounter with the place in the fourth grade. I also cannot remember when I lost my interest in these events – perhaps in my adolescent years in the high school (illus. 62). Food was a big problem then. To take part in a National Day parade one had to get up really early and walk really far – all the way across the city from east to west. But for several years only very little food was provided at the end of the march. There was a serious famine in the early 1960s and everyone was starving. But the food ration was not increased even on a National Day. I remember this because one of my classmates complained after a parade and was criticized for 'learning nothing from seeing Chairman Mao during the National Day celebration'.

It is difficult to remember something after you have lost interest in it. So I have little recollection of the parades that I participated in during my college years, although these events were closer in time than my boyhood experience. What I remember about these later parades are bits and pieces, trivial and ironical. One such fragment surfaces from 1964, when I was a sophomore. Since my college – the Central Academy of Fine Arts – was under the jurisdiction of the Ministry of Culture, we were ordered to walk in the Grand Artistic Army, which always constituted the most colourful contingent of a National Day parade. For this role we dressed up like folk dancers wearing embroidered costumes and white turbans. It would still have been ok if the trousers I was issued were not three sizes too small. To make them look decent I had to create a pair of suspenders on the spot. When I 'marched' through the Square shouting slogans, I was actually struggling with the crotch of my trousers dangling between my knees.

But there was a time before such boredom and meaninglessness – a time when a National Day parade was still exciting and energizing; so I remember much more about it. One such moment was 1959. The whole nation was in a fever during the Great Leap Forward, a political campaign that promised the instant arrival of a Utopian society. There was unlimited food for everyone; villages renamed themselves People's Communes; radios and newspapers reported industrial and agricultural miracles as daily news. Young students like us stopped taking classes, and instead devoted ourselves to smelting steel and breeding high-yield grain in the school's backyard. I was thirteen then and had just entered the junior division of the 101 High School in Beijing. After Chen Baokun, the art teacher, discovered my artistic talent, he put me to helping make revolutionary murals inside and outside the school. (Seven years later, I heard that Mr Chen was killed by the school's Red Guards at the beginning of the Cultural Revolution.)

In early September the school held a competition to select the best design for a float, which would be the centrepiece of the school's procession in the forthcoming National Day parade in Tiananmen Square. Many of us made fantastic, impractical plans. (Mine was a moving steel monument vaguely resembling the Eiffel Tower. With my whole class standing on its various levels, it was in turn carried by a team of trucks that my school certainly did not possess.) The

62 A photo of the author in 1961, embellished with the photo studio's 'Tiananmen' logo.

competition produced no winner; and the school's float took the conventional, bullet shape of a space shuttle. But my disappointment soon turned to delight when I was assigned to help make the float. Over three weeks we used bamboo stalks to construct a frame for the shuttle's body, pasted it over with layers of rice paper, and finally painted it silver with a red star. All the while we imagined that we would carry it through Tiananmen Square on National Day, with one of us sticking out from the cockpit.

Another prospect made the parade even more enticing: on 1 October we would wear the new school uniform for the first time. The uniform's design, reportedly derived from a famous Russian military school, was unique among all high schools in Beijing. I was particularly attracted by the hard-top hat usually worn by army officers. We received the uniform on 30 September. Immediately several of us ran to a local photo studio to have our pictures taken. The next day was exhausting, but we were so proud of our looks we even forgot lunch. I heard people talking about us and saw reporters aiming their cameras at us. We were told before the parade that we could see Chairman Mao when we passed the Square – he would be the tallest of all the leaders on Tiananmen. I believed that I did see him: slowly walking above Tiananmen's balcony he kept waving his hand at us. But after the parade we debated whether the Chairman wore a hat that day.

Two weeks later I heard that the new issue of the *Renmin huabao* (People's Pictorial) was in the school library. I ran to look at it: I had this conviction that our photos must have been included in the magazine's coverage of the National Day parade. I searched in vain for our space shuttle and ourselves in each picture, looking so hard that some pictures were permanently imprinted in my mind. When I began to research this book I went back to this issue of the *People's Pictorial* on a dust-covered shelf in the Harvard-Yenching Library. There it was, still familiar but having assumed a different meaning.

A mainland Chinese of my generation (that is, the generation schooled in the 1950s and early '60s) often has difficulty seeing the People's Republic of China as part of a larger historical process or pattern, and is often shocked to find links or parallels between New China and old China. An official myth, though dated, still retains force: it claims that because Mao and the Chinese Communist Party rejected the idea of 'evolution' and chose instead the path of 'revolution', they could turn the sociopolitical system of old China upside down; the outcome of their success in 1949 was a China ruled by the people and for the people. A routine subject of history textbooks and exhibitions, this myth also owes much of its survival to a set of political rites conducted in Tiananmen Square: commemorations to the revolution, celebrations of the victory of the people, and endorsements of the Party's political agendas.

During the first decade of the People's Republic, two grand parades were conducted each year, one for International Labour Day on 1 May, the other for the National Day on 1 October. Mao reviewed them all. The Labour Day parade was cancelled after 1959 owing to the country's extremely stringent economic

63 An anti-Vietnam War demonstration in front of Tiananmen, photographed by Marc Riboud in 1965. The demonstrators are from the Central Academy of Art, the author's Alma Mater.

condition after the disastrous Great Leap Forward. The National Day parade alone persisted to display 'a bright, progressive socialist country' and 'a confident, unified revolutionary people'. Around the same time, a series of large-scale rallies took place in the Square to support 'a global revolution against American imperialist hegemony'. Unlike those anti-government demonstrations before 1949, however, these were government-sponsored activities aimed at attacking external enemies and endorsing official policies (illus. 63).[10] Top Party leaders, sometimes Mao himself, cheered the marchers from Tiananmen's balcony; these rallies were therefore the Party's instruments to mobilize revolution. For the same purpose, when Mao started the Cultural Revolution in 1966, he ascended Tiananmen eight times in three months from August to October to review the assemblies of 1.1 million Red Guards, who travelled to the Square from all over the country to receive his instructions (illus. 64). During the following years, the Cultural Revolution brought about endless class struggles to destroy 'all enemies of the revolution' and pushed the country to the verge of civil war. Consequently, representations of a unified, harmonious people went out of fashion, and even the National Day parade stopped after 1970. It was not until fourteen years later, in 1984, that the new chairman, Deng Xiaoping, reinstalled this political rite (illus. 65): as a survivor of the political persecution during the Cultural Revolution, Deng saw a great National Day parade as the best demonstration of the country's resurgence after the decade-long chaos. The National Day celebration that year, in which Deng reviewed the military forces and gave a public speech, self-consciously mirrored the founding ceremony of the People's Republic in 1949. Deng's precedent was again followed by the next chairman, Jiang Zemin, fifteen years later at the fiftieth anniversary of the People's Republic. The grandest National Day parade ever staged in the Square, this ceremony in 1999 was hailed as a defining moment of the Jiang Zemin Era in the country's modern history (illus. 66).

64 Mao review-
ing Red Guards
on 18 August
1966.

This brief review makes it clear that, among all the parades, rallies and assemblies in the post-1949 Square, none is more fundamental to the regime than the National Day celebration. While other ceremonies have had their specific goals and timing, this rite transcends such particularity and can be constantly updated to represent progress and renewal. It frames the history of New China as a self-contained unit: its unambiguous origin in the founding ceremony of the People's Republic turns everything before it into a 'negative history', and anyone taking part in this ceremony automatically joins a 'positive history' of the country. Meticulously planned and conducted, a National Day celebration is also supposed to be spontaneous. Indeed, many news photos covering the event are intended to represent such spontaneity: old soldiers hold back tears when their former army divisions match through the Square;

65 Deng Xiaoping
reviewing armies
on 1 October
1984.

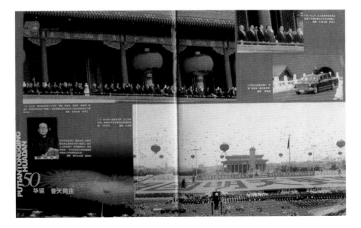

66 Jiang Zemin reviewing mass parades on 1 October 1999.

excited Young Pioneers jump up and down while waving flowers at the leaders. These images are no fakes.

To relate a post-1949 National Day celebration to a pre-1949 event – say, the warlord Zhang Xun's grand ritual in 1917 to commemorate his restoration of the imperial order – is therefore not only counter-intuitive (from the point of view of the current regime) but can also be infuriating (to those participants emotionally involved in the parade). To make such historical connections implies an analytical position external to 'the people' as both the subject and object of a National Day parade. It is precisely at this juncture that my account of the event shifts from personal remembrance to historical reconstruction. From this second perspective, a post-1949 National Day parade, like many other things found in the present-day Square, is rooted in historical precedents. Indeed, since a ruling power – whether traditional or modern – always creates an idealized image of the ruled to legitimate itself, it comes as little surprise that such a representation was conducted in Tiananmen Square long before the founding of the People's Republic.

Because the T-shaped Square in traditional Beijing was a walled compound inaccessible to ordinary people, this representation took place in an open space immediately outside the southern end of the compound (illus. 67). Called Qipanjie or Chessboard Street, it was a 'square' 365 metres each side, paved with granite slabs and surrounded by stone railings (illus. 68).[11] Three factors made this place a unique 'political space' in pre-modern China. First, it was juxtaposed with the southern gate of traditional Tiananmen Square and shared the gate's symbolism. This gate was destroyed in 1958 to make room for the Monument to the People's Heroes, but its image – a plain, single-storey structure with three passageways – is preserved in old paintings and photographs (illus. 69). This rather understated image is deceptive, because the building formerly possessed an extraordinary significance as the 'gate of the state' (guo men), a symbolism confirmed by the changing of its name under different regimes. As mentioned earlier, it was called the Gate of the Great

Ming during the Ming and the Gate of the Great Qing during the Qing. This political symbolism continued even after the dynastic history ended: as soon as the Republic was established in 1911, the new government renamed it Zhonghuamen, or the Gate of China, to signify China's rise to the rank of a modern nation. Lying south of this gate, Chessboard Street was the first 'public space' outside the imperial domain, a location that made all the activities taking place there into symbolic displays of the imperial power.

67 Plan of traditional Beijing:
1. Chessboard Street
2. Gate of the Great Ming/Qing
3. Tiananmen.

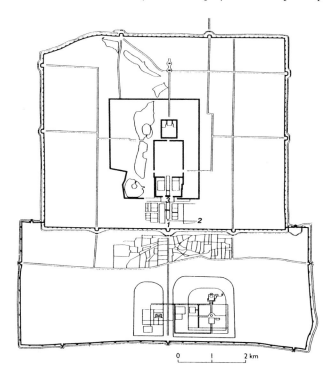

68 Chessboard Street in the early 20th century.

69 Gate of the Great Qing in the early 20th century.

Second, paired with the 'gate of the state', Chessboard Street divided the Imperial Passage into two sections. The section inside the gate coincided with the central axis of the Imperial City and the Forbidden City; the section stretching southward from Chessboard Street was shared by the emperor and his subjects (see illus. 67). In other words, whenever the emperor left the Imperial City to make a ritual sacrifice or to inspect the country, he would go through Chessboard Street. Once he reached this space he would be (symbolically) among his subjects and assume the identity of a 'public leader'. In retrospect, we realize that the walled Tiananmen Square functioned as a liminal space: it belonged to neither the Imperial City nor the Inner City, but provided a transition from the royal palace to the society at large – from Tiananmen (i.e., the gate of the Imperial City) to the 'gate of the state' and Chessboard Street beyond.[12]

Third, as mentioned in Chapter One, during the Ming and Qing dynasties two groups of government departments flanked the walled Square to the east and west. Those to the east dealt with civil affairs; those to the west handled military and security matters (see illus. 11). Chessboard Street not only connected these two branches of government and symbolized their unity, but also provided a crucial route for Beijing's east–west traffic. This last role was especially important to the city's daily activities owing to Beijing's layout: because the Imperial City blocked off more than two-thirds of the east–west streets, to travel from the east part of the Inner City to the west part a Beijing resident either had to circle around the northern end of the Imperial City or go through Chessboard Street (see illus. 67). Taking advantage of the place's reputation as the 'throat' of Beijing's traffic, merchants set up temporary stands there to sell various goods, and the place was ordinarily crowded with travellers and shoppers.

Chessboard Street therefore assumed multiple functions and linked different spaces. It was a meeting point of the imperial and public domains as well as an intersection of two kinds of movement – that of the emperor along the north–south Imperial Passage and that of ordinary people between Beijing's east and west sides. Governed by a ritual calendar, its appearance was transformed whenever the emperor went to sacrifice to Heaven, earth, stars or agriculture in ritual structures outside the Inner City, or when the yearly Grand State Assembly was held inside the Imperial City. At these moments, Chessboard Street was emptied and cleaned, and imperial guards set up colourful banners to mark the occasions. Travellers and merchants returned after a ceremony was over, and the place resumed its role as the 'throat' of Beijing's traffic, once again filled with people and enlivened by their activities.

This introduction to Chessboard Street provides a basis for re-reading a famous passage by the Ming historian Jiang Yikui, which has been cited by virtually every author in discussing this space.

> The chessboard-like Heavenly Avenue outside the Gate of the Great Ming manifests the image of the hexagram *li*, and connects the government branches to the left and right. All types of people under Heaven – gentlemen and commoners, workers and merchants – come here with official credentials. As they all gather here the place becomes extremely crowded; the lively noise continues from morning to night. This is indeed an extraordinary scene of prosperity at the gate of the state.[13]

This passage has often been used to identify Chessboard Street as a busy commercial district, 'like a thriving marketplace one finds today'.[14] But in actuality it internalizes a perception that frames the place as a highly politicized space, where an idealized ruling authority is juxtaposed with an idealized subject. Jiang clearly associates Chessboard Street with imperial power: not only does he call it a 'Heavenly Avenue' but, according to the *Yi jing* (Book of Changes), the image of the hexagram *li*, which he claims that the place manifests, denotes 'the great man' who, 'by perpetuating his brightness, illuminates the four quarters of the world.'[15] A crucial significance of this place, according to him, is therefore to manifest the emperor's power and wisdom over the whole country. This understanding was shared by another Ming scholar Xie Jin, who inscribed a couplet on the 'gate of the state' facing Chessboard Street: 'The sun and the moon brighten the virtue of Heaven; mountains and rivers glorify the imperial home.' This couplet won admiration from Emperor Yongle, the founder of Ming-Qing Beijing.

94

Equally important, Jiang Yingkui considers the 'extraordinary scene of prosperity' on Chessboard Street an indication of the country's general socio-economic condition, and identifies those who travel to the place as representing 'all types of people under Heaven', meaning the whole population. It is interesting that he notes that these people wore 'official credentials'. It seems that the 'extraordinary scene of prosperity' he describes, while supposedly spontaneous and unmediated, is actually under state surveillance.

Writings like this do not simply record what someone actually saw, but also proscribe what ought to be seen. In Jiang's account, the crowd gathered on Chessboard Street is already categorized into 'gentlemen and commoners, workers and merchants' – classes and occupations as structural elements of a larger social entity known as 'the people' (*min* or *baixing* in traditional Chinese). The 'extraordinary scene of prosperity' he finds there is already a display, construed and experienced as the manifestation of a higher order of reality, of which it is but a tangible expression (illus. 70). His account thus embodies an anonymous vision that instantaneously endows the place and its constituents with explicit political meaning and value.

A similar logic governs the perception and reception of a National Day parade in the People's Republic of China, but the totalizing vision in Jiang's account is now distributed to specific participants in the ceremony and assumes different points of view. A parade (*youxing* in Chinese), as the word's dictionary definition suggests, is a large-scale ceremonial procession conducted in a public space and under the inspection of a superior leader. A National Day parade converges two principal gazes, one from the procession and the other from the inspecting leader, into a dynamic exchange; the shared 'vision' that emerges from this exchange then endows the ceremony with a coherent meaning as a supreme representation of the people.

One big change after 1949, of course, is the anthropomorphization of the ruling power, which has now become immediately recognizable in Mao's huge portrait on Tiananmen's façade, doubled with Mao's (and his successors')

70 A detail of a Ming painting by Zhu Bang, showing people of different classes and occupations meeting in front of the southern gate of Beijing's Inner City. For the full composition, see illus. 123.

bodily appearance above Tiananmen's rostrum during a National Day celebration. Other changes concern the size and form of a mass assembly in the expanded Square: it is several thousand times bigger than the crowd on the old (and now vanished) Chessboard Street, and takes the form of an organized ceremonial procession. As has been discussed in the preceding Chapter, these new forms of representation do signify important changes in the conception of political authority. But as constituents of a 'meeting' between high and low, we wonder how much has altered in their basic roles in a ritual communication: like the 'extraordinary scene of prosperity' displayed on the old Chessboard Street at the emperor's front door, the colourful pageantry in the new Tiananmen Square has continued to help forge symbolic ties between the ruler and the subjects (now called the leader and the people).

Practically speaking, due to the considerable distance separating the inspectors on Tiananman and the masses below, any actual communication between these two groups of participants in a National Day celebration is impossible. A poster created after the first National Day celebration in 1949 conveys just such a visual experience: like a distant mirage, Tiananmen looms over an ocean of parading masses, who cheer at the monument with an empty rostrum (illus. 71). Ironically, the difficulty in visual communication during the ceremony made it an urgent task to invent such communication: when 'vision' was absent in reality it had to be constructed in art and literature. It is therefore no coincidence that as soon as mass pageantry became a routine practice in Tiananmen Square after 1949, 'seeing Mao', and especially 'being seen by Mao', became a dominant subject of visual and literary representations of the National Day parade.

A series of ten photos in a 1950 issue of the *People's Pictorial* is an early result of this kind of creativity. Recording scenes during the National Day celebration that year (i.e., the first anniversary of the People's Republic), these images occupy a spread (illus. 72). The largest picture in the series represents marchers in the parade, cheering and waving towards someone outside the picture frame. The subject of their enthusiasm is shown in another photo to the upper left: Mao stands on Tiananmen's balcony and waves back to the marchers. The downward angle of the first photo effectively emphasizes the immensity of the crowd. Equipped with a telephoto lens, however, the photographer is also able to capture the ecstatic expressions on nearby marchers' faces. The second photo is much smaller, and Mao's remote figure cannot be immediately discerned. Magnified by his portrait hung directly below him, however, the presence of the Great Leader never becomes questionable. Placed at the upper left corner of the spread and overlapping with the larger photo, this smaller photo assumes a commanding position and defines a vantage point. Shot from a stand constructed especially for the occasion, this picture has a level, symmetrical composition, in contrast to the downcast perspective of the large photo, which implies Mao's gaze from above.[16] Juxtaposed as a pair, these two photos create the illusion of two gazes responding to each other: whereas the marchers become ecstatic upon seeing Mao (or Mao's portrait), Mao also sees them from Tiananmen's balcony. The intentionality of this design is also revealed by the

71 Anonymous, *National Day Celebration in the Square*, 1950.

72 Images of the 1950 National Day celebration in *People's Pictorial*, October 1950.

captions of the two photos: 'Chairman Mao on Tiananmen waves at the 400,000 people in the rally' for the upper left picture, and 'Chairman Mao sees the masses who wave to him with great enthusiasm' for the lower right image.

The remaining eight photos in the series, further reduced in size, are arranged along the left and bottom of the spread to surround the first two pictures. Not coincidentally, they all serve a dual purpose to represent specific components of the parade and to construct Mao's omnipresent gaze. This purpose is again stated explicitly in their captions, which all describe the parade through Mao's perception. (This arrangement thus clinches the role of the upper left image as the vantage point for other pictures. Its caption summarizes the collective meaning of the whole series.) The captions of these eight photos, from left to right, read: (1) 'Chairman Mao sees the young generation'; (2) 'Chairman Mao sees the growing force of peace'; (3) 'Chairman Mao sees a forest of portraits of Grand Marshal Joseph Stalin'; (4) 'Chairman Mao sees a forest of portraits of Prime Minister Kim Icheng and Chairman Ho Chi Minh'; (5) 'Chairman Mao returns a salute to this old man'; (6) 'Chairman Mao must have seen the flowers in your [that is, the young pioneer in the picture] hands'; (7) 'Chairman Mao sees these female students who will soon present flowers to him'; and (8) 'Chairman Mao sees these waist-drum players'. While all these descriptions subject the images to an authoritative gaze that is absent in the images themselves, two of the captions – the fifth and sixth – accomplish more. The photos that they accompany show, respectively, the close-up of an old man shouting slogans and that of a boy waving paper flowers. Framed by the captions as 'exchanges' between these individuals and Mao, these two scenes highlight the collective purpose of the photo series to forge an expected communication between the marchers and Mao.

Serving the same purpose but with a different emphasis, reports on mass parades in Tiananmen Square have often focused on people's 'actual experience' in participating in the ceremony. This focus of representation was established not long after the founding of the People's Republic, as demonstrated by a magazine article written in the mid-1950s about a group of young Communists in Beijing, who formed a Youth Service Centre to help people. Their contribution to New China earned them an opportunity to parade through the Square. The article details the lasting impact of this event on them, as the writer reports:

> When these young people marched through Tiananmen Square, they saw Chairman Mao waving his hand at them. In response they cheered in ultimate excitement. When the parade was over, one member of the group told her comrades: 'Chairman Mao is really great: he even stood in the rain to wave to us.' Another said: 'For a whole year I had been waiting for this moment. Today I finally saw Chairman Mao.' A young housewife in the group told her fellow members: 'Never even in my dreams did I imagine that I could participate in such an extraordinary event, with so many people as my friends and comrades. I swear that I heard Chairman Mao shout to me: "Long life my young fellow!"'[17]

For the next twenty years, until Mao stopped reviewing the National Day parade from Tiananmen,[18] writings like this proliferated after each occasion; their predictable dominance over the media during such periods became part of the holiday ritual and helped regulate the political lives of Chinese people. The repetition of similar stories and experiences was never considered a problem. On the contrary, such repetition became an important means in promoting a heightening 'Mao cult', which began to control China's political culture from the mid-1950s. This cult, in turn, contributed greatly to producing an increasingly uniform, anonymous people. The stories and experiences told and retold after each National Day parade, in fact, made Mao a prerequisite for the masses to identify themselves as 'the people'. As exemplified by the magazine article cited above, the marchers were instantly uplifted by Mao's gaze to a new level of spirituality: under this imaginary gaze, they were no longer scattered individuals but had become part of an immense body of 'friends and comrades', a body that had Mao as its head and brain.

The growing uniformity and anonymity of the masses explains two important changes in the visual presentation of a National Day parade: first, a parade quickly developed from a loosely synchronized 'walk through' into a rigidly programmed procession. Second, a sustained pursuit for visual spectacles transformed a parade into an elaborate mega-performance, representing a formidable force of the people while erasing any sign of individual existence. Much inspiration for both changes came from the Soviet Union, which China held as her example in all spheres of social progress in the early and mid-1950s. Leaders of the two countries routinely visited one other on state holidays, inspecting mass parades from Tiananmen or Lenin's mausoleum. Especially in the early 1950s, parades in Moscow's Red Square provided ready-made models for parades in Beijing's Tiananmen Square.

   The 1952 National Day celebration in Tiananmen Square marked the beginning of this new programme, providing a blueprint for later parades. The ceremony started at 10 a.m. After the National Anthem was performed and a 100-gun salute was fired, Zhu De, the chief commander of the People's Liberation Army, reviewed the military forces and reported to Mao that 'the army is ready to defeat all enemies'. Mao's acknowledgment of the report then introduced the parade in seven successive sections:

   The 'three divisions of the army' in the order of the infantry, the navy and
      the air force.
   A ceremonial vanguard headed by 1,000 railroad workers carrying flags
      and a huge model of the national emblem, followed by 1,500 waist-
      drum performers and again by 15,000 Young Pioneers, who represented
      the country's Communist future [illus. 73].
   A team of 90,000 industrial workers.
   A team of 20,000 farmers.
   Teams representing government institutions, schools, merchants and
      Beijing residents.
   The 'Grand Athletic Army' formed by 3,000 athletes.
   The 'Grand Artistic Army' formed by 5,000 artists.

Like the 'extraordinary scene of prosperity' that Jiang Yikui observed on the old Chessboard Street, this modern representation of the people again relied on categorization: what one saw in the parade was not a shapeless 'mass', but a classification of social classes and types – workers, farmers, intellectuals, merchants, etc. – that formed a structured, hierarchical whole. The order of the groups' appearance in the parade indicated the degrees of their importance to the state: thus industrial workers – the leading class in the People's Republic – marched first after the ceremonial vanguard; farmers and other groups followed because they subjected themselves to the workers' leadership. The parade thus derived its internal structure from Mao's prescription of a socialist society based on Marxist-Leninist sociology. This structure of a National Day parade has remained basically unchanged to this day, although the size of the parade has continued to grow, and subsections have been added to reflect new political tenets and technological developments.

A major characteristic of the later parades – one that has given lustre to these events – is their incessant pursuit of visual spectacles. The 1952 parade again marked a new departure in this direction: with huge models and placards as focal images, the sections of the procession were shaped as geometric patterns of varying colors. Three years later the Grand Artistic Army in the

1955 parade generated much excitement with a spectacle unseen in the previous National Day celebrations: the 7,000 dancers in this section performed *A Great Union of Nationalities* when they matched through Tiananmen (illus. 74). At the centre of each dance formation was a float supporting a tableau from a drama or ballet, with famous actors and actresses arranged as 'living sculptures'. The 1957 celebration introduced yet another visual form: several thousand people were lined up in the Square to construct two large characters, 'Guo qing' ('National Celebration'), picked out in bouquets of flowers. This last event had a particular importance in the history of the National Day parades for three reasons: it made the Square south of Chang'an Avenue a primary space for visual presentations; it started the tradition of using living people to construct patterns; and it restricted the audience of such presentations to the leaders on Tiananmen, since the constructed patterns could be seen only from their angle (see illus. 66).

All these experiments and innovations prepared for the 1959 National Day celebration. Taking place at the height of the Great Leap Forward, this holiday also gave the regime an opportunity 'to demonstrate the extraordinary achievement of the Chinese people in the first ten years of the People's Republic'. My earlier discussion of the Square's history has shown that the preparations for this celebration went far beyond a National Day parade and included the expansion of the Square from 54,000 to 400,000 square metres and the construction of the Ten Great Buildings. (For a discussion of this last project, see below.) The parade, however, served to bring all such accomplishments into sharp focus. The

74 The 'Grand Artistic Army' in the 1955 National Day parade.

following excerpt from a report, based on the memories of some planners of the National Day ceremony, describes the laborious planning process of the ritual occasion and the planners' major concerns, expressed in the rhetorical language characteristic of this type of writing. Interestingly, a total, still image of the Square assumed an overwhelming importance that even surpassed the parade. The reason is that, as we read in the report, this image would remain under Mao's eyes during the entire ceremony.

Tiananmen Square had been completely transformed by the tenth anniversary celebration. Old buildings, including two brick gates and wooden archways on Chang'an Avenue, the vermilion walls of the old Square, and houses along the nearby streets, had been erased from the map. In their places had arisen the Great Hall of the People and the Museum of Chinese History, and the Square had become the largest space for public gatherings in the world. These changes made it possible to plan a much grander National Day celebration.

Several government departments joined Beijing's Communist Party Committee to take charge of the planning process; the dominant purpose was to conduct a perfect holiday ceremony and to make the Square truly magnificent and stunning. The parade had to be more spectacular than ever, and had to reflect the country's extraordinary achievement in its first decade under the leadership of Chairman Mao and the Party. It also had to express Chinese people's unmatched confidence and strength in their effort to create a socialist society.

Tiananmen Square is the main location of the holiday celebration. Spreading in front of Tiananmen and the accompanying reviewing stands, during the entire ceremony it would lie under the eyes of Chairman Mao, other government and Party leaders, and honourable guests from all over the world. The organization and presentation of the masses in this place would determine the outcome of the whole event. Any mistake in this place would be immediately recognizable and cause irreparable damage.

Because the Square has such importance, how to conduct a visual display in this space became a primary task for the Headquarters of the National Day Celebration. Discussions started in June 1959 and all sorts of proposals were made. Based on these proposals, Xin Yi and Wu Yuan, principal administrators of the Headquarter, decided to station 100,000 people in the Square. Those in the middle would construct a large pattern of the national emblem, flanked by the dates 1949 and 1959.

After the higher authorities granted this concept, a team of planners designed the method of making the pattern. According to their plan, along the north edge of the Square and flanking the ceremonial band, Young Pioneers would form a decorative band with multi-coloured flowers, wreaths and balloons. College students would construct the national emblem in the middle of the Square. Industrial workers would form the two dates. Staff members of government institutions would stand along the west side of the Square, while representatives of Beijing residents would be lined up along the east side. These two groups of people would construct two additional decorative bands east and west, framing the national emblem in the middle. Nineteen large balloons, rising 60 metres above the ground, would project the Square's shape in the sky. The fourteen balloons on the east, west and south sides would carry twelve banners, each with a slogan announcing a current agenda of the Party. The five balloons on the north side (and hence directly facing Tiananmen) would be shaped like traditional red lanterns; the five large characters suspended from the balloons would form the sentence 'Long Live Chairman Mao!' More than 5,000 smaller balloons of different colours would be released at the beginning and end of the ceremony. At the final moment of the day's celebration, all 100,000 people in the Square, upon a signal, would surge toward Tiananmen and cheer Chairman Mao [illus. 75].[19]

The report then details various technical challenges and the solutions to them. Indeed, using 100,000 living human bodies to make a picture was no simple task. The 'foremost challenge' that the report emphasizes over and over, however, was how to make this picture visible from Mao's standpoint on Tiananmen's balcony. Many experiments were conducted, and a huge model was made to ensure the calculation. 'Where there is a will there is a way', continues the report,

> based on Tiananmen's height and the angle of Chairman Mao's gaze (which would meet the Square at a 15-degree angle), the planners were finally able to decide the perspective of the picture. Members of the Headquarter of the National Day Celebration inspected the model and all considered it a major step toward the final success.[20]

The result was indeed impressive: in an area 274 metres east to west and 232 metres north to south (63,568 square metres in total), 19,441 people made up the national emblem, 32,661 formed the two dates, and the remaining 50,000 plus people constituted the background and decorative frames.[21] Next day the image they constructed appeared in newspapers throughout the country, and was praised as a major proof of Chinese people's 'unmatched confidence and strength in their effort to create a socialist society.' An unstated fact, however, is that none of the 100,000 people in the Square could see the picture with their own eyes during the National Day celebration – they were the material employed to make the picture.[22]

Exhibition Architecture

Thinking about the early 1950s, it seems that everything new and exciting came from the Soviet Union and anything from the Soviet Union was new and exciting. Repeated over and over in schools, parks and on streets was the slogan: 'The Soviet Union's Today is Our Tomorrow'. It was both exhilarating and uncanny to see your own future written on someone else's face, especially when this 'someone else' had yellow hair and pink skin. Nevertheless, the future suddenly became tangible and attainable. It was displayed in all sorts of propaganda posters and pictorials about the Soviet Union: the proud, broad-shouldered workers and peasants conquering the world with their invincible machines; the radiant, uniformed Young Pioneers marching through Red Square; the shining red star on the Kremlin's soaring clock tower – images that inspired admiration and encouraged imitation.

My mother, along with all her female colleagues in the Central Academy of Drama, immediately permed her hair into numerous curls to resemble those robust Russian heroines. Sometimes she asked me to keep her company when she went to 'do her hair' (*zuo toufa*) in a newly opened beauty salon not far from my home (called *Yileye*, 'Happiness and Relaxation'). It was an infinitely long and complex ordeal, during which her hair was divided into tiny batches, wrapped with pieces of paper and rolled onto special hairclips, each terminating in an electric wire and heated for a seemingly endless period. Her image in this last process is permanently printed in my mind: with her head suspended on a forest of electric wires hanging down from the ceiling, she sat motionless while reading a book on Shakespeare. (She was trained at Mills College and Mount Holyoke as a Shakespearian scholar.) I either read the comic books I brought with me or drew some pictures. But most of the time I simply stared at her strange image reflected in the mirror in front of her. Occasionally she would raise her eyes from her book and call out in an alarmed voice, and the hair stylist would run over to free a batch of her hair from a particular hairclip, which had begun to smoke.

Fused with my memory of my mother's hairstyle during that period was a kind of dress that people called a *bulaji* (a phonetic rendering of the Russian word). It had short puffed sleeves, a buttoned-up collar and a wide, floating skirt, and was always made of colourful fabric with cheerful patterns, again associated with the 'revolutionary spirit' of the Soviet Union. People went to buy such cloth in new shops called the Patterned Textile Company (*Huashabu Gongsi*), in which rolls of cloth of varying colours and designs were displayed above and behind long counters. I liked to go there to see and touch the cloth, especially the seersucker kind that bore geometric patterns on a puckered surface. Before the 1950s my mother used to wear *qipao* (a kind of tight, Chinese-style dress) made of plain, blue cloth. To me it was elegant but too serious. I liked to see her in cheerful *bulaji*, joking and laughing with her female colleagues, also dressed in *bulaji* but of different patterns and colours.

(Later on I learned that neither the permed hairstyle nor the *bulaji* were particularly Russian. Since the entire Western world had closed its doors to China, however, the Soviet Union and other socialist 'brother countries' provided the only channel for us to know anything foreign. Thus when my uncle, an oil painter who had studied art from a German teacher before 1949, wished to learn the Impressionists' methods in rendering colour, he visited a large Russian art exhibition [housed in Beijing's Workers' Palace] day after day to copy some landscape paintings. He didn't consider this way of learning a disadvantage, because Soviet artists, as he was told, had surpassed French Impressionists by 'utilizing' the latter's techniques in creating a much better, socialist art.)

Then came one of the most exciting events in the early 1950s, which elevated all admiration for the Soviet Union and expectations of it to an unprecedented height: the construction of the Soviet Union Exhibition Hall outside Xizhimen – the north-western gate of Beijing's city wall – from 1953 to 1954.[23] Excitement prevailed among Beijing's residents when the building gradually emerged under scaffolding. Rumours travelled fast about how many kilos of pure gold were used to gild its towering spire, and what intriguing mechanism lay hidden underneath its circular theatre. Finally the building opened with an enormous exhibition, showing off the Soviet Union's wondrous achievement in all aspects of its economic, cultural and social life. People competed to put their names on the waiting list to get in; but my father managed to obtain tickets for the whole family not only to see the show, the first week after it opened, but also to dine and watch a ballet in the exhibition compound.

To me that was an unforgettable trip filled with wonderful surprises. Although my father had described to us at length the magnificence of the building, which he had already visited on a restricted tour, I still fell spellbound when our bus passed Xizhimen's heavy, solemn gate and I suddenly saw a golden spire soaring above the surrounding sea of flat tile roofs. I had never seen anything so tall and dramatic, and had no idea that architecture could be so beautiful and sensual. The magical effect of the building increased as we approached: in front of the exhibition hall, an open plaza was embraced by the graceful curve of a gallery consisting of sixteen interconnected arches, each crowned with the emblem of a republic in the Soviet Union (illus. 76). Water spurted from a large fountain at the centre of the plaza, spreading outwards to form a crystal tent.

Entering the exhibition hall and travelling through its many rooms, I was less excited by the numerous machines and models on display than the rooms themselves, which were decorated with opulent gold mouldings and stained-glass windows. The most beautiful rooms were in the Moscow Restaurant, located in the west wing of the exhibition compound. Here, massive bronze-coloured columns bore lively images of animals. Ornate carvings in the different shapes of snowflakes projected from the ceiling. The main banquet hall had a reflecting pool in the middle. Large oil paintings on the walls depicted dense, misty Siberian forests; a mother bear led some baby bears to drink in a luminous spring. After dining in this magnificent place we went to see the ballet. Once again I was overpowered by the architecture – the theatre was an immense round space illuminated by crystal chandeliers. Seated far away from the stage, I saw only the dancers' tiny white bodies leaping and turning. But the music of Swan Lake was familiar; my mother and sister never failed to turn on the radio when it was broadcast. Exhausted, I fell asleep before the enchanted princess made her first appearance.

Although since then I have learned that the Soviet Union Exhibition Hall is a derivative, exposition-type building of little historical significance, I haven't been able to recapture the sensation I felt on that trip, even from some of the greatest monuments I have visited in different countries and cities. My only comparable experience – but of a different sort – was acquired on the tenth anniversary of the People's Republic in 1959. Earlier I recounted my participation in that National Day parade and events associated with it. Returning from the parade, two of my closest friends and I made an impromptu decision: we would make a pilgrimage to the Ten Great Buildings on foot that night.

   The Ten Great Buildings – a series of state-sponsored structures to be completed in Beijing in less than a year before the anniversary – had a magical effect on us throughout 1959, since they seemed to stand for everything the Great

76 Capital
Exhibition Hall
(former Soviet
Union Exhibition
Hall) in 1957,
Beijing.

Leap Forward was about. Now, looking back, it is clear that what attracted Chinese people to the Great Leap Forward was exactly its impracticality and theatricality: it was a Utopian vision posing as a socio-economical programme, a fantasy materialized in performances. Especially to young students like us, it transformed boring school life into endless games and play. We loved to spend night after night smelting steel in primitive furnaces that we had built ourselves – in effect converting usable steel products back into their original material. We enjoyed reading the industrial and agricultural miracles reported in newspapers, and composed similar tales for writing assignments. We cheered the government decision to 'eliminate the four evils' (i.e., rats, sparrows, flies and mosquitoes), a campaign that inspired all sorts of ingenious methods to destroy petty insects and animals. It was most fun to catch sparrows, birds said to have an abnormal appetite for grain. The most effective way to kill them, it turned out, was to have the whole population of Beijing stationed everywhere and making noise simultaneously – blowing horns, beating washbasins, firing firecrackers. Because sparrows could only fly short distances, they would simply drop dead from exhaustion if they couldn't find a place to land.

In the same spirit we cheered the decision to construct the Ten Great Buildings, which, as we heard, would set world records in both architectural grandeur and speed of construction. Our interest in the project was encouraged by the school, which organized a special tour for us to visit the famed Architectural School of Tsing-hua University, which was entrusted with the design of some of the buildings. Spirited young architects there showed us a model of the National Theatre, and proudly told us that they had designed the building and made the model in less than two weeks. We were duly impressed and were later disappointed when this structure disappeared from the list of the Ten Great Buildings: it was not going to be built after all.

My school, a boarding school called 101 High, was located in Beijing's northwest suburbs, some 20 kilometres from the centre. The three of us sneaked out of the school around 10 p.m., when the campus fell silent, and started to talk only after we reached the street outside. Wearing our new uniform and the hard-top cap, we marched down the street in military style, singing every revolutionary song we knew over and over. But this exercise soon exhausted us and forced us to slow down our pace. Finally, after stopping many times, we arrived at Tiananmen Square at 2 a.m. After walking the whole day (including the parade) we could now barely stand. But as we looked at the monuments around us we felt like heroes. The Square was covered by half a million people during the day and could hardly be seen; now it was nearly empty and belonged to us alone.

We sat down in front of the Monument to the People's Heroes, speechless and transfixed. Afterwards we walked along Chang'an Avenue to the Beijing Train Station, one of the Ten Great Buildings. Having heard so much about its grand escalator – the first such device in China – we were eager to try it ourselves. We rode the escalator up and down some twenty times, and left the building at dawn. We slept all the way back to school on buses.

The 'Ten Great Buildings' Project

Carried out from 1958 to 1959, this project was the second major effort in Beijing to legitimize the new state by constructing monumental architecture. It was a logical extension of the Monument to the People's Heroes: unveiled in 1958, this earlier monument honoured the past – the martyrs who had dedicated their lives to liberating the Chinese people. The Ten Great Buildings, on the other hand, honoured the present by demonstrating the achievement that a spirited people had made in merely a decade since their liberation. The sequence of these two groups of monuments attests to a historical pattern that can be traced back to at least the eleventh century BC: ancient texts record that the Zhou's conquest of the previous Shang dynasty was followed by a period of stabilizing the new rule and pacifying the whole country. Only after this period of consolidation did the Zhou celebrate its victory through various activities, including constructing a capital and new ritual structures. For this reason, the Zhou king who conquered the Shang was given the posthumous title Wu, meaning 'martial' or 'military'; the king responsible for constructing the new capital and buildings was called Cheng ('accomplishment').

To Mao and other leaders of the People's Republic of China, a similar moment of accomplishment was reached before the regime celebrated its tenth anniversary in 1959. During the decade from 1949 to 1958 they mobilized a series of campaigns to stabilize the new-born country. In the domain of domestic economy, the First Five-Year Plan was inaugurated in 1953 and, according to official statistics, achieved a dramatic increase in industrial production across a broad sector of goods; the quota set for the five-year period was attained one year early, in 1956.[24] The same year also witnessed the abolition of private ownership: all businesses became, either partially or entirely, the property of the state. Citing these and other signs of progress, Mao declared in the eighth congress of the Chinese Communist Party, held in September that year: 'The transition from neo-democracy to socialism has now been completed; Chinese history has entered a new period of developing an all-round socialist society.'

This then led to the Great Leap Forward. Rejecting any economic theory and long-term planning as backward conservatism, this campaign relied instead on the 'revolutionary enthusiasm' of the masses – it was believed that a spiritually transformed people could create an economic miracle with little help from modern science and technology.[25] The Great Leap Forward began in January 1958. In September Beijing's mayor Peng Zhen announced an important decision: to celebrate the forthcoming tenth anniversary of the People's Republic, Ten Great Buildings, or *Shida jianzhu* in Chinese, would be designed, constructed and completed within one year.

Unlike the Monument to the People's Heroes, the Ten Great Buildings are functional structures serving various political, cultural and civil purposes. They can be considered political monuments and 'exhibition architecture' owing to their inherent symbolic and ceremonial tasks, their strategic locations in the capital and their expositional architectural style. Significantly, half of these structures are museums and exhibition halls, including the Museum of Chinese History (see illus. 86), the Museum of Agriculture (illus. 77), the Military Museum (illus. 78), the Cultural Palace of the Nationalities (illus. 79) and the National Art Gallery (illus. 80).[26] The other five – the Great Hall of the People (see illus. 88), the Beijing Train Station (illus. 81), and three guesthouses for foreign leaders, overseas Chinese and minority Chinese – also contained special exhibition spaces and abundant works of art. Such overwhelming interest in 'display', an interest also made obvious by the buildings' architectural styles, which emulate traditional monuments in both Chinese and European traditions, resulted from a sense of accomplishment and the desire to demonstrate it. If the Monument to the People's Heroes had helped the leaders of New China to redefine Beijing's centrality, now they were ready to reorientate the entire city by constructing groups of prominent landmarks.

For this purpose, the locations of the Ten Great Buildings were highly significant (illus. 82). Positioned along major traffic roads running east to west, these buildings – gigantic, cement structures such as the city had never seen – finally transformed the old Beijing into a new city by radically altering its orientation and appearance. As mentioned earlier, traditional Beijing was characterized, first of all, by its symmetrical layout centred on a north–south axis (see illus. 10). A major change during the early twentieth century was the opening of the city to east–west traffic, which became possible when the imperial power fell. Especially after 1949, Tiananmen, the front gate of the Imperial City, became Mao's platform to review mass rallies. Running east–west in front of Tiananmen, Chang'an Avenue increased in both width and length, burying the old north–south Imperial Way underneath. This transformation was completed in 1959: with seven of the Ten Great Buildings constructed on either side of Tiananmen, Chang'an Avenue was now the site of most of Beijing's monuments and manifested the capital's splendour. This avenue then became the axis of the new Beijing.

Although no official rationale was provided to explain the locations of the Ten Great Buildings, the correlation between a structure's identity and location suggests two possible factors in selecting its site. First, it seems that differences existed between the ten buildings in terms of their political priority and determined the buildings' 'closeness' to Tiananmen. Of the ten monuments, the two grandest and most important – the Great Hall of the People and the Museum of Chinese History – are located across Chang'an Avenue from Tiananmen to define the east and west limits of Tiananmen Square. Five less privileged monuments (the Cultural Palace of the Nationalities, the Military Museum, the Beijing Train Station, the State Guest House and the Hotel of the Nationalities) stand a little away, but still along Chang'an Avenue.[27] As for the National Art Gallery and the Hotel of Overseas Chinese, their locations on a parallel avenue to the north attest to their even lower status in the political hierarchy.

Second, the groupings and locations of the Ten Great Buildings seem to correspond to the distinctions made in the official social theory between the 'economic foundation' and the 'superstructure', and between 'primary' and 'secondary' elements of the superstructure. All the seven monuments along

Chang'an Avenue are dedicated to politics, law, history and military force – crucial aspects of the 'primary superstructure'.[28] The avenue to the north, the name of which is derived from the May Fourth cultural movement, provides a collective site for institutions and places related to art, literature, education and entertainment – elements of the 'secondary superstructure'. Along this second avenue, therefore, one finds the Palace Museum, the famous parks Beihai and Coal Hill, the old Beijing University, the Bureau of Cultural Relics, the National Art Gallery, the National Library and the Ministry of Culture. A third avenue runs from east to west across the northern part of the city. At its

110

79 Cultural Palace of Nationalities, Beijing, completed in 1959.

eastern end stands the Museum of Agriculture (illus. 77); at the western end is the old Soviet Union Exhibition Hall (illus. 76), which was turned into a major industrial exhibition site.[29] These two buildings at the city's rear thus stand for the 'economic foundation' of the country.

It would be wrong, however, to think that the Ten Great Buildings were merely static representations of the ideology and structure of the state. Rather, their construction process (especially their speedy completion in ten months) was taken as a supreme demonstration of the basic tenet of the Great Leap Forward, that a mass movement mobilized by Communist ideology could overcome any

80 National Art Gallery, Beijing, completed in 1962.

difficulty to achieve victory. To Zhang Bo, a principal architect of the project, its success owed much to a military strategy that the People's Liberation Army developed during the civil war, called *jizhong bingli da jianmiezhan* ('concentrating one's military strength to conduct a battle of annihilation'). Applied to the Ten Great Buildings project, it means utilizing all available means and resources to accomplish a seemingly impossible task.[30] A recently published report shows how this strategy was practised literally throughout the project.[31]

According to this document, the Party's decision to construct the Ten Great Buildings was delivered to Beijing's municipal government on 5 September 1958. Three days later, more than a thousand architects and engineers in the capital were apprised of this decision at a grand 'mobilization meeting'. Even before this meeting, on 7 September, a list of architectural experts around the country had already been drafted and telegraphed to sixteen provinces and cities, ordering them to report to Beijing by 10 September. Upon their arrival they were told, together with their Beijing colleagues, that they had five days to come up with initial designs for the buildings. After this task was accomplished, a second round of the designing process took another five days, resulting in more than a hundred drawings. These drawings were reviewed on 20 and 21 September by Beijing's municipal leaders, whose opinions became the basis for a third round of revisions. When the minister of the Ministry of Culture (Qian Junrui) and the chairman of the National Association of Literature and Arts (Zhou Yang) came to examine the results on 26 September, however, they found the designs still too conservative and traditional. Attributing the problem to the architects' 'professional baggage', they suggested bringing in younger architects and students, whose lack of experience would promise fresh, unconventional thinking. This suggestion was supported by Premier Zhou Enlai, and a set of new designs was made collectively by old and young architects in three days.

112

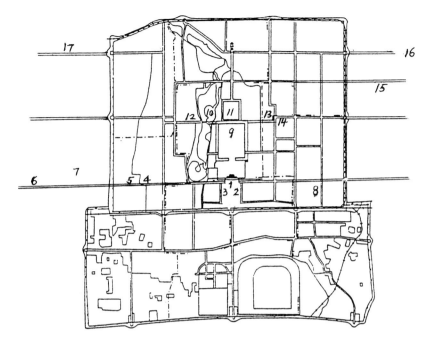

82 Locations of the Ten Great Buildings and other monuments in Beijing:
1. Tiananmen
2. Museum of Chinese History
3. Great Hall of the People
4. Cultural Palace of the Nationalities
5. Hotel of the Nationalities
6. Military Museum
7. State Guest House
8. Beijing Train Station
9. Palace Museum
10. Beihai Park
11. Coal Hill
12. Beijing Library
13. National Art Gallery
14. Hotel of Overseas Chinese
15. Workers' Stadium
16. Museum of Agriculture
17. Capital Exhibition Hall (former Soviet Union Exhibition Hall)

Under a zealous, demanding political leadership, such collective teamwork characterized the whole architectural campaign. In fact, owing to the project's extremely tight schedule (all the ten buildings were supposed to be completed in August 1959), final designs for a structure were never achieved before the construction work started. In many cases, plans were constantly altered as a building took shape. This was especially clear in the case of the Great Hall of the People, an enormous, complex structure that presented many technical challenges: debates about the layout and engineering of its above-ground section continued even after the foundation work was finished.[32] But the unlimited supply of manpower and materials – conditions made possible by the highest level of government – eventually enabled the construction team to meet the deadline. We are told that 6 major architectural institutes and universities oversaw the details in designing the structure,[33] 34 large companies around the country made it their top priority to provide architectural materials and equipment, and more than 10,000 experienced workers, artists and craftsmen were brought to Beijing to build and decorate the monument.

This short review makes it clear that the conception of the Ten Great Buildings project as a 'mass movement' (*qunzhong yundong*) originated with the political authorities: it was the Party that determined the project's objective and deadline, and mobilized the whole country to meet the task (illus. 83). But this logic is deliberately twisted in the numerous official reports of the project, which all emphasize the initiative and spontaneity of the project's participants and define it as a 'mass movement' based on these criteria. Hailing the project as a supreme demonstration of the revolutionary spirit of the Chinese people, the authors also stress its educational purpose: the construction of the Ten Great Buildings enabled the workers and architects to discover their own strength and creativity, hence consolidating their self-identity as 'revolutionary masses' (*geming qunzhong*). The following statement from a report by Zhao Dongri, the chief architect of the Great Hall of the People, is an example of this rhetoric:

> As soon as the Party announced its decision to restructure Tiananmen Square and to construct a series of monuments, including the Great Hall of the People, architects and construction workers around the country welcomed this glorious assignment with great confidence, actively taking part in a national competition to design the buildings and throwing themselves into a mighty collective campaign of architectural creation.
>
> The buildings' architects, designers, and sound, lighting and electric engineers came from Beijing, Shanghai, Nanjing, Wuhan, Tianjin and other cities and provinces. The participants in the campaign included men and women, young and old, and workers, students and professors. In merely a single month, they came up with numerous initial proposals. In the case of the Great Hall of the People, 84 floor plans and 189 elevation plans were proposed. The final design emerged from careful, collective discussions and extensive revisions of these proposals. Only through such collective effort could the construction begin on time, and could the construction team accomplish this glorious task entrusted to it by the Party.
>
> All the participants in the campaign displayed immense initiative and creativity, making great contributions to the cause of socialist architecture. At the same time, by taking part in the campaign they also received a profound socialist education. Their revolutionary awareness was heightened, and they built a new foundation for themselves to achieve even greater victory.[34]

It is interesting to think about the source of this kind of description and reasoning – a rhetoric that conceives the construction of a monument as a spontaneous, collective expression of a people for a shared political cause. Mao's interpretation of Marxist historiography definitely provided an immediate theoretical foundation: as cited in the epigraph of this Chapter, he considered the people to be 'the motive forces of world history'. But many examples from ancient Chinese history also show startling parallels, suggesting deeper roots of this rhetoric in traditional political discourse. Once again, the initial archetype was set up by the Zhou in the first millennium BC. A sacred hymn performed in its ancestral temple, known as the Ling tai ('Spiritual Terrace'), traced the Zhou's rise to dynastic power. The hymn begins with King Wen constructing the terrace near the capital, Hao, and ends with the victory of his son, King Wu, in conquering the Shang. Interestingly, it describes the construction of the structure – a holy place where the Zhou kings received the mandate to rule – as a collective, spontaneous effort of the Zhou people, and especially emphasizes the speedy completion of the project:

114

When he built the Spiritual Terrace,
When he planned it and founded it,
All the people worked at it,
In less than a day they finished it.

When he built it, there was no goading;
Yet the people came in their throngs.
The king was in the Spiritual Park,
Where doe and stag lay hid.[35]

The Zhou, the last archaic society in Bronze Age China, fell in the third century BC. What followed was an intense struggle to establish a bureaucratic system under imperial rule. This new political order was given a symbolic, architectural form: Ming tang (Bright Hall).[36] It was said that this mysterious building was invented by ancient sages as the most authoritative symbol of sovereignty, but its form and structure had been forgotten by the end of the Zhou and had to be restored. A person able to accomplish this historical mission would prove himself the legitimate successor of the former sage kings; his success in rebuilding Bright Hall would be a definite sign of Heaven's approval of his ruling mandate. A Han dynasty text glorifies the building in these words:

Bright Hall is constructed for the emperor to observe Heaven and seasonal orders, to carry forward the virtuous ancestral rites, to confirm the contributions of royal predecessors and feudal lords, to declare the principles of honouring the old, and to promote the education of the young. Here, the emperor receives feudal lords and selects learned scholars in order to illuminate the regulations. Here, living people come to demonstrate their special skills, and the dead are offered various sacrifices according to their merits. Bright Hall is also the Palace of Great Learning, equipped completely with the four academies and all the government departments. It is like the North Pole, which stays in its own place while countless stars surround it and a myriad creations assist it. Bright Hall is thus the origin of administration and education, and the source of changes and transformations. It brings all things into its unifying light, and this is why it is called Bright Hall.[37]

More than one Han emperor attempted this monument in the second and first centuries BC, but it was Wang Mang (a royal relative who finally replaced the Han with his own dynasty Xin) who succeeded in rebuilding it, based on exegeses of Confucian texts. Recorded in historical writings and rediscovered during a recent archaeological excavation, Wang Mang's Bright Hall had a complex, three-storey building set in a courtyard 235 metres square. Further surrounded by a circular moat, 360 metres in diameter, the whole architectural complex must have taken months or even years to complete; its highly abstract, geometric structure must have resulted from minute calculation and careful design (illus. 84, 85). But this is not what the historical records tell us: a contemporary document – a memorial that praises the hall as a manifestation of Wang Mang's extraordinary virtue – characterizes its construction as a spontaneous and speedy act of the people: more than a hundred thousand commoners and Confucian scholars gathered south of the capital Chang'an, of their own accord, and completed the hall in twenty days.[38] Clearly, this memorial, like the monument itself, was part of a larger political project that facilitated Wang Mang's advance to the throne.[39]

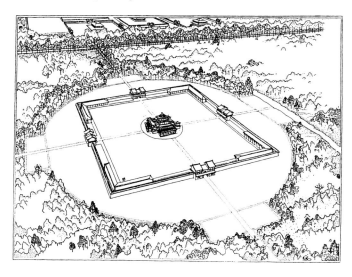

84 A reconstruction of Wang Mang's Bright Hall, early 1st century AD.

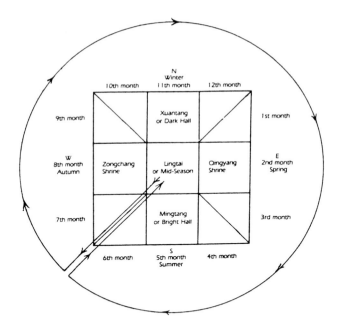

85 A diagram
showing the
twelve rooms of
Bright Hall and
the imperial
positions during
the twelve
months.

The Great Hall of the People and the Museum of Chinese History

The flagships of the Ten Great Buildings, these two mammoth structures formed a pair in 1959 to flank the newly restructured Tiananmen Square (see illus. 17). Their symbolism was also complementary: as mentioned in the first Chapter of this book, facing each other east–west, they added to the Square a second axis of juxtaposition between past and present (see diagram on p. 35). The first axis, linking Tiananmen and the Monument to the People's Heroes, juxtaposed living Communist leaders with their predecessors. (Significantly, on National Day and other important occasions, huge portraits of Marx, Engels, Lenin, Stalin and Sun Yat-sen were erected in the Square, joining the Monument to face Tiananmen to the north.) The Great Hall and the Museum of History shifted the focus of representation from leaders – representatives of the people – to the people themselves. Entering the Museum, one immediately encounters a gilded inscription of Mao's famous motto: 'The people, and the people alone, are the motive forces of world history'. As for the Great Hall of the People, its name (chosen by Mao) identifies its supposed owner and user.

These two monuments constitute an imbalanced pair, however. Zhou Enlai did not bother to elaborate on a crucial instruction he gave on 6 October 1958, while reviewing the sixth round of designs of the Ten Great Buildings: 'The Museum of History and the Great Hall should be basically symmetrical. But whereas the Great Hall should be solid, the museum should be empty inside, with less floor space.'[40] A simple comparison demonstrates how literally this instruction was carried out: roughly identical in external dimensions (the Great Hall is 336 metres north–south and 174 metres east–west; the Museum is 313 metres north–south and 149 metres east–west), the former's floor space (171,800 square metres) almost triples the latter's (65,152 square metres). It is possible that the premier made the instruction based on practical concerns: it might be too costly or time-consuming to build the Museum the same size as the Great Hall. But it is also clear that in his mind, the Great Hall would serve actual state functions; the Museum needed to match it only in appearance, not in substance. This of course does not mean that he deemed the Museum unimportant. Rather, its importance was mainly symbolic and could be expressed by an architectural design that took the building's image as its point of departure.

In this way, the Museum of Chinese History exemplifies a primary feature of the five exhibition halls among the Ten Great Buildings: their emphasis on visual monumentality over their usefulness as actual exhibition sites. In other words, what they exhibit are mainly their own architectural appearances; the exhibitions they held were often confined in narrow, crowded galleries. Standing in front of the Museum of History, for example, a visitor was dwarfed by an immense colonnade 100 metres wide and 33 metres tall, which creates the illusion of an oversized façade (illus. 86). Examining the building's elevation and floor plans, we find that such illusionism actually constitutes a general strategy in designing the monument: extending the colonnade, long exhibition halls define the museum's exterior boundaries, outlining a sprawling structure that is largely empty inside (illus. 87.1). The same strategy guided the designs of the other Ten Great Buildings. Many of them are topped by pavilions with traditional, glazed tile roofs – expensive architectural features of little practical use (see illus. 77–81). Each building impresses the onlooker with a broad, pyramid-shaped front. But this grand frontal image is disproportional to the building's pitiful depth, and disappears completely if one views the building from the side. Each structure occupies a large area, but its complex floor plan serves only to maximize the exterior surface (illus. 88).

In terms of interior space, all these museums and exhibition halls have large, richly decorated foyers for ceremonial activities. The galleries, in contrast,

86 Museum of Chinese History, Beijing, completed in 1959.

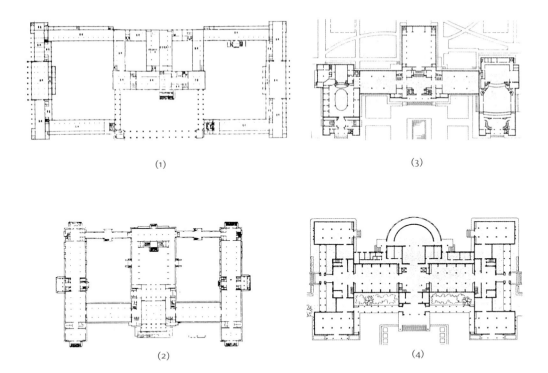

(1)

(3)

(2)

(4)

are unadorned and rigid, conceived as monotonous, uniform containers of exhibition items displayed on walls and in glass cases. Until 2002 the Museum of History consisted of two institutions, the Museum of Chinese History and the Museum of Revolutionary History, under a single roof. The two permanent exhibitions on display in its two symmetrical wings, one on traditional Chinese history and the other on modern Chinese history, constituted a continuous historical narrative. They were divided by the year 1840, the date of the First Opium War, which marked China's entrance into a global, colonial era. Before a museum reform was introduced in the 1980s,[41] both exhibitions featured abundant explanatory captions and illustrations; their content was dictated by a standard version of Chinese history compiled by official historians and sanctioned by the government. Written in a language suitable for people on different educational levels, this official history was taught on every grade level from primary school to graduate school, and guided historical representations in any artistic form. As specific educative institutions, the exhibitions in the Museum of Chinese History thus functioned 'as repositories of the already known', in Tony Bennett's words: 'They are places for telling, and telling again, the stories of our time, ones which have become a *doxa* through their endless repetition.'[42]

Such 'stories of our time' were actually about any time – the whole of Chinese historical scholarship in the 1950s and '60s was dominated by Mao's

87 Floor plans of four of the Ten Great Buildings: 1. Museum of Chinese History 2. Military Museum 3. Cultural Palace of the Nationalities 4. National Art Gallery

teaching that 'the past must serve the present' (*gu wei jin yong*). Schooled in this didactic tradition, the curators in the Museum of Chinese History were not concerned about the fidelity of their representation of the past 'as it really was'. Rather, they worked hard to contextualize the exhibitions within a current historical discourse and its associated ideological affiliations – a tactic that Patrick Wright has termed a 'past–present alignment'. As he explains:

> This alignment makes it possible to think of historical development as complete, a process which finds its accomplishment in the present. Historical development is here conceived as a cumulative process which has delivered the nation into the present as its manifest accomplishment. Both celebratory and complacent, it produces a sense that 'we' [i.e., the visitors as the people] are the achievement of history.[43]

Although such 'alignment' is a general characteristic of representations of national histories around the world, Beijing's Museum of Chinese History was completely uninhibited about this tactic when it was first built in 1959. It openly rejected the function of a history museum as a neutral sheltering space of historical knowledge, and its exhibitions aggressively pressed visitors to internalize a familiar story about the struggle and triumph of the people – a story that started from Primitive Society and ended with the establishment of the People's Republic of China. 'Like the reader in a detective novel', writes Bennett, 'it is toward the end point that the visitor's activity is directed . . . For the visitor, reaching the point at which the museum's narrative culminates is a matter of doing as much as of seeing. The narrative machinery of the museum's "backtelling" took the form of an itinerary whose completion was experienced as a task requiring urgency and expedition.'[44]

At the end of the exhibitions in the Museum of Chinese History, the visitor reaches a point between past and present. To find the present – the consequence of the people's struggle and triumph as shown in the exhibitions –

88 Great Hall of the People, Beijing, completed in 1959.

89 Principal auditorium in the Great Hall of the People.

he needs to turn his eyes toward the monument across the Square: the Great Hall of the People (illus. 88).

89 Principal auditorium in the Great Hall of the People.

Unlike the Museum of History, which holds more courtyards than gallery space, the Great Hall is packed with rooms behind its colonnaded façade, including a Great Assembly Hall for Ten Thousand People (illus. 89), a State Banquet Hall for 5,000 guests to have a sit-down dinner, a Grand Friendship Hall of 2,500 square metres, a Small Assembly Hall furnished with 600 armchairs, and more than 50 reception and conference lounges on different levels and of different sizes. The building is multi-functional and can be used for any important event, but it is its primary identity as the location of the National People's Congress and the home of the Congress' Standing Committee that has determined its architectural form and decoration. Generally, its design reinforces three interconnected significances of the building as an officially sanctioned monument for 'the people' of the People's Republic: (1) it represents the various regions and ethnic groups of the country; (2) it represents the country as the union of these regions and groups; and (3) it represents the Party as the leadership of this union.

The first significance is realized primarily by a group of 34 Regional Halls (*Difang ting*) named after the country's 34 provinces, autonomous regions and municipalities. Although much smaller than the auditoriums and often neglected in scholarly discussions, they possess an indispensable role in the monument's representation of China and the Chinese people. Here is how an official guide to the Great Hall introduces these rooms:

These halls are designed and decorated by artists and architects from different parts of the country. They collect in one place the local or regional cultures from across the country, concentrate and exhibit the natural

90 'Regional
products' in
Hunan Hall, one
of the Regional
Halls in the
Great Hall of
the People.

scenery and cultural life of the local people, and symbolize the unity and unification of the Chinese nation.[45]

The rooms thus have a significance much greater than their function as meeting places of representatives of various regions during the National People's Congress. To state this significance plainly, they stand for local people by classifying them into a political geography, thereby reinforcing this political geography and its associated administrative system. The chief means of this representation is to display a region's famous scenery and/or products in a room named after this region. Thus, huge paintings in the Beijing Hall and Hong Kong Hall showcase the Forbidden City in broad daylight and Victoria Harbour on a starry night. Antique bronzes in the Hunan Hall and Shaanxi Hall boast of the ancient cultural heritage of these two provinces (illus. 90). The Xinjiang Hall displays 'the largest Oriental carpet in Beijing', made by Uygur craftsmen. The Tibet Hall covers its walls with Thangka-like murals. Produced by artists and artisans past and present in different localities, these images and objects are gathered in the Great Hall to symbolize the allegiance of these regions to the central government.

Although official documents invariably interpret these rooms in terms of the Party's effort to establish a 'socialist unity' of regions and nationalities, students of Chinese history easily find in them vestiges of an ancient 'trib-ute' system, which started from the very beginning of China's dynastic his-tory. 'The Tribute of Yu', a treatise in the *Book of Documents*, records that when Yu founded the first Chinese dynasty, the Xia, he divided the country into nine provinces, each defined by natural boundaries and ranked by its contribution of revenue. The rest of the text identifies the people of each region and their 'special goods', which constituted their tribute to the ruler of China.[46]

Another text, also referring to Yu's unification of the country but employ-ing an allegorical language, tells about his creation of a set of tripods (ritual vessels), which then became the most important symbol of political authority in ancient China:

> In the past, when the Xia dynasty was distinguished for its virtue, the
> distant regions put their things into pictures and the nine provinces sent
> in copper as tribute. The tripods were cast to present those things. One
> hundred different things were presented, so that the people could distin-
> guish divine from evil … Hereby a harmony was secured between high
> and low, and all enjoyed the blessing of Heaven.[47]

The idea that the tripods legitimated the implementation of a centralized power over the whole country is expressed symbolically: these ritual vessels bore the 'things' of various regions, possibly their emblems or totems. The act of sending their things to the Xia demonstrated these regions' submission to Xia authority. The engraving of their things on the tripods meant that they had entered into a single political entity. After the tripods were made, all these regions were iden-tified as 'divine', whereas all enemy tribes and kingdoms (whose things were

91 Central Hall in the Great Hall of the People, with one of the two clocks on the walls showing standard 'Beijing time'.

absent from the tripods) were sanctioned as 'evil'. This political process is also signified by the tripods' materiality and manufacture: the precious copper used to make them was sent from the 'nine provinces'. When the copper was mixed and cast into a single set of vessels, it was understood that those who presented the material were also assimilated into a single unity.

Embracing the 34 Regional Halls as well as their collections of regional goods and images, the Great Hall of the People, like the ancient tripods, can also be considered a coercive representation of diverse peoples as a unified body. To reinforce this symbolism of the monument, specific images and objects are staged in strategic locations in the building to highlight the idea of national unification. One such group of objects is a pair of clocks in the Grand Central Hall (illus. 91). This spacious room (75 metres wide and 48 metres deep) connects the building's main entrance with the Grand Assembly Hall on the first floor. All members of the People's Congress must cross it before entering the auditorium. As they do so, they are received by the clocks installed on the two side walls, calibrating their watches according to the clocks' standard 'Beijing time'. Significantly, unlike other large countries in the world that are divided into multiple time zones, the People's Republic of China has only a single time zone: every region in the country, from Manchuria to Xinjiang, takes Beijing time as its local time. The clocks in the Great Hall of the People thus serve to dismiss regional differences and impose a strict measure of uniformity upon the local.

National unity is again the central theme of a painting entitled *This Land So Rich in Beauty*, a line from Mao's 1956 poem 'Snow' (illus. 92). At 5.5 metres tall and 9 metres wide, it is the largest of all the paintings hung in the Great Hall, and its position above the grand stairway leading to the banquet hall makes it the focal image of the entire building. I have mentioned that pictures in the Regional Halls invariably depict local scenes. Such geographical specificity disappears in *This Land So Rich in Beauty*, created jointly by Fu Baoshi from Nanjing and Guan Shanyue from Guangzhou. It is said that after several early drafts by these two artists were rejected, Chen Yi, Minister of Foreign Affairs and a poet-general, helped them conceptualize Mao's poem. He told them that the beauty of the nation must transcend local reality, and the painting should synthesize different places and times:

> It should depict lands on both sides of the Great Wall, the full length of the Yellow River, the snowy north-western plateaus, the luxuriant landscape of the south and the remote Eastern Sea. The idea is that this painting should incorporate features of China's four quarters as well as different scenes of the four seasons. Only then can it compress the magnificent landscape of the motherland in a single composition.[48]

Inspired, the two artists created a composite landscape in what has been hailed as a masterpiece of Chinese socialist art. This landscape is brightened by a red sun rising in the east, an obvious allusion to the Party's leadership over the country.[49]

92 Fu Baoshi and Guan Shanyue, *This Land So Rich in Beauty*, mural in the Great Hall of the People, 1959.

Another image of comparable significance in the Great Hall is the red star on the ceiling of the grand auditorium (see illus. 89). From the beginning, the size and design of this auditorium – the largest and most important space in the building – became the topic of constant discussion and debate. Although the intention of building a 'ten-thousand-people auditorium' surfaced early on, some architects questioned such an excessive scale. The original idea finally prevailed, however. The reasons were found in the auditorium's symbolism as an architectural manifestation of the Chinese nation and people, as Zhao Dongri articulated in a report published immediately after the completion of the monument:

> A basic fact is that our country is a great nation with 650 million people. Consequently, we have a large number of people's representatives and heroes. For them to gather together to discuss important state affairs and to exchange their experience and heroic deeds, we need an auditorium that can hold 10,000 people and a banquet hall that can entertain 5,000 guests. Of course, auditoriums and banquet halls of such size have never been, and could not have been attempted in the past; nor do they exist in the present world. [We have built them] because of the immensity of our country and because we live in a socialist era, which surpasses all other historical eras.[50]

If the auditorium itself symbolizes China and her people, the design of its ceiling emphasizes the Party's unchallenged authority over the country:

> The auditorium's expansive, curved ceiling alludes to the infinite space of the universe. In its centre, an illuminated red star made of plexiglass stands for the leadership of the Party. The star emits radiating rays of

golden light, and is encircled by gilded sunflower patterns and again by waves outlined with recessed light. The message of the decorative scheme is clear: all the people unite themselves around the Party, following the Party to advance the revolution from one victory to another.[51]

However pompous and ideologically driven, these words are not merely political propaganda. The reason is that in 1959 many Chinese, including a majority of the architects and designers of the Great Hall of the People, still held a romantic notion about the revolution, genuinely believing that they were creating a society of the people and for the people. The Great Hall and other monuments from the era were joint products of this popular idealism and the Party's political agenda. But when the Chairman Mao Memorial Hall was built seventeen years later in 1977, such earlier hopes for prosperity and trust in the Party had largely been destroyed by the Cultural Revolution, making this new monument an opportunist event motivated by purely political needs.

The Chairman Mao Memorial Hall

No other time in my life has been as depressing and hopeless as 1975–6, the final years of the Cultural Revolution. It was like a deadly plague had finally arrived, consuming anything left in a battered battlefield. Paralysed, we watched its coming in terror but couldn't even escape. Few people were brave enough to call it a plague; most people internalized it – you saw it in their sullen faces and suspicious eyes, symptoms of what old folks called a 'death aura' (si qi).

All along we had been hearing about deaths – deaths in prisons and labour camps, deaths in violent conflicts between 'revolutionary factions', and deaths by suicide. But we now learned of deaths, not only through rumours, but also from the front page of the newspapers and TV broadcasts: the plague had reached the leaders residing deep inside Zhongnanhai, finishing them off in a relentless, methodical procession.

It started with Dong Biwu, a founder of the Chinese Communist Party and President of the People's Republic since 1968. He died in April 1975, followed in December by Kang Sheng, a long-time chief of secret police and one of the most feared campaigners of the Cultural Revolution. The next month saw the death of Premier Zhou Enlai amidst the contempt of his ultra-leftist enemies. A few months later Zhu De died. The father of the Red Army, he was equal to Mao before 1949 in the Communist leadership. His death in July 1976, to many people, foreshadowed Mao's own demise two months later. By this time the mournful, tear-jerking National Dirge, broadcast whenever a 'state death' (guo sang) was announced, had become part of normal life. But people still cried – and cried again. It was difficult to know what they were crying for.

Unknowingly, death came to determine the course of history and the fate of the people, and funerals became chief sites of emotional expression and political discourse. Thus when a memorial service for Zhou Enlai was rejected by the hateful Madam Mao and her comrades, a grassroots movement emerged in the guise of a mass funeral for the deceased prime minister. Thus to many participants in this movement, Mao's death accidentally saved them when it stopped a political persecution of Zhou's sympathizers.

It was therefore with a strange, mixed feeling that we joined the construction of Mao's memorial hall. To us he was still a larger-than-life, visionary figure. But his vision had lost human proportions and nearly destroyed the country. Organized by our work unit to participate in so-called voluntary service, we went in teams to Tiananmen Square to transport bricks and plant trees. We were promised that we would see Mao's remains when the memorial hall was completed. But only 26 years later did I get there, when I had to finish my research for this book.

Few comments will be made here about the Chairman Mao Memorial Hall: three detailed official reports on its structure, decoration and construction have enabled a number of Western scholars to write on it.[52] But above all, this monument is insignificant, even for documenting the Party's beliefs and policies in the post-Mao era. This era began with Mao's death in September 1976 and the subsequent fall of the Gang of Four headed by his wife Jiang Qing. Hua Guofeng, the man responsible for arresting Jiang, was installed as the Party Chairman. In modern Chinese history, Hua's short rule bridged the Cultural Revolution with the reform era of Deng Xiaoping, which formally began in 1978.[53] To many of his contemporaries, Hua was a product of the Cultural Revolution and a believer in Mao. Most tellingly, he legitimated his position as Mao's successor solely on the basis of a private arrangement that Mao had made on his deathbed – allegedly on a scrap of paper Mao wrote to him: 'With you in charge I am at ease'. He evoked Mao's words whenever possible on public occasions, and named himself the chief editor of a new volume of Mao's writings, published in 1977 with great fanfare. But as historians have noted, all of these may have been an elaborate political façade, thoughtfully constructed to sustain public support. Hua actually made some initial economic and political reforms, but did so only under a Maoist cloak.[54]

93 Chairman Mao Memorial Hall, completed in 1977.

The huge Memorial Hall of Mao in Tiananmen Square, which Hua spared
no expense to build in 1977, served the same pragmatic purpose (illus. 93).[55]
Its inherent pragmatism, in turn, dismissed any experimentation and innova-
tion in its conception and design. Reports of this monument once again
boasted of its speedy completion in six months, its construction as a collective,
spontaneous effort of the revolutionary masses, and its minute political symbolism down to every detail in its decoration (illus. 94, 95). Modelled upon earlier
writings on the Ten Great Buildings, however, these formulaic descriptions were

96 Mao's statue in the Chairman Mao Memorial Hall, 1977.

now clichés even to their writers. If these reports served any real purpose, it is that they concealed the reactionary nature of the monument, which in reality abandoned the earlier rhetoric of representing the people. What it displays is Mao, and only Mao. The monument is therefore a product of the Mao cult in the post-Mao era, a ghost posed as divine.

Entering the Memorial Hall from the north, one faces a white marble statue of Mao seated in an armchair, backed by a huge tapestry showing a panorama of China (illus. 96); the design probably combines ideas derived from the

97 Mao's corpse in the Chairman Mao Memorial Hall.

Lincoln Memorial in Washington, DC, and the painting *This Land So Rich in Beauty* in the Great Hall of the People. Behind this worship hall is a window-less chamber, in which (in imitation of Lenin's mausoleum in Red Square in Moscow) Mao lies in a crystal casket for public viewing (illus. 97). A number of reception lounges surround the chamber and the worship hall; poems and paintings displayed in these rooms constitute a narrative of Mao's revolution-ary career, just as similar displays characterized countless exhibitions during the Cultural Revolution. Outside the Memorial Hall, four groups of heroic sculptures in socialist realist style allude to Mao's leadership during successive periods of the Chinese revolution, in a manner derived from the carvings on the Monument to the People's Heroes.

Ellen Laing, in her discussion of the Memorial Hall, points out that the construction of this monument physically closed off Tiananmen Square and made this space a 'repository of political symbolism signifying a closed Chapter in the history of the Chinese Communist Party and the People's Republic of China'.[56] My discussion here suggests that the monument also closed off the Square ideologically and artistically: representing and glorifying death, it defies any former idealism and imagination even in constructing a Com-munist political space.

Monumentality of Time: From Drum Tower to 'Hong Kong Clock'

This Chapter investigates the relationship between political time and political space in Beijing. More specifically, it focuses on three different ways of public time-telling in the city's history. Each way was associated with a particular type of monumental architecture, which in turn indexed a particular system of technology, public space and political power. Among them, the Drum Tower (together with the Bell Tower) built on Beijing's axis facilitated imperial control over a tightly sealed urban space. While this tower was silenced in 1900, European-style clock towers mushroomed in central Beijing around the turn of the twentieth century: both events signified a crucial shift in China's historical temporality from a traditional empire to a modern nation-state. Finally, a giant digital clock was erected in Tiananmen Square in 1986 to count down the remaining days and seconds before Hong Kong's return to China; its relentless computation of a shortening time span generated nationalist exhilaration as well as local anxiety. Since these three types of structures and instruments have all been connected with Tiananmen Square (either surrounding it, attached to it or projecting from it), the Square is recognized as the origin or originator of public time; its absolute authority over the city and the country is strengthened by this particular significance. To the ordinary residents of Beijing, however, the various methods, equipment and architecture of time-telling are imbued with their personal memories and have inspired local stories.

The Hong Kong Clock and post-1989 Tiananmen Square

When I first saw the Hong Kong Clock (or 'Xianggang zhong', as Beijingers called it) in Tiananmen Square in 1994, it displayed a bright digital number of 1,055: the days remaining until the resumption of sovereignty over Hong Kong on 1 July 1997. When I returned to the Clock in 1996, the number had changed to 298, then 297, 296 . . . (illus. 98); and my response to it had also changed from ridicule to a tightening sense of expectation: the Clock – in fact a giant timer – seemed to tick louder and louder.

There was another difference in 1996: more 'clock-watchers', mostly in small groups and all Chinese, appeared before it. Judging by their clothes and dialect, some of them probably came from Hong Kong or Macao; others were mainlanders travelling to the capital from the provinces. Many visitors posed in front of the Clock to have their pictures taken (illus. 99); some were grim-faced while others laughed and joked. A young man said to his female companion in a heavy Shandong accent: 'Yinian hou zanmen yeneng qu Xianggang warwar le' [A year from now we can also go to Hong Kong to have fun]. I looked around and wondered what brought these people there: they seemed to have little in common in terms of origin, culture, profession or even citizenship. But at that moment we had all linked ourselves to a single measure of time and space, since all of us had come to Tiananmen Square to see the Clock, and the Clock would show the same number in every snapshot taken that day.

Between 1994 and 1997 Tiananmen Square was given a new centre of gravity, as the Hong Kong Clock – a giant digital timer installed on the façade of the Museum of Chinese History on the east side of the Square – attracted domestic

98 The Hong Kong Clock in Tiananmen Square, 1996.

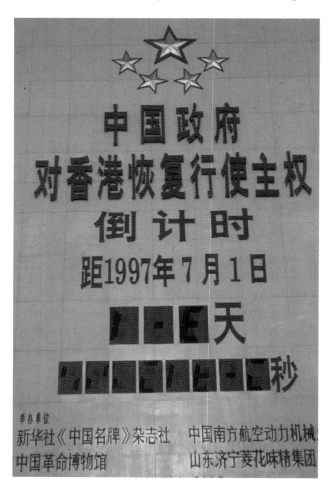

99 Visitors to the Hong Kong Clock having their pictures taken, 1996.

and international attention, and as an increasing number of visitors travelled from all over the world to see it. One wonders what lay behind this fascination: the Clock had little aesthetic appeal, and its exaggerated size still fell short of evoking genuine awe. Rather, what was tantalizing about this official installation was its implication of an unrealized (and hence uncertain) reality, an idea that seemed at odds with the existing monumental complex in Tiananmen Square. In fact, one may argue that people were attracted to the Clock precisely because it problematized an existing order: what a visitor encountered was not only a digital clock, but a renewed Square, whose symbolic structure and political significance had inevitably been modified by the Clock's insertion.

The Square during these years had the same 'hardware' as in 1977. As discussed in previous Chapters, the four monuments surrounding the Square formed two symmetrical pairs, each juxtaposing the present with the past in a symbolic historiography. Tiananmen, the grandstand of the living Chinese leaders in state ceremonies, was opposite Mao's Memorial Hall; the Museum of Chinese History faced the Great Hall of the People (see illus. 18, 19). This structure thus defines a particular system of *political time* – a temporality that internalizes a political ideology and agenda.

Within this symbolic structure, history – a systematic account of events in a temporal order – is given its most authoritative narrative form in China. Through the inscriptions and relief carvings on the monuments and through the exhibitions in the Museum of Chinese History, the static juxtaposition of the past and the present is transformed into a logical process linking the past to the present. The concept of political time is therefore historicized and particularized. Selected figures, images and dates punctuate the 4,000-year-long Chinese history in stages; but the periodization is retrospective, with the self-professed purpose to prove the inevitability and legitimacy of Communist rule. In particular, as mentioned earlier, this periodization underscores the bipartite structure of the Museum of Chinese History, which consists of two institutions – the Museum of (traditional) Chinese History and the Museum of Revolutionary History – under a single roof. The former houses an exhibition of ancient Chinese history up to 1840; the latter displays the 'revolutionary history' of the Chinese people after this date.

Sustained by the Square and its monuments, in 1996 this official historiography still seemed steadfast and all-powerful. On the other hand, almost half a century had passed since Mao wrote his inscription on the Monument to the People's Heroes, and the exhibition in the Museum of Chinese History was close to 40 years old.[1] In fact, no permanent monument had been added to the Square since 1977, after the establishment of Mao's Memorial Hall as the final closure of the Cultural Revolution. That the Square had actually stopped growing for almost two decades was itself a significant phenomenon. (Indeed, for a person like me who grew up in Beijing and witnessed the transformation of the Square from a walled tunnel into 'the largest square in the world', it would have been hard to believe that it would one day cease to expand.) This is not to say, of course, that the government had paid less attention to the Square: it had become such a sensitive political spot after the 1989 student movement that more money had been spent each year to guard it, renovate its monuments and keep it as a sparkling showpiece.[2]

But all such attention – protection and renovation – had only helped to transform the Square from a 'bright symbol of New China' to a collection of well-maintained relics from a bygone era. In other words, the whole symbolic system of the Square was reframed in a larger historical narrative: although the Square still retained its intrinsic political symbolism and historical evolutionism, this system itself had become a creation of the past and was contrasted with a fast-changing present. The pre-1977 monuments in the Square remained 'living symbols' of the People's Republic only to the extent that they embodied, as official propaganda continued to assert, 'the fundamental ideology of the Communist Party', which China was obliged to retain even though it had become quite a different country by the 1990s.

The Hong Kong Clock was the first long-term (though still temporary) structure added to Tiananmen Square in the almost twenty years after 1977, and its construction highlighted new historical conditions and problems. Most important, before the installation of the Clock, the Square with its monuments and statues symbolized an eternal political order that denied any change. But as a political timer, the Hong Kong Clock pointed to a future moment as the projected result of an ongoing process; its rapidly changing numbers indicated the passage of time. The addition of the Clock to the Square thus inevitably created a dilemma: on the one hand, it was constructed to support Communist historiography in general and to facilitate a current political programme specifically. On the other hand, with its inherent signification of impermanence and transformation, the Clock was destined to challenge the Square's supposed permanency and immortality. The first aspect constituted the intention of the Clock; the second aspect resulted from historical forces beyond intentionality and pointed to the Clock's deeper meaning.

Although never documented in words, the placement of the Clock on the façade of the Museum of Chinese History reveals an unmistakable effort to insert this new addition into the established symbolic structure of the Square. A three-point explanation for this location can be deduced from Maoist historiography. First, this location corresponds to the division between the museum's two wings, the south wing dedicated to traditional history and the north wing to modern history; the Clock thus implies the year 1840, which separates these two historical phases and the corresponding wings of the museum. Second, in this location the Clock confirms the concept of 'democratic revolution', defined by Mao as the Chinese people's struggle for the country's independence beginning in 1840. It also predicts the victory of this struggle: the return of Hong Kong (a Chinese city ceded to a foreign power by the first unequal treaty) will symbolically conclude this revolution.[3] Third, that the Clock blocks the museum's entrance symbolizes the incompleteness of this historical process.

To create this historical enclosure from 1840 to 1997 was also the purpose of the written passage on the Clock's 9-metre-high face:

THE CHINESE GOVERNMENT
RESUMES EXERCISE OF SOVEREIGNTY OVER HONG KONG
CLOCK COUNTING BACKWARD
TO JULY 1 1997
X X X DAYS
X X X X X X X SECONDS

This passage, on the other hand, was unreadable because it changed every second. What the Clock registered, therefore, was the present, but a fleeting present that was meaningful only because it was unstable. The Clock provided the days and seconds left before 1 July 1997; we wonder why hours and minutes were not given. The answer must be that the rapidly running numbers of seconds, although of little use for actual time-telling, most acutely (and dramatically) conveyed the impression of the fast disappearance of the present and hence the fast approach of an anticipated future.

Although called a *zhong* or 'clock', the Hong Kong Clock resembled a giant document. This seems a purposeful design, since its features, including the rectangular shape, the thin, flat surface, the five-star heading and the 'black-characters-on-white-paper' (*baizhi heizi*) style of the written message all imitate an official document, or, more precisely, an official certificate. But this document is not yet finalized. It is still in the making and its function as a certificate is only implied, not consolidated. To realize this function it must gain the stable form necessary for a document, which can be achieved only when the Clock's changing number stops at zero. The Clock would then freeze and its message, THE CHINESE GOVERNMENT RESUMES EXERCISE OF SOVEREIGNTY OVER HONG KONG, would become eternal. The identity of the Clock as a timepiece would then cease; instead it would certify the identity of a space. This also means, however, that while the Clock is still ticking, the concepts of political time and political space are still being negotiated. The Clock, although created to ensure the result of this negotiation, also highlights the Utopian nature of its goal, because political time and political space must always be interdependent; the notion of a 'timeless' space turns politics into religion.

The Drum Tower and the Politics of Traditional Time-telling

This meditation on the historicity of the Hong Kong Clock leads to a larger issue: the changing relationship between political time and political space in Chinese history. In particular, in what way(s) did this 'post-modern' digital clock continue or alter the systems of public time-telling in pre-modern and early modern China? How did the earlier systems help regulate systems of public space? And, more closely related to this book, how were these systems related to Tiananmen and Tiananmen Square in pre-modern and modern Beijing? This section focuses on the Drum Tower and the accompanying Bell Tower. Like the Hong Kong Clock, these two buildings announced time to the public and were connected to Tiananmen; but they employed a different technology to control a different space.

Historians of Chinese architecture are used to studying traditional Beijing from its two-dimensional layout (the map in illus. 10 exemplifies this interest). As a result, an important feature of the city has escaped most discussions of its design: during the five-and-a-half centuries of the Ming and Qing dynasties, the Drum Tower and the Bell Tower were the two tallest structures standing on Beijing's central axis (illus. 100), exceeding the emperor's primary throne hall, the Hall of Supreme Harmony behind Tiananmen, by more than 10 metres.[4] But the real difference between the towers and the throne hall was still not their height but their visibility: while the Hall of Supreme Harmony was concealed inside the layers of walls of the Imperial City and the Forbidden City, the Drum Tower and the Bell Tower were exposed to public view. In fact, among all imperial buildings in Ming-Qing Beijing, these two towers were the only ones that can be called 'public monuments'. Even today, their towering appearance above the surrounding commercial and residential buildings generates a strong impression of architectural monumentality (illus. 101).

The Drum Tower and Bell Tower are the subject of a wide range of literary works, including official documents, commemorative inscriptions, government archives, travelogues, memoirs and folk-tales. Checking this literature, however, we find that private memoirs and local stories say little about the buildings' magnificent architectural imagery, but are animated by a strong sensibility to sound – the beating of the 24 drums and an enormous bell installed above the towers.[5] In contrast, official documents and inscriptions

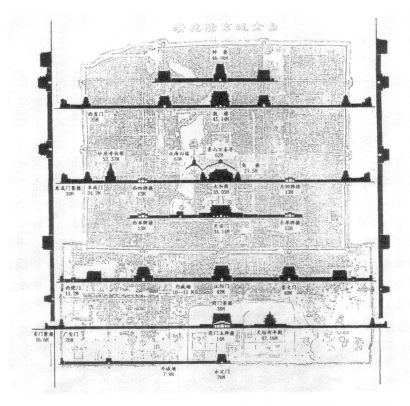

100 Heights of major structures along the central axis in traditional Beijing.

rarely mention sound but are mostly concerned with the towers' cosmological significance and political symbolism.[6] One wonders why there is such a difference and what this difference means. The easiest but perhaps most reliable answer is that the official documents were issued by people who built the towers to practise their control over public time-telling, but the memoirs and folk-tales were created by people whose everyday lives were directly affected by the sound issuing from the towers. The official documents often associate the intention of the towers with visual presentation; the memoirs and folk-tales often associate the towers with acoustic presentation. The different content and focuses of these two kinds of literature indicate two contrasting aspects of the towers' meaning.

A well-known description of the rhythmic sound of the drums, for example, comes from a private memoir written by a Beijing resident, which reports a popular saying in old Beijing: 'Eighteen fast beats, eighteen slow beats, and there are yet another eighteen beats that are neither fast nor slow.'[7] A popular Beijing folk-tale, on the other hand, was inspired by the sound of the bell, which was considered peculiar.[8] It relates that when the Yongle emperor ordered a bell to be cast in the early fifteenth century, the foundry master failed repeatedly to obtain a perfect casting. The emperor was furious and threatened to execute the incompetent man. The foundry master's daughter heard about this. To save her father's life, she jumped into the huge mould when the molten metal was poured into it, thus making herself a permanent part of the bell. Her father made a desperate clutch at her, but only caught hold of one of her shoes. This time the bell was perfectly cast. But to the ears of Beijing's residents, it ever since gave forth the sound 'Xie!' – the sound of the Chinese word for 'shoe' – as if the girl kept looking for her missing personal belonging whenever the bell was struck.

I first learned this story not from books – although I did read it later (with some noticeable discrepancies) in modern collections of Beijing folk-tales. The person who told it to me was my old nanny Ma Yulin, a middle-aged 'bannerwoman' (qiren) of Manchu descent. Her father, as she told me with some pride, worked for the last Qing emperor as a guard of the imperial gold storehouse. For some reason I always thought that the storehouse was located inside the beautiful Summer Palace in the western suburbs of Beijing. Nanny Ma's stories about her father were filled with intimate details that both fascinated and embarrassed me. Once she told me that, like everyone working in the storehouse, her father had to strip naked as a baby after each day's work and jump three times in front of a superior, to prove that he hadn't hidden the emperor's gold in some unspeakable places. She laughed so hard when she was telling me this episode that both my mother and sister ran out of their rooms to ask what was going on.

She moved in with my family when my parents were transferred from Nanjing, after Beijing became the capital of the People's Republic. My father came with the Academia Sinica's Institute of Economy; my mother was invited to teach in the newly established Central Academy of Drama. I passed my fifth birthday – the first one in Beijing – in November 1950. Both my parents wore Western-style spectacles, which Nanny Ma thought to be ornaments of fanciful intellectuals. I always suspected that she secretly considered my parents aliens, who had even travelled to America on a boat. She herself had never left Beijing and, as far as I know, had never gone beyond the northern part of the city centred on the Drum Tower and the Bell Tower.

Like most Manchus in Beijing, Nanny Ma's family declined after the fall of the last dynasty – the Qing established by the Manchus. She did have a husband, a dwarf who sold boiled beans on the street, but she never wanted to have him near her. My parents explained to my sister and me that she had an 'arranged marriage', which sounded terrible to us. Now and then her husband would turn up at our door. Whenever this happened she would hide herself inside her tiny room crying, while my father would go out, sending him away with some money.

Her room was located at the south-west corner of our courtyard compound. It was so small that its only contents were a bed, a small dresser and a tap-water fountain. But to me it was the cosiest part of the entire house, and I spent countless hours there watching her combing her long black hair, and listening to the stories she told in a soft, drawling voice. Besides shopping for the household she rarely went out. But if she decided to spend half a day away, the time was always Sunday morning and the destination was always the marketplace behind the Drum Tower. On such occasions I tried hard to keep her company, mainly because my parents would never take me there, a quintessential section of old Beijing filled with food stands, antique stalls and jobless Manchus wandering around with birdcages in hand.

It took about fifteen minutes to walk from our house to the Drum Tower. Before leaving home, Nanny Ma would spend hours arranging her hair and painting her eyebrows. Then we would walk along the Back Sea and go through the Slanting Pipe Lane. At the end of the lane we would be able to see the Drum Tower, emerging abruptly about a hundred yards to the left. After reaching the place behind the tower, Nanny Ma would circle around, greeting acquaintances by making a strange gesture, putting both hands on one side of her waist and bending her knees two or three times. She would then take a long time to inspect each food stand, deciding which one was cleanest and used the freshest ingredients that day. She always ordered a bowl of fermented bean soup called *dou zhi* and four small dishes of pickled vegetables. This was the only part of the trip I didn't enjoy: she once offered me some bean soup; it was so incredibly stinky that I immediately spat it out on the ground. She was not offended, however. Later she told me that only a real Manchu knew how to appreciate *dou zhi*.

After the brunch she would usually spend some time there chatting with her acquaintances. I would watch a monkey circus show or read a few comic books at one of the bookstands (it cost 1 cent to rent a book to read on the spot). Afterwards we would walk to the Bell Tower to see an enormous iron bell next to its entrance (illus. 102). It was the bell made by the Yongle emperor (which was later replaced by a new bell during the Qing); and it was on one of these occasions that Nanny Ma told me the story of the foundry master's daughter.

I have started my discussion of the Drum Tower and Bell Tower with folk remembrances and stories, not with emperors' edicts or government documents, because this unofficial literature preserves a vanished aspect of the towers that easily eludes a historical study: these two buildings, though physically intact, are now completely silent; to a modern observer their meaning seems entirely to depend upon their form and decoration. In other words, with their audible aspect gone, their visual aspect has become the most obvious evidence for their historical significance. It is true that a modern art or architectural historian can happily observe and analyse the architectural features of the towers, and can also reconstruct their histories based on archives that record their repeated construction and restoration. But in such research he runs the danger of allying himself with the patrons and designers of the towers – his emphases on the buildings' architectural design and intended symbolism seem to echo theirs too closely. What is absent in these emphases is how the towers, and more specifically the sound issuing from their balconies, actually worked and what they evoked.

One is reminded of this absence when one realizes that the towers are now soundless and hence lifeless. This reflection leads to a two-fold methodology that guides the following discussion of the Drum Tower and the Bell Tower. First, to understand their historical monumentality a modern historian cannot rely on their physical properties and archival records alone, but must also try to resurrect – to 'listen to' – their vanished sound, and to imagine the social interactions and spatial transformations activated by such sound. Second, a main method to resurrect this vanished sound is to activate the memories of the 'historical listeners' – memories of ordinary Beijingers preserved in personal memoirs and folk-tales. It is difficult to find a better metaphor for remembrance than a vanished sound recalled. But the sound from the Drum Tower and the Bell Tower was special and indeed monumental

– a sound that dictated the daily lives of millions of people for several hundred years.

First constructed in 1272 by Kublai Khan in Dadu – the Great Capital of the Yuan dynasty on the site of present-day Beijing – the Drum Tower has since been reconstructed and repaired many times.[9] Its current form and location basically preserve those of the early Ming Drum Tower, commissioned by the Yongle emperor before he moved his court to this northern city in 1421. A magnificent wooden-framed structure, it is 45.14 metres high and covers an area of 7,000 square metres, painted entirely vermilion except for the green roof tiles and the bluish decorative bands below the repeated eaves (illus. 103). The lower storey of the tower, actually the tall base of the entire structure reinforced by thick brick walls, raises the upper storey to 30 metres above the ground, from where one may look down and find traditional Beijing at one's feet. The single enormous room on the upper storey originally housed 24 drums, each with a round drumhead 1.5 metres in diameter and covered with cattle skin. Now all the original drums save one have disappeared; so have the bronze clepsydra (waterclock) and other chronographs that imperial officials used to determine the time to beat the drums. A new set of drums has recently been made. But these are silent replicas created to showcase a perished past for the sake of a burgeoning business: the tower has

141

become a major tourist attraction in Beijing, and its lower level now houses a giftshop.

The Bell Tower stands a short distance north of the Drum Tower (illus. 104). The history of this second tower can also be traced back to the early Ming – Kublai Khan's Bell Tower, now untraceable, was located slightly to the east. Unlike the Drum Tower, which remains a timber-framed building, the Bell Tower was turned into a brick and stone structure in 1745 – a decision made by the Qianlong emperor of the Qing dynasty after the original wooden Bell Tower was destroyed by fire. In front of the building the same emperor also erected a large stone stele, on which he inscribed a long text that he composed to commemorate the 'renewed harmony between Heaven and earth' achieved by rebuilding the tower (illus. 105). It is possible that Qianlong, a ruler famous for his penchant for art, also redesigned the Bell Tower for aesthetic and symbolic reasons: the new building has a sober and elegant look that both contradicts and complements the flamboyant Drum Tower. The Drum Tower is voluminous and powerful; the Bell Tower is slender and elegant. Its height of 46.96 metres (even greater than the Drum Tower's) attests to an unmistakable attempt to achieve verticality. The Drum Tower is *yang* and masculine; the Bell Tower is *yin* and feminine.

Like the Drum Tower, the Bell Tower is also a two-level building, the first storey of which serves as a tall base. An enormous bronze bell (5.5 metres tall and 6.3 tons in weight) is hung inside a vault in the centre of the upper storey, left open so as not to block the sound of the bell. In the case of the Drum Tower, however, doors built all around the upper storey were left wide open when the drums were beaten on regular hours, so the sound could reach every corner of the city.

Every day at the *wu* hour, beginning about 7 p.m., the 24 drums were struck, followed by the bronze bell. The rhythmic sound was divided into sec-

103 The Drum Tower in Beijing, first constructed in 1272; the photograph was taken in the early 20th century.

(NO. 23) THE DRUM PAGODA, PEKING. 樓鼓京北

104 The Bell
Tower in Beijing,
first constructed
in 1272 and
rebuilt in 1745;
the photograph
was taken in the
early 20th
century

tions of various paces. As summarized in the popular saying cited earlier, each
sequence started with eighteen fast beats, was followed by eighteen slow beats,
and then concluded with eighteen medium-paced beats. This sequence was
repeated twice to make a total of 108 beats. Responding to the sound from the
two towers, imperial guards stationed at the nine gates of Beijing's Inner City
struck the chimes or bell installed in each of the gate-towers.[10] With this joint
call, all the gates of the Inner City were closed, local police shut the 'street
gates' and people also locked their doors. The same performance of the drums
and the bell was repeated next morning at the *yin* hour, about 5 a.m.: the night
was officially over and it was time for the city to wake up. So, with another
round of joint striking of drums and bells, the city gates slowly swung open;
markets started to receive customers; and high-ranking officials departed to
attend court meetings. Between these two moments – that is, between 7 p.m.
in the evening and 5 a.m. in the early morning – the Drum Tower kept silent
and only the Bell Tower announced the nightly hours.[11]

This schedule seems strange to a modern observer: the drums and bell
thundered only from evening to morning, and announced time to Beijing's
residents only when they were supposed to stay home and sleep. To understand this seemingly bizarre custom is to understand the working of the two
towers and, indeed, a predominant system of public time-telling in pre-modern
China. I have surveyed the history of this system in another essay;[12] Beijing's
example discussed here allows us to summarize two basic roles of this system.
First, the joint striking of the drums and bell controlled urban spaces by activating Beijing's gates – not only the main city gates but also all other gates
throughout the imperial capital. One type of gate, no longer seen in present-day Beijing, was the 'street gate', of which there were 1,219 in number.
These divided the city's traffic routes into short, isolatable sections. Several
members of the British Macartney mission of 1793 mentioned this device in

their reports and memoirs. Lord Macartney himself wrote: 'At night all the streets are shut up by barricades at each end and a guard is constantly patrolling between.'[13] The unified actions of these and other gates implied a daily transformation of the city's spatial structure: when all the gates were closed in response to the evening striking of the drums and the bell, not only was the walled city isolated from the outside, but all the walled spaces within the city – palaces, offices, markets, temples and private homes – turned into enclosed and dissociated units. Roads and streets became empty and ceased to connect the city's various sectors into a dynamic whole.

Traditional Beijing thus underwent a ritualized dormancy on a daily basis, and each period of its inactivity was framed and reinforced by the joint sound of the drums and bell. This primary role of public time-telling, to mark the beginning and end of the nightly curfew, was complemented by the second role of public time-telling, to punctuate each night into five equal divisions for the night watches (a role performed by the Bell Tower alone). The joint striking of the drums and bell at dusk was known as *ding geng*, meaning literally 'the beginning of the night watch'. The following bi-hourly beatings of the bell then marked 'the first night watch' (*chu geng*), the 'second night watch' (*er geng*), and so on until the drums joined the bell again to announce the beginning of the next day at the 'fifth night watch' (*wu geng*). Between *ding geng* and *wu geng*, municipal night watchmen, equipped with long poles with iron hooks on top, patrolled the streets in groups of two or three.[14]

Unlike public bells in medieval Europe, which were 'drivers of actions' and 'goads to effective, productive labour', according to David S. Landes,[15] the Chinese Drum Tower and Bell Tower ensured peace through the long night.[16] This particular function of the towers, in turn, raises questions about the role of their architectural imagery. I have mentioned that the Drum Tower and the Bell Tower were the two tallest buildings standing on Beijing's central axis during the Ming and Qing dynasties. Their striking visual images, however, did little to reinforce their public function of telling time. In fact, since these two buildings emitted sound only from dusk to dawn, their sound and their architectural image were to a large extent mutually exclusive: they were heard at night and seen during the day. Their imposing but silent presence during the day realized the political control of time. From the point of view of the imperial authority, the towers could realize such control because they focused public perception and brought about a sense of unification and standardization.

This particular role for the monumentality of the towers is clearly stated by the Qianlong emperor, in a text that he ordered inscribed on the stele erected in front of the Bell Tower in 1747 (illus. 105):

My divine capital is as broad as the ocean, and it possesses all sorts of goods. Its run-through avenues intersect with streets and lanes, and a large, well-off population dwells there. But when things multiply opinions become diverse. Unless an instrument is created to unify people's minds, synchronization of dawn and dusk cannot be achieved. The effectiveness of such an instrument is determined by its physical size. This is why this

105 The stele of 1747 commemorating the rebuilding of the Bell Tower in 1745.

tower must be constructed as a multi-levelled building of unusual height: only in this way can its solemn image be seen far and near. Moreover, the Drum Tower and the Bell Tower will form a pair, guarding the Forbidden City to the rear.[17]

The last sentence in this quotation refers to the position of the two towers relative to the imperial court, and further signifies the buildings' social identity and political symbolism. Unlike all other imperial structures in Beijing, the Drum Tower and Bell Tower stood outside the royal domain and were accessible to anyone who lived in or travelled to the city. The area centred on these two towers was one of the busiest commercial districts in the city. Many records of old Beijing describe at length the many restaurants and shops one could find here. The authors of these records also unanimously emphasize the attraction of this area to people of different professions and social classes. While the artificial lakes south-west of the towers offered educated people quiet places for literary gatherings and relaxation, teahouses and open-air performances attracted commoners, women and children.

It is important to realize that the identity of the Drum Tower and the Bell Tower as a centre of Beijing's urban popular culture was already implied in the city's symbolic structure (illus. 106). By locating these two buildings outside

106
A 19th-century Chinese map of Beijing, showing the locations of
1. the Forbidden City
2. the Throne Hall
3. the Drum Tower and the Bell Tower
4. Tiananmen
5. Di'anmen or the Gate of Earthly Peace

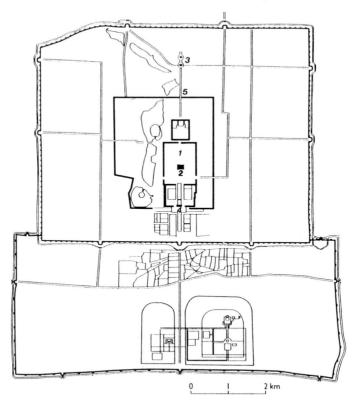

Di'anmen, the designer of Beijing consciously associated them with the element *di* ('earth') as opposed to *tian* ('heaven'). Di'anmen, or the Gate of Earthly Peace, was the north or rear gate of the Imperial City (illus. 107), while the south and front gate of the Imperial City was the famous Tiananmen or the Gate of Heavenly Peace. These two gates constituted an opposed *yin-yang* pair: the area outside Di'anmen was a public space populated by the subjects of imperial rule, while Tiananmen symbolized the emperor as the master of the whole population.

As a designated centre of Beijing's public sphere, the Drum Tower and the Bell Tower both counterbalance the Forbidden City and were subordinated to it. The political dominance of the Forbidden City over these two towers was most acutely expressed by locating the towers at the northern end of Beijing's central axis. The symbolic centre of this axis was a series of throne halls inside the Forbidden City; the two towers were therefore understood as a far-reaching projection of imperial power from the throne halls into the public domain. One of the throne halls is Jiaotai Dian, or the Hall of Union. The hall realized its significance as the nexus of imperial power by displaying two groups of objects (illus. 108). The first group consisted of the emperor's 25 official seals in golden boxes. The second group included two enormous clocks flanking the

107 Di'anmen
(the smaller
building in the
mid-ground)
before its destruc-
tion in 1955–6. In
the distance is
the Drum Tower.

108 Interior of the Hall of Union in the Forbidden City.

109, 110 The two clocks in the Hall of Union.

throne: a traditional hydraulic clock to the left of the throne and a Western-style mechanical clock to the right (illus. 109, 110). These two timepieces were placed here for symbolic, not practical, reasons. The idea was that through controlling the knowledge of time, the emperor could internalize the intrinsic movement of the universe. He could therefore rule the world without using force. That is why in this hall two large characters hung above the throne read 'Non-action' (*Wu wei*), an ancient political philosophy now facilitated by Western science. While this throne hall demonstrated imperial control over time-keeping, the Drum Tower and the Bell Tower manifested imperial power over time-telling. Time was politicized and monumentalized in both places, but through different symbols and architectural forms.

The Clock Tower and the Invasion of a Modern Temporality

For 3,000 years Chinese political theory held that harmony between time and space was the foundation of rulership over a unified country. This idea was first established in the *Book of Documents*, one of the Confucian Classics written during the second and first millennia BC. The book begins with the famous 'Canon of Yao', which records that Yao, a legendary emperor in the time of Great Harmony, established a system that allowed him 'to compute and delineate the sun, moon and stars, and the celestial markers, and so to deliver respectfully the seasons to be observed by people.'[18] In this system, time was conceived from and framed within the 'four ends' of the world, and the mythological emperor could thereby define his position at the centre of this temporal/spatial structure known as China. It was also believed that it was the emperor's duty to announce this standardized, canonical time to his subjects on a regular basis, thereby bringing order and peace to the world.

This basic conception and function of time gave birth to two separate systems of technology known as time-telling and time-keeping. Readers who connect public time to Big Ben outside the Houses of Parliament in London will have trouble distinguishing these two systems, because in that case a single clock, which moves and sounds automatically, performs both roles. But in the ancient Chinese system two sets of equipment were employed in separate places for these two purposes. Time-keeping relied on horology and astronomy, which allowed the government to regulate seasons, months, days and hours. In his *Science and Civilization in China* Joseph Needham emphasizes over and over the political significance of time-keeping to a Chinese emperor.[19] Hellmut Wilhelm considers ancient Chinese astronomy and horology a secret science of priest-kings.[20] Time-telling, on the other hand, conveyed a standardized official time to a large population. The principal instruments for this purpose were the Drum Tower and Bell Tower. These towers were not 'clocks', because they did not compute time and did not record the passage of time. They came alive only at designated moments, when they amplified signals from an official clock and transmitted these signals to the public. What

the towers presented to the public, therefore, was not a continuous, even and unidirectional movement of time, but an official schedule of projected operations and recurring events.[21]

For centuries, the sound of the drums and bell dictated to Beijing's residents when to work, rest, open the city gates or retreat into individual courtyard compounds: this was the schedule of a community in a tightly walled city. What the sound signified was an eternal repetition recognized as time itself. This way of telling and knowing time in Beijing was finally challenged by European 'self-ringing bells' (*zimingzhong*), which arrived in China through two different channels: foreign tribute and invasion. The challenge imposed on the Chinese system of public time-telling thus also meant a challenge from a different kind of political space.

As tribute, a European mechanical clock satisfied the recipient's desire by offering not only a private timepiece but also a fancy visual presentation and an array of entertaining accessory functions: sounding bells, playing melodies, singing birds, parading little automated figures. They were revered by the

Chinese emperor and the nobility. 'The Imperial Palace', wrote Father Valentin Chalier from Beijing in the 1730s, 'is stuffed with clocks . . . watches, carillons, repeaters, organs, spheres and astronomical clocks of all kinds and descriptions – there are more than four thousand pieces from the best masters of Paris and London, very many of which I have had through my hands for repairs or cleaning.'[22] It is doubtful whether these Western instruments had any significant impact on China's modernization, however. Most were status symbols and playthings;[23] a few large ones were paired with traditional astronomical water clocks in the Palace to symbolize the emperor's continuing mandate in a 'modern' world (see illus. 109 and 110). It is even true that a 'clock tower' was built, but it was located inside the emperor's Summer Palace outside Beijing and had therefore no public function at all (illus. 111). Another example, a temporary Western-style building with a clock on it, was made on the occasion of the birthday of the Qianlong emperor's mother (illus. 112).[24]

Ironically, these fancy European clocks, often designed and decorated to suit Chinese taste, became a distinct target when foreign troops looted the great palaces in Beijing in 1860 and again in 1900.[25] But again, the destruction of some large clocks (including the one in the Summer Palace) and the return of some portable ones to European markets left little impact on Chinese society.

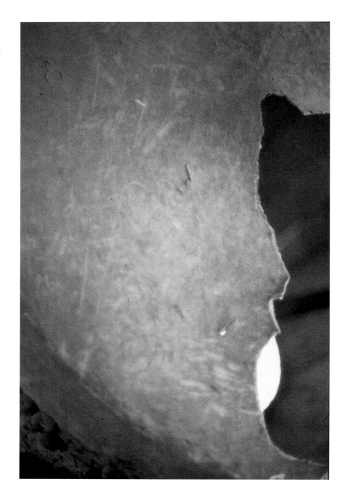

113 A drum in the Drum Tower showing bayonet cuts, said to be made by soldiers of the Eight-Power Allied Forces in 1900.

Around the same time, however, two real changes in public time-telling were brought about by foreign military and economic invasions, and profoundly altered the definition of political space in China. First, the old Drum Tower in Beijing was silenced. During the invasion of 1900 to suppress the Boxer Rebellion, soldiers of the Eight-Power Allied Forces (sent by Britain, France, the United States, Japan, Germany, Italy, Austria and Russia) occupied the tower and slashed the leather drumheads with bayonets (illus. 113).[26] After the Republic of China was founded, the building was renamed Realizing Humiliation Tower, and a Municipal Centre for Common Education was established on its lower level.[27] The tower thus acquired the identity of a witness to the 'crimes of foreign devils' and to a major national humiliation. This change in the building's significance was intimately related to China's transformation from an ancient empire to a modern nation-state. As part of this transformation, the Drum Tower was among the architectural sites used to arouse people's consciousness of the calamities befalling their country. (Not coincidentally, the

152

ruins of the Yuanming Yuan Garden, left from the destruction of the joint forces of the British and French armies in 1860, also attracted wide public attention from the mid-1920s, before finally becoming not just a particular war ruin but a nationalist monument.) Before this moment, the memory that the 'living' Drum Tower evoked, using Pierre Nora's words, was 'an integrated memory – all-powerful, sweeping, un-self-conscious, and inherently present-minded – a memory without a past that eternally recycles a heritage, relegating ancestral yesterday to the undifferentiated time of heroes, inceptions, and myth.'[28] The silence forced upon the tower made it a 'modern' monument: not only did it now serve a contemporary political agenda, but its changing monumentality implied the uprooting of its traditional 'integrated memory' by a historical narrative based on events and happenings.[29]

Second, around the same period, time was announced by mechanical clocks installed on Western-style public buildings that appeared with increasing frequency in Chinese cities. Many Chinese viewed such clocks and clock towers as amazing achievements of modern technology. The fascination with them is revealed in pictures and literary descriptions, both found in popular lithograph pictorials, which were the earliest modern form of mass media in China. Among these pictorials, the two earliest ones were the *Dianshizhai huabao* (Dianshi Studio Pictorial) and the *Feiyingge huabao* (Fleeting Shadow Pavilion Pictorial), both published in Shanghai and illustrated by Wu Youru, a skilled painter best known for his vivid depictions of news events both inside and outside China. In the early twentieth century, the most popular Chinese pictorial was probably the *Tuhua ribao* (Pictorial Daily), published every day instead of every ten days, as the two earlier ones had been. Images of Western-style clock towers are abundant in all these publications; the accompanying texts reveal the appeal of the painted subjects. A picture by Wu Youru, for example, has the title 'A Great Self-ringing Clock' and this explanation (illus. 114):

> Western inventions have become increasingly intricate and incredible, and increasingly accurate and clever, demonstrating a technological development that advances every day. There is now a large self-ringing clock in Shanghai's French Concession. It is more than several *zhang* high, and its sound can be heard several *li* away. Those ignorant Confucians are all amazed by this creation, which they have never seen or heard.[30]

But instead of depicting this new invention in Shanghai, Wu Youru painted a clock tower in Britain – an authentic Western building that provided the French Municipal Council Office in Shanghai with a model. He did portray the French Council clock tower in other pictures, but here the building acquires a different meaning. Instead of demonstrating the superiority of Western science and technology, these images associate the clock tower with a repressive foreign power. In a picture in the *Dianshi Studio Pictorial*, for example, a large Chinese crowd is gathered outside the Council Office, gesticulating and shouting (illus. 115). Several of them lie on the ground, apparently killed

114 'A Great Self-ringing Clock', a lithograph by Wu Youru (d. 1893).

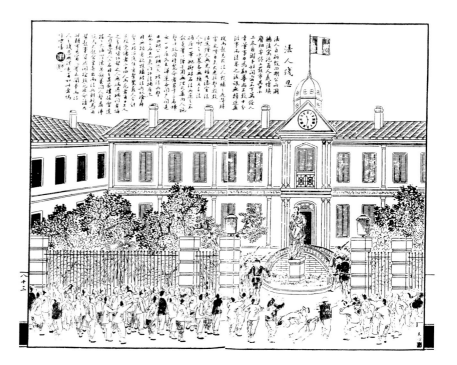

115 'The Cruelty of Frenchmen', a lithograph by Wu Youru.

by the French soldiers who hold guns while rushing out of the office gate. The explanatory text details the event: responding to the destruction of a neighbourhood building by French police, more than tens of thousands of Shanghai residents held demonstrations; some of them destroyed the electric streetlights in the French Concession and threw stones at the French police station. The French authorities retaliated by sending soldiers to the street, killing seventeen people and wounding many more. Filled with grief and indignation, Wu Youru wrote at the end of the text: 'Alas! Who could believe that Frenchmen could be as ruthless and unreasonable as this?' In a symbolic gesture, he also inscribed the picture's title, 'Ruthless Frenchmen', next to the clock tower of the council office with a French flag on it.

In fact, Western clock towers aroused negative sentiments among native Chinese as soon as such buildings appeared in China, long before the Shanghai incident in the late nineteenth century. It was such sentiment that prompted the Qing scholar Yang Congqing to write his book *A General Description of Beijing*, an exploration of the city's rich architectural tradition that also allowed him to reject the newly arriving Western science and ideology. The book begins with this autobiographical account of the author about his first encounter with a 'Western bell tower': when he was still a young man he visited his father, a Confucian scholar who was then serving as secretary to a Manchu prince in the imperial capital. One day he passed the area near the city's south-west gate, called Xuanwumen, and was startled by the ringing of bells in broad daylight. When he returned home he reported this anomaly to his father. 'My late father told me that the sound came from the self-ringing bell on top of a Catholic church. He then sighed deeply and said: "These people from the West will eventually bring calamities to this country."'[31] Yang Congqing never forgot his father's words.

In this account Yang did not say that he actually saw the clock tower on the Catholic church. The sound of the clock startled him because he, or any other eighteenth-century Chinese, never expected that time would be announced to the public in the middle of the day. It is a curious question whether the Western-style clock towers, which steadily increased in number in Chinese cities from the eighteenth century onwards, actually provided an effective means of public time-telling – that time would be announced to the city's residents when they were not sleeping but working, entertaining themselves and moving around. The answer is negative: a study of their locations reveals that these clocks were not built in residential areas and did not constitute a practical system of public time-telling in Beijing.[32] Rather, clock towers typically appeared in places that were rich in symbolism and associated with political and economic institutions. As examples, three prominent clock towers were constructed in the early twentieth century to surround traditional Tiananmen Square. The first one, on top of the city's first railway station, was located immediately outside the Front Gate south of Tiananmen (illus. 116). The other two belonged to two banks that flanked the traditional Tiananmen Square from east and west (illus. 117). Displaying their intimidating height and advanced technology, these Western-style clock towers not only surrounded the most prominent political

116 Beijing Train Station with its clock tower, c. 1900.

space in traditional China but also overpowered it. To the city's ordinary residents, however, these startling public symbols of modernity did little to change their daily life. The technology of mechanical clocks eventually entered their lives only through more specific and individualized connections: through desk clocks and wall clocks installed in their living and working spaces, and through pocket watches and wristwatches that they carried about. Until these moments finally arrived, however, a twentieth-century Chinese relied on the most ancient way of knowing time – observing the sun's movement.

117 A foreign bank (now the People's Bank) near Tiananmen Square with its Western-style clock.

Before I finally possessed a watch in the tenth grade, I was accustomed – and indeed quite skilled – at estimating time from shadow. This was made easy by Beijing's layout, since almost all streets ran north–south and east–west. When the shadow of a north–south wall shortened and was about to disappear, I knew that it was time for lunch. Partly for this reason, I found an ideal spot to read lengthy novels during the winter vacation – my favourite pastime in that grey, idle month. The place was at the south side of the pavilion on Coal Hill. There, below the building's tall foundation, the chilly wind from the north was completely blocked off, and the air was so warm on a bright day that I could even take off my cotton-padded coat. The spot also offered a visual feast: right before my eye was the sea of yellow roofs of the Forbidden City (illus. 118). I could see all the way from Shenwumen to Tiananmen (the northern and southern gates of the City) and the layered rooflines of the six principal palaces in between. Until I got my first watch, however, these ancient buildings also served the role of a sundial. Even on a cloudy day, their changing shadows told me the passage of time.

My memories of those pre-watch days also have a less nostalgic side: for several years until 1961 the ultimate object of my desire was a watch. At that time, watches were still uncommon even among grown-ups in China; none of my schoolmates possessed this luxury object. When I reached the first year in junior high school, however, I did find a way to enjoy a watch, even very briefly. It started when several classmates and I discovered that we could borrow watches from our parents for the final exams in a semester. Our reason was compelling: we could achieve better grades if we could control time better. Since I attended a boarding school and returned home only at weekends, this meant that at the end of each semester I could have a watch for a whole week. Both my parents wore watches. I was most thrilled if I could convince my father to lend me his watch, which was slim and had a metal strap. My mother's, although Swiss-made, was fatter.

It is difficult to explain why wearing a watch was so exciting. To earn better grades was clearly a pretext, and I suspected that my parents could see through me just as easily as I could convince them. Perhaps it was because to me, a teenager in a boarding school famous for its revolutionary heritage, a watch was

118 Looking at the Forbidden City from the top of Coal Hill.

such a personal object and its allure came from so many directions: a beautiful ornament, a fancy toy, an intricate piece of scientific equipment, a ready-made status symbol. But exactly for the same reasons we had to abandon our 'watch-borrowing' ritual in 1960. Around that time, political education began to loom large in the school's curriculum. The principal teacher of our class, an alert Party member, detected 'bourgeois ideology' in our desire, and prohibited students from wearing watches in the classroom at any time. (To her credit, those who borrowed watches from their parents were naturally from better-off, mostly 'bourgeois intellectual', families.)

My predictable reaction to this prohibition was an even stronger desire for a watch. My mother finally agreed to buy me one. But this decision came at a wrong time: in the aftermath of the Great Leap Forward campaign, China was going through one of the hardest times in her history. There were widespread famines and great shortages of almost everything. Not only food, but all sorts of goods, from cloth, furniture and bicycles down to soap, toothpaste and toilet paper were rationed. Watches were no exception. My mother first made several trips to Tianqiao (the location of Beijing's largest second-hand market) to find a used watch for me. When this attempt failed, she finally managed to trade various coupons, which she had saved for months, for a 'watch coupon'.

I can never forget my feeling – torn between exhilaration, gratitude and guilt – when I followed her to a department store to purchase my first watch. It was made in Shanghai and called 'Shanghai'. I cherished it for almost ten years. After I became a staff member of the Palace Museum in the early 1970s, the 'watch coupon' was finally abandoned, and quartz watches appeared on the market for the first time. I was once again mesmerized by this amazing object. I bought one from my savings, paying a price that equalled two months' salary, and for days kept looking at the changing digital numbers in its rectangular window. The watch was made in Hong Kong.

Back to the Hong Kong Clock: 'Counting Down' as a Means of Political Control

Attached to churches, banks, customs houses, railway stations and Western-style schools, the late nineteenth- and early twentieth-century clock towers were modern intruders in an old Chinese city. They provided tangible references to an alien system of time and space, and offered the most concrete and convincing evidence for the superiority of Western science, thereby legitimating the growing existence and dominance of foreign powers in China. Such clock towers did not simply replace the traditional Drum Tower and Bell Tower (the latter stopped ringing in 1924), because they served entirely different purposes and helped to construct different political spaces. Whereas the Drum Tower and Bell Tower protected a tightly walled city, clock towers destroyed such enclosure and connected a traditional Chinese city like Beijing into a huge colonial network marked by a chain of Western 'self-ringing clocks' in London, Singapore, Shanghai and Hong Kong (illus. 119). This social

119 The clock tower on Queen's Road in Hong Kong, photo taken by M. Miller in the 1860s.

network realized the Enlightenment design of a universal scheme of time and space. Indeed, if in 1600 the Chinese saw the first self-ringing clocks and world maps as Western curiosities, in 1900 they found themselves governed by such clocks and maps, which had reassigned their country – the Central Kingdom – to quite a different place in a global time-space legitimated by science. In David Harvey's words, in this process China and similar countries 'were deterritorialized, stripped of their preceding significations, and then reterritorialized according to the convenience of colonial and imperial administration.'[33]

A Western-style clock on a foreign bank in Beijing or Shanghai, therefore, signified the dominance of a new technology, which, according to Robert A. Adams, should always be thought of as a social-technical system: 'What underlies and sustains technological systems is partly institutional and partly technical, partly rooted in material capabilities and possibilities and partly in human associations, values, and goals.'[34] The traditional, parallel systems of timekeeping and time-telling became obsolete when a public clock moved and struck by itself. This fascinating, automatic timepiece freed time-keeping from imperial control. It also changed the nature of public time-telling altogether: instead of issuing an official timetable, it presented an 'objective' time that was believed to be homogeneous and universal. The smooth and ceaseless movement of its hands further offered a powerful cue for reorganizing human thought and action sequentially. If the punctuality of the Drum Tower was linked to traditional history constructed as a succession of dynasties and reigns, the mechanical clock helped the Chinese reconceptualize history as a teleological evolution.

This concept of totalizing and self-expanding time was adapted by Chinese Communist historiography and entered the commonsense of Chinese urban culture (through the eventual availability of personal watches and clocks). But it was challenged by the Hong Kong Clock. It is most important to realize that the Clock not only purported to mark the end of China's colonial history; its horology and ideology indicate a new technological system, which implicitly challenges the Enlightenment design of universal time and space. This challenge should not simply be understood in terms of the general modernist or postmodernist breakdown of Enlightenment order.[35] Rather, the Clock fuses both pre-colonial and post-colonial techniques of time-telling into an anti-colonial discourse to serve a nationalist polity. On the one hand, the Clock rejects the concept of universal time by resuming the logic of an imperial Drum Tower: it again presents an official schedule to an internal audience (that is, to the people of Hong Kong as subjects of the People's Republic of China). On the other hand, the Clock negates the notion of linear and continuous time by abolishing the movement of a mechanical clock. Its liquid crystal display of days and seconds are strictly momentary and self-sustaining. These flashing numbers dissociate the Clock from a durable mechanical or architectonic construction, instead linking it to a large family of computer screens, terminals, consoles and other electronic signboards, which many writers have related to the intensifying fragmentation and compression of time and space in the postmodern era.[36]

Whereas an earlier Western-style mechanical clock united time-keeping and time-telling, the Hong Kong Clock reintroduced tension between the two. The Clock's political content – the 'timetable' it delivers – was determined by Beijing, but its digital technology was associated with Hong Kong. Indeed, when the first generation of commercial quartz watches were offered by Japanese firms in the 1970s and early '80s, many were actually manufactured in Hong Kong, where labour was cheap and exchange rates were favourable.[37] By 1990 this small island exported 590 million such watches each year to every corner of the world.[38] Such products created a sensation in Beijing around the end of the Cultural Revolution: though pitifully dim and unstable, the hour and minute shown numerically in a small rectangular window offered the most convincing proof of Hong Kong's advanced technology. In a broader sense, this 'window' allowed the Mainland public to have its first glimpse of Hong Kong's 'modernity' after many years of separation.[39]

Twenty years later a Hong Kong quartz watch could hardly generate any excitement, even in the Chinese provinces, but Hong Kong's technological superiority remained incontestable and continued to stimulate the fantasies of Mainlanders. The Hong Kong Clock, established in 1994 in Tiananmen Square and employing a digital display reminiscent of the 'window' on a Hong Kong quartz watch, thus did more than count down Hong Kong's remaining days as a British colony: what was being calculated was also the days before China annexed its technology as its own property. Ackbar Abbas told me he found this 'a situation unprecedented in the history of colonialism: the colonized state is in a more advanced [technological] position than the colonizing state.'[40] This interpretation, which casts China's regaining Hong Kong as a colonizing process within a nationalist framework, leads me in the final section of this Chapter to investigate the circumstances of the Clock's invention to uncover its implicit colonialist agenda and intention.

One thing is clear: although the Hong Kong Clock's legal foundation was the Joint Declaration between the Chinese and British governments of 1984, it was only established ten years later in 1994. Its delayed appearance meant that the Clock, rather than being an instantaneous celebration and confirmation of the treaty, responded to political changes during the decade after 1984 and, more urgently, to the political situation of 1993–4. Michael Yahuda has reviewed the diverse problems involved in the 'Hong Kong issue' during these ten years.[41] Some of the most important events and processes surface from his narrative and draw our attention.[42] The most important change concerning the Joint Declaration itself was Hong Kong people's growing suspicion towards it. The initial, if guarded, optimism that greeted the Declaration gradually gave away to an apprehension about how the Beijing government would interpret and apply its terms. Negotiation between China and Britain continued, but was more often than not handicapped by profound ideological differences as well as misunderstanding and distrust. In the midst of such prolonged diplomatic struggle, the 1989 pro-democratic movement occurred. Eager to see China moving towards a democratic society, people in Hong Kong gave their spiritual and financial support to the hunger-striking students. But they were soon as disillusioned as they were stunned by the massacre of the pro-democratic students in Tiananmen Square. With horror and disbelief, they watched on live television as tanks and soldiers killed peaceful demonstrators. Their response was to hold their own demonstration: a million people (which amounted to 20 per cent of the total population of Hong Kong) marched through the centre of the island in protest (illus. 120; see also illus. 28); on their mind was not only the tragedy in Beijing but also their own fate after 1997.

Beijing's attitude towards Hong Kong was also changing. The strong support and sympathy that the student movement received from Hong Kong caused the central government to view the territory as a source of subversion and a potential threat to political order in the People's Republic. This conclusion did not surprise the Chinese leaders: for almost ten years they had been watching closely and nervously the transformation of Hong Kong's socio-political system. Since the 1970s, a strong middle class, including a large group of professionals, had emerged and heavily influenced Hong Kong's cultural, economical and political scenes.[43] The 1984 Sino-Anglo treaty and the 1989 Tiananmen Square massacre further stimulated this group's self-awareness of its social responsibilities, and, on a broader scale, stimulated the people of Hong Kong to pursue their own cultural, social and political identity. It is commonly held that, from

120 Candlelight memorial rally in Hong Kong's Victoria Park, 4 June 1989. In the middle is the *Goddess of Democracy* stone wall.

the end of the Second World War until the early 1980s, the majority of the Chinese population in Hong Kong showed little interest in participating in politics or the business of government – interest that was strongly discouraged by the British colonial government.[44] This situation changed dramatically after 1984: the majority of Hong Kong people actively participated in meetings, elections, protests and other public activities. In a poll taken in 1982, more than 60 per cent of Hong Kong residents identified themselves as 'Chinese'; but in 1988 nearly two-thirds of the population professed stronger ties to Hong Kong.[45] As Yahuda has remarked, 'The difference between the two polls reflects the concerns after 1984 to demarcate Hong Kong and its way of life from that of the mainland to whose sovereignty it would soon revert.'[46]

New political groups emerged in Hong Kong and some went on to become political parties.[47] Largely supported by professionals and other members of the middle class, a new generation of politicians tried hard to define a 'Hong Kong position' independent from both China and Britain. Their main goal of establishing a workable democracy in the territory before the return to Chinese sovereignty attracted many people in Hong Kong. The strong support of this rising political force was demonstrated in the first direct election to the Legislative Council in 1991. Twelve of the eighteen seats were won by candidates of the United Democrats headed by Martin Lee (whose Democratic Party grew out of the 1989 All Hong Kong Alliance in Support of the Chinese Patriotic Pro-Democracy Movement); another three seats went to independents sympathetic to their point of view; and none of the candidates close to Beijing won a seat.

This election, together with the 1992 'Patten Proposal' (a plan for democratic reforms in the territory, proposed by the newly appointed Hong Kong Governor Chris Patten), drew angry responses from Beijing. In a series of furious attacks, Chinese newspapers called Patten, *inter alia*, a prostitute and snake, and Martin Lee a subverter and foreign spy. Seventeen rounds of negotiations between China and Britain were held in 1993 but ended in failure. In July Beijing moved to establish an alternative centre of power by appointing a 57-member Preliminary Working Committee to prepare for the transfer of Hong Kong. In October an earlier speech of Deng Xiaoping was published, reminding people of the official rationale for the Tiananmen massacre. In it Deng warned: 'Don't ever think that everything would be all right if Hong Kong affairs were administrated solely by Hong Kong people while the Central Government had nothing to do with the matter.' He asked: 'Isn't it possible that something could happen in the region that might jeopardize the fundamental interests of the country? . . . what if they [i.e., pro-democratic Hong Kongers] should turn their [anti-Communist] words into action, trying to convert Hong Kong into a base of opposition to the mainland under the pretext of "democracy"?' Under such circumstances, he concluded: 'We should have no choice but to intervene.'[48] As if to respond to Deng's harsh words, in December the Legislative Council in Hong Kong voted the final package of the Patten Proposal into law, with effect from 30 June 1994. This vote was countered by a formal notification from Beijing, which asserted that Hong Kong's Legislative Council would be dismantled after 1 July 1997 and replaced by a 'legal representative institution'. These dates should now be familiar: on 30 June 1994 the Hong Kong Clock was unveiled in Tiananmen Square and began to count down the days and seconds to 1 July 1997.

Viewed in this context, the Clock was a political statement as well as a strategic gesture. Its timely establishment implied the sense of urgency and danger felt by Chinese leaders at that moment. The Clock, in fact, materialized Deng Xiaoping's warning against Hong Kong becoming an anti-Communist base 'under the pretext of "democracy"'. With its exaggerated size and appearance of a legal certificate, the Clock reasserted the schedule for Hong Kong's return and expressed the determination to realize this goal by any means, including military intervention. Located in Tiananmen Square, it sent out signals from the heart of the Communist political machine. The Clock was not just 'a public reminder to the people of Hong Kong that they were due to be embraced by the motherland under the leadership of the Chinese Communist Party before too long.'[49] It actually transgressed the current China-Hong Kong boundaries and exercised power over the people on the other side of the border. The Clock gained such power from its location and from its way of counting and telling time.

In a sense, the Clock continued the tradition of public time-telling in imperial China, which regulated the life of royal subjects by imposing on them a programmed schedule. But instead of presenting a timetable that was regular and repetitive, the schedule delivered by the Clock was designed for a single occasion. More specifically, it measured a particular transitional period and framed this period as a shrinking duration of 'negative time' before zero. On the surface, the Clock ran towards zero to indicate that the day of Hong Kong's return was approaching. On a deeper level, it meant that the existing Hong Kong as part of the colonial past would reach its end in due course. 'Counting down' was thus a powerful symbol of (and an effective means for) termination and revolution: the old Hong Kong would die and a new Hong Kong would be born at point zero. Before that point, Hong Kong belonged to a 'counter-history' that had to be measured backwards. After that point, Hong Kong would be given a 'positive time' synchronized with the rest of the country. 'Counting down' thus provided a structure for constructing history.

The Hong Kong Clock was a political timer. As a timer, it dwelled on the concept of 'end' or 'expiration' and generated anxiety. The implied viewers of the Clock were the people of Hong Kong, because only to them did this concept have concrete meaning. I was struck by the fact that many people in Beijing seemed quite indifferent towards the Clock located right in their neighbourhood, but individuals thousands of miles away in Hong Kong seemed to hear its ticking even in their dreams. So many articles and speeches in pre-1997 Hong Kong contained exclamations such as 'Time is running out!' or 'We don't have much time left!' There was a tendency for writers and speakers to calculate the remaining days before 1 July 1997 in an increasingly publicized manner; in so doing they seemed to accept the Clock's logic to see the future as the end.[50]

As an official instrument, the backward-counting Clock sharply demarcated Hong Kong's two alternative identities, either as 'foreign colony' or as 'an integral part of the socialist motherland'; this place was denied a third identity.[51] Hong Kong's existence before 1997 was conceived as a continuation of the past, represented by the disappearing days and seconds on the Clock. As I am writing, however, six years have passed since the Clock stopped running; and one can see more clearly the artificiality of such a notion of 'past' or 'future' imposed on a people or place by a political authority. The nature of the Clock as a means of political control and manipulation has also become more apparent: following its removal on 1 July 1997, Tiananmen Square had regained its original balance to represent once again an unchanging Communist order.

Art of the Square:
From Subject to Site

This Chapter investigates artistic responses to Tiananmen Square, not just representations of it but also interactions with it. It is predictable that a prominent official space like the Square would produce and inspire canonical images in official art, as will be demonstrated by a review in this Chapter of some of the most important paintings on the subject made under government patronage from the sixteenth century onwards. It is also not surprising that, when an unofficial art finally emerged in post-Mao China, it would turn the Square into a combat zone, challenging the place's authority in order to realize its own unorthodox identity. As a piece of evidence, a poster of a Beijing website of experimental art features an image of Tiananmen Square and labels it a 'space of avant-garde' (illus. 121), demonstrating the site's importance in the formation of an alternative, contemporary art tradition.

In this process, the role of the Square in artistic expression has changed from the subject of pictorial representations to the location of site-specific performances and simulated installations. The main force underlying this transformation is the intensification of an iconoclastic movement in Chinese art. Whether created during the Ming/Qing period or in the People's Republic, government-sponsored paintings of the Square have typically mystified this space and, in turn, contributed to the place's 'aura' in an imperial or totalitarian political culture. Consequently, early generations of unofficial artists made the effort to demystify this space through creating 'counter images'. Still conceived and produced as two-dimensional representations, these images were iconoclastic accounts of what had been deemed sacred – Tiananmen, Mao's portrait, the Square and its monuments, and 'the people'. Often deliberately modelled upon canonical paintings, these images aimed to debase their official prototypes.

The introduction of contemporary art forms from the West, including performance, installation and multi-media art, has provided new possibilities for unofficial artists to engage with the Square. Indeed, the wide adoption of these forms since the mid-1990s has radically changed the position of the Square in Chinese art, from something to be depicted (whether positively or negatively) to something to be responded to. It is another instance of how a socially conscious avant-garde realizes its political intent through manipulating visual forms. In this case, the site-specificity of new works points to a 'return of the

121 Tiananmen
Square: *Space
of Avant-garde*,
advertisement of
newyouth.beida
website, 2000.

記念. Xu Hao 対更
新的貢獻。但色
角不在中間、呈
采仍具有权威

122 Anonymous,
*The Forbidden
City*, hanging
scroll painting,
16th century,
colour and ink
on silk.

real',[1] as the artists re-conceptualize Tiananmen Square as an actual place of political/artistic activities and discourses. Created after 1989, however, these performances and simulated installations have had a distinctly traumatic over-tone: in their active interactions with the Square, the artists have inevitably responded to a failed pro-democracy movement and its memory.

Representing Authority

Several Ming-dynasty paintings depict the Forbidden City in nearly identical compositions. In a version created after a major renovation of Tiananmen in 1562, the central section of the Forbidden City along the north–south axis is set out in strict symmetry from a bird's-eye view (illus. 122).[2] A man dressed in official garb stands next to Tiananmen, the first of a series of elaborate imperial buildings portrayed in the picture. He is Xu Hao, Minister of the Department of Construction, who oversaw the renovation, and the painting commemorates his involvement in the architectural project.[3] This is probably why the painter depicts the buildings in the manner of an architectural draw-ing, displaying minute structural details with exaggerated clarity. But unlike a conventional commemorative painting, which usually makes the subject of commemoration its focus, here the Forbidden City is given an unambiguous centrality and dominance. With its major gates and audience halls unfolding one above another along the picture's vertical axis, the imperial city, although devoid of human existence, manifests the authority of its (invisible) occupant: the emperor.

A similar painting by Zhu Bang, also dating from the sixteenth century, employs the same composition for a different representational purpose: it mystifies the Forbidden City rather than revealing it (illus. 123). Rising clouds half-cover and isolate the palace gates and halls, replacing the solid ground in the first painting to connect individual buildings into an implicit architectural system. The painter thus takes a metaphor literally – the Forbidden City is truly the 'heavenly court' (*tian ting*) of the Son of Heaven. To reinforce this message, he also juxtaposes the Forbidden City with an 'earthly realm' outside Beijing's front gate, depicted at the bottom of the painting. The Forbidden City, as a celestial palace, is distant and mysterious; but this second place is located on earth and animated by people and their lively activities. Here we see travellers who have just arrived and dismounted from their horses, and servants conversing with one other in a relaxed manner. It is an idealized world, though: men and women, as well as people of different social status and occupations, live in harmony and mutual respect. To this end, the central scene of this section, which shows officials and a gentleman politely greeting each other before Beijing's front gate, highlights the section's significance.[4]

Images in this lower section remind us of Jiang Yikui's description of the Chessboard Street outside the imperial domain. As I have discussed in Chapter Three, this Ming scholar-official identifies Chessboard Street as a public space of social intercourse, where 'all types of people under Heaven' converge in

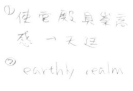

123 Zhu Bang, *The Forbidden City*, 16th century, hanging scroll painting, colour and ink on silk.

最大、紅牛間 →

front of the 'gate of the state' (see pp. 94–5). I have also explained in Chapter Two how the layered walls and gates of the Forbidden City served to increase the emperor's mystique through intensifying the sense of distance between the inner and the outer (see pp. 57–9). In a remarkably succinct way, this Ming painting brings these two spaces and their associated representational modes – inside and outside, concealing and displaying – into an ordered whole. The result is a symbolic representation of a political structure dominated by imperial authority.

The image of Tiananmen takes on a unique role to facilitate this hierarchical representation. Although the painter positions the Hall of Supreme Harmony, the principal palace in the Forbidden City, at the top of the painting as the summit of the heavenly court, he depicts Tiananmen as the largest architectural structure and places it at the exact centre of the composition. In this way, Tiananmen serves as a double-edged signifier both to conceal and reveal imperial power: as the gate of the Imperial City it also projects the emperor's aura to the society at large. It must be no coincidence that the painter extends Tiananmen's wings into straight walls, separating the painting into two rigid halves. It must also be no coincidence that he uses the same technique to subdivide the lower half, and depicts 'all types of people under Heaven' outside Zhengyangmen, Beijing's front gate. The zone between Tiananmen and Zhengyangmen, where traditional Tiananmen Square lies, is thus conceived as a transitional space. Accentuated by a passageway in the middle and a ceremonial usher to one side, this space reinforces Tiananmen's symbolism as the link between the inner and the outer, the emperor and his subjects.

If the 'hanging scroll' format provided the painters of these two Ming pictures with a suitable means to represent political hierarchy in a vertical composition, the 'handscroll' format was employed by a group of Qing court painters to render Emperor Kangxi's (reigned 1662–1722) expedition to southern China in 1689 as a continuous 'moving picture' consisting of twelve scrolls.[5] The work is monumental: the twelve scrolls together form a composition more than 200 metres long and double the width of a standard handscroll painting.[6] With such extraordinary dimensions, the painting could not possibly be handled and viewed by any individual viewer. Rather, it was created to preserve the emperor's political legacy for posterity.

The first scroll starts with scenes representing the departure of the imperial entourage from Yongdingmen, the southern gate of Beijing's Outer City. Accompanied by hundreds of officials, guards and attendants on horseback, Kangxi proceeds to cross a royal hunting park (Nan yuan). The gate of the park painted at the end of the scroll marks the southern limit of the capital area. The next ten scrolls depict major political and ceremonial activities that the emperor carried out on his journey across China from north to south: he inspects flood control work at the Yellow and Huai Rivers, makes a grand ritual sacrifice to Heaven at sacred Mt Tai, pays homage to the tombs of previous dynastic founders, and celebrates the prosperity of southern cities such as Suzhou and Hangzhou. The last scroll in the set depicts his return to the imperial palace, described by a written preface at the beginning of the scroll:

> With respect we have painted this twelfth scroll. His Majesty has completed his ceremonial southern expedition. The Yellow River flows in its proper course, and the people behave in exemplary ways. His Majesty's visit has transformed the local regions, nourishing the whole country with his divine virtue. Thus he is now holding the *ru bi* ceremony to re-enter the imperial city. All the way from Yongdingmen to Wumen, Beijing residents sing and dance, welcoming him as his entourage passes. All the hundreds of ministers and officials greet the imperial procession in ecstasy. [This scroll depicts] the magnificent capital, the lofty palatial buildings, the luxuriant vapour of the place, and the auspicious clouds that flow in from the four directions to shield [the throne hall]. In this way, the painting

ru bi ritual

124 Wang Hui and others, the twelfth scroll of *Emperor Kangxi Returning to the Forbidden City from his Southern Expedition*, after 1689, handscroll, ink and colour on silk. Reversing the normal viewing sequence of a handscroll, the emperor's procession proceeds from left to right, and from the bottom register to the top register.

will serve as a record of the sage rule of the Son of Heaven for ten thousand years.[7]

A major discrepancy exists between this preface and the painting itself, however: whereas the text describes Beijing residents' spontaneous celebration of the emperor's return, the picture represents nothing of the sort (illus. 124). In fact, it shows that the public road from Yongdingmen to Zhengyangmen (that is, the road linking the southern gates of Beijing's Outer and Inner Cities) has been blocked off and cleared for the imperial procession. All the shops facing the road are closed, their doors and windows tightly shut. Only beyond this barrier do we see scattered people in houses and on the streets.

Clearly, this public road has been temporarily transformed into a forbidden space. This is exactly the meaning and function of the *ru bi* ritual, conducted when a ruler re-entered the palace after touring the country.[8] This painting thus demonstrates that in traditional China the 'imperial domain' was actually a flexible concept, the boundaries of which changed on different occasions. It could be defined by Tiananmen (during an edict-issuing ceremony when imperial subjects received the edict under the gate), by the Gate of Great Ming or Qing (which overlooked the usually busy, public Chessboard Avenue), by Beijing's Inner City gate (as shown in Zhu Bang's painting discussed above) or by the Outer City gate (as during Emperor Kangxi's *ru bi* ceremony).

170

From the first scroll in the set to the eleventh, the emperor's procession proceeds consistently from right to left, synchronizing with the motion of unrolling the scrolls. But the procession turns around in this last scroll and moves from left to right – a conventional visual trope in traditional Chinese art for homecoming. Another visual trope, identified in the scroll's preface as images of 'luxuriant vapour' and 'auspicious clouds', helps the painter, first, map the ritual site and, second, establish a hierarchical structure internal to the imperial territory.

First, whereas vapour and clouds embrace only the Forbidden City and the Inner City in Zhu Bang's painting discussed above (see illus. 123), here they frame the entire ritual site, starting from the gate of the Outer City. Second, this Qing painting represents two kinds of vapour or clouds connected with two different spaces: clouds with curvilinear contours frame the scroll's left half, and then transform into clouds of rigid, horizontal shapes at the exact conjunction of Chessboard Avenue and the Gate of Great Qing. The first kind of clouds is associated with a public space that has been temporarily integrated into the imperial domain; the second kind signifies the permanent imperial space starting from Tiananmen Square. Passing the U-shaped Wumen, the front gate of the Forbidden City, clouds of the second type suddenly thicken, and become pervasive after the Gate of Supreme Harmony. Consequently, the emperor's throne hall behind this gate is almost completely concealed behind such 'auspicious clouds'. This building, the Hall of Supreme Harmony, is thus only alluded to, not actually represented. Depicted at the right end of the scroll, it is the final stop on the emperor's journey. The message is clear: once having re-entered the hall, the emperor would become 'invisible' again and rule China from this place where no human sight could reach.

All three of these paintings created in pre-modern China, whether in the single-frame hanging-scroll format or in the multi-frame handscroll format, represent political authority through framing an empty centre. Even in the last example, where Emperor Kangxi is actually portrayed at various places inspecting his country, it is the mysterious, nearly invisible Hall of Supreme Harmony that ultimately manifests the imperial authority. This representational mode became obsolete in Chinese art when the country entered the modern era. As I have discussed in Chapter Two, nationalist leaders of twentieth-century China eagerly embraced a Western model to have their likeness represented and delivered to the public. In addition to formal portraits displayed in public spaces and publicized through mass media, historical paintings were commissioned to immortalize their pivotal roles at crucial moments in modern Chinese history. Unlike the Kangxi scroll, which depicts the emperor as a tiny figure among many, these paintings share the interest of a public portrait to boast of a larger-than-life image of a political leader; what separates them from a portrait is their inherent theatricality: the leader is always represented as the central character of a historical drama.

The most celebrated and influential work of this genre in post-1949 China is undoubtedly Dong Xiwen's *The Founding of the Nation* of 1952–3 (illus. 125). An oil painting 4 metres wide and 2.3 metres high, it represents the very

125 Dong Xiwen, *The Founding of the Nation*, 1952–3, oil on canvas.

moment when Mao Zedong, standing on Tiananmen's balcony, proclaimed the establishment of the People's Republic of China. Behind Mao are other top leaders of the new country, including, from left to right, Lin Boqu, Zhou Enlai, Zhu De, Liu Shaoqi, Song Qingling, Guo Moruo, Dong Biwu, Zhang Lan and Gao Gang. Standing close to one other while keeping a respectful distance from Mao, they form a collective backdrop to emphasize Mao's unchallenged prominence.

Whereas the accuracy of these leaders' likenesses was corroborated by the leaders themselves (who were invited to examine the painting before it was exhibited and published), official art critics have hailed the painting as a masterpiece of Chinese socialist art mainly for its stylistic originality. From this second perspective, the painting has been praised for its successful 'nationalization' (*minzu hua*) of the foreign medium of oil painting. The evidence includes Dong's selection of typical 'national objects', such as the red lanterns and the Chinese-style carpet; the painting's striking contrast of bright colours, which betrays influences from folk art, especially from traditional 'New Year's painting'; and the flat, crisply outlined figures and objects – images akin to those found in woodcut prints.[9] These observations are not off the mark: Dong Xiwen himself expressed on many occasions his desire to forge a national style of oil painting; and for this purpose he spent three years at Dunhuang studying traditional methods of rendering shape and colour.[10]

With their dominant interest in the 'nationalization' of the painting, however, these critics have dismissed other innovations made by the artist, which may have had a greater impact on Mao's approval of the work. It is reported that upon the painting's completion it was delivered to Zhongnanhai, where Mao lived, to be examined by Mao in person. After gazing at it for a long time, Mao finally nodded and said: 'It is a great nation. It is really a great nation.'[11] Apparently he was more interested in the painting's content than its style; and in terms of content he was looking not only at the leaders (including himself) on Tiananmen, but also at the masses in the Square. I would suggest that herein lies the most important decision made by Dong Xiwen: to him, *The Founding of the Nation* had to represent the leaders and the masses in the same composition, and for this purpose he had to find clever ways to manipulate reality.

In the painting, Mao's authority is established by his central position, his extraordinary physique (he is at least half a head taller than the other leaders) and by the artist's creative use of perspective. Whereas Dong Xiwen portrayed the other leaders at about eye level, he painted Mao's head and upper body from a slightly lower angle to emphasize the loftiness of the founder of New China. But here he ran into a difficulty: from this angle it would be impossible to see the space under Tiananmen; what could be seen would be only Mao's silhouette against an empty sky. To solve this problem, Dong Xiwen artificially raised the horizon, so the entire Square could come into view. To make this manipulation less obvious, he also intensified the foreshortening of the balcony, making the floor's perspective consistent with that of the Square. Furthermore, he omitted a column to Mao's right to maximize the view of the Square, and coloured the vast sky above the Square crisply blue and adorned it with bright, white clouds, although in reality the day was gloomy, with no sunshine.[12]

The result of this series of manoeuvres is an unobstructed view of the two spaces above and below Tiananmen: this composite scene is absent in any photograph of the event, which could focus only on one space or the other, never both (see, for example, illus. 66 and 72). But the painting's representation of these two spaces and their associated human subjects is not even-handed, since it embodies Mao's view in depicting the people: looking down from Tiananmen, the Square resembles a vast ocean; on its surface red flags and banners wave and float. The leaders atop Tiananmen are portrayed as convincing individuals; the parading masses in the Square derive strength from a collective anonymity. The combination of the two – above and below, the leaders and the people – constitutes a comprehensive representation of New China. It was this representation that led Mao to say: 'This is really a great nation'.

The 'afterlife' of this painting is well known: it has been constantly revised according to China's changing political circumstances (illus. 126).[13] Less than a year after its completion, Gao Gang, the man portrayed immediately to Mao's left, lost his position in the government and committed suicide. He was consequently expunged from the painting; an enlarged chrysanthemum partly filled the resulting empty space. Then, when Liu Shaoqi and Lin Boqu were purged during the Cultural Revolution, their images were likewise erased, with Liu's head transformed into that of Dong Biwu. A reverse process took place after the Cultural Revolution: the work was altered – not simply restored – to facilitate new political needs (illus. 127). Whereas the reappearance of Liu Shaoqi and Lin Boqu in the painting recognized their rehabilitation, 'a previously unidentifiable figure in the back row', as Julia Andrews has noticed, 'now looks vaguely like the young Deng Xiaoping.'[14]

Instead of presenting a definitive, unchanging image, therefore, this painting has been the site of a metamorphic process of re-presentation.

Nonetheless, despite the changes made over the past half a century, the painting's basic composition and central character have remained unaltered: Mao has always been the man announcing the founding of the nation, and the event has always been represented as a grand meeting between the people and their leaders. With the current version prominently displayed in the Museum of Chinese Revolutionary History, this painting signifies the Party leadership's changing personnel as well as the persistence of its fundamental ideology.

The Founding of the Nation is the only canonized painting on the subject in the People's Republic of China. As such, its monumentality in official art is

128 Sun Zixi,
*In Front of
Tiananmen*, 1964,
oil on canvas.

ensured by its singularity. It is also the only painting that represents the two
spaces above and below Tiananmen while internalizing Mao's view. Other
painters have tried to juxtapose these two spaces, but have invariably shifted
their viewpoint to the Square. Consciously or unconsciously, they identify
themselves with the 'revolutionary masses' in the Square and subject themselves to Mao's gaze from Tiananmen. A representative of this second composition, an oil painting that has become a counterpoint of many 'avant-garde'
attacks on Tiananmen Square since the 1990s, is Sun Zixi's *In Front of
Tiananmen* (illus. 128). Painted and published in 1964, it was soon singled out
by official critics as an outstanding example of socialist realist art,[15] and was
praised especially for its successful deployment of national forms in creating
this art, a goal that had been championed by official painters and theoreticians
from the early 1950s. If Dong Xiwen's *Founding of the Nation* of 1952–3 was
the first major artwork created with this aim, Zhou Yang, a principal spokes-
man on cultural policies at the time, made this goal an official demand the
same year:

> We request that the contents of literary and art works represent the
> people and express the thoughts of the new age, and that their forms
> express the style and vigour of the nation . . . All writers and artists
> should diligently study their own national literary and artistic legacy
> and take the continuation and development of the national heritage's
> excellent tradition as their mission.[16]

Created a decade later, on the eve of the Cultural Revolution, *In Front of
Tiananmen* realized such a demand in an almost graphic manner. Stylistically
it both follows and exaggerates Dong Xiwen's effort to 'nationalize' oil painting.
Compared to *The Founding of the Nation*, its colour scheme and perspective

system are further simplified to heighten the painting's symbolic value. The spatial depth is much reduced; the composition is now nearly symmetrical. A few bright colours are used extensively as flat, unmodulated patches applied to distinguish basic shapes. The artist self-consciously borrowed elements from Chinese folk art, and such stylistic borrowing served to enhance the work's content, which is, in Zhou Yang's words, to 'represent the people and express the thoughts of the new age'.

At the centre of the painting, directly in front of Tiananmen, a group of figures poses for a photograph. Judging by their clothes and physical features, they come from different regions and include cadres, workers, peasants and students. The group consists of nine men and three women. Although most are in their twenties, a few exceptions help to extend the group's coverage to include older and younger generations. Most of them smile broadly at the spectator – or at an implied camera in front of them. This implication is made explicit by two other groups in the painting. Much reduced in size, the group to the right consists of six sailors from the navy, while a dozen or so figures of different nationalities form the group to the left. The juxtaposition of these two groups reflects certain formal concerns, since the painter clearly intends to contrast the sailors' uniforms with the varied, colourful minority costumes. But these and other contrasts between the figures serve only to emphasize their sameness: despite their differences in ethnicity, age, gender and occupation, they have all come to the Square and are taking photographs in front of Tiananmen.

This painting offers a textbook case to study Chinese socialist realist art in the early 1960s, because it internalizes a deepening paradox in this art at the time. On the one hand, the scene depicted in the painting is 'realistic' because it is based on reality: since the 1950s Tiananmen Square had become the most popular spot in the country for people to have their portraits taken, either by themselves or by professional photographers (these two situations are represented in the painting by the soldiers and minority figures, respectively). On the other hand, the scene is deliberately unrealistic because it is an artificial construct created by distilling common situations into an abstraction – a process known as *dianxing hua* – 'to typify' reality in an artistic representation. An essential component of theories on socialist realist art at the time, this process aims to reveal the substance of larger social-historical phenomena for socialist causes, and to create paintings as vehicles of political ideas. As a result of this process, *In Front of Tiananmen* shows portraits but not individuals: we see different figures but know nothing about their names and lives. Instead of revealing individuality, the figures' differences serve to index large social categories based on ethnicity, gender, age and occupation. These figures can therefore together represent the 'People-as-One', a constructed social body that Claude Lefort considers the foundation of totalitarianism.[17] At the same time, the figures' grouping and positioning also signify a hierarchical structure internal to this collective social entity: among the three groups in the painting, the central group stands for the union of workers and peasants, the leading classes in the People's Republic, and also represents the Han Chinese – the dominant nationality in the country.

But are 'the people' – even as an abstract notion – the central subject of the painting's representation? To answer this question, it is important to note that, although the painting follows the general format of a group portrait, it reverses the relationship between figures and background in a conventional group portrait. In other words, although the figures in this painting are supposedly the main subject of representation, they are deliberately reduced in size and confined within the lower register of the composition. Although in theory Tiananmen constitutes the figures' physical environment and provides the backdrop for their picture-taking, in actuality it dominates the whole composition. In particular, the artist positions Mao's portrait at the painting's exact centre. From this place on Tiananmen's façade, Mao not only dominates all the people in the Square, but also looks straight into the eyes of any viewer of the painting.

Four artists already mentioned were professors at the Central Academy of Fine Arts in the 1950s and '60s – China's top art school at the time and my alma mater. Among them, Zhou Lingzhao painted Mao's first Tiananmen portrait in 1949 for the country's inauguration ceremony; Dong Xiwen completed *The Founding of the Nation* in 1953; Liu Kaiqu headed a team of sculptors from 1953 to 1958 to design the relief carvings on the Monument to the People's Heroes; and Sun Zixi painted *In Front of Tiananmen* in 1964. They were all there when I entered the Academy in 1963.

Founded by Xu Beihong in 1946,[18] the Academy had a small campus but a large and distinguished faculty. It was said that of the 50 top artists in the country in the late 1940s and the '50s, forty were recruited by Xu and his successors to teach in the school. Some of these artists were educated in Paris or Tokyo; others were home-grown products. They were then joined by a new generation of painters and sculptors trained by Russian professors in the mid- to late 1950s. Over the years the school also routinely expanded its faculty by recruiting its best graduates. Whereas teachers in the four studio art departments (oil painting, traditional painting, graphic art and sculpture) were all artists, those in the fifth and last department (art history and art criticism) were scholars and theoreticians of different types, including a former film director well-known in 1930s Shanghai, a street performer turned folk art specialist, and several Russian-trained theorists and historians of Western art.

The Academy's architecture was as eclectic as its faculty. (I say 'was' because the school has relocated and most of its buildings have been torn down.) Local residents traced the history of the site to a large compound of imperial guards in the last dynasty; and indeed during the 1960s the street in front of the school was still called Jiaoweiying, or Camp of Honour Guards. Also according to local lore, the camp was taken over by warlords and officials after the Qing fell. Among its new owners, Li Zongren, who later became a president of the Republican government, installed electric lights and plastered ceilings in the camp's traditional timber houses. During the Second World War Beijing was occupied by Japanese troops. A two-storey, cement building with a U-shaped floor plan was constructed alongside the timber houses to provide classrooms for a Japanese elementary school. After the war the school was handed over to the Republican government and turned into an art college. Some people say that Xu Beihong painted 100 horses – he was famous for making such images – in exchange for the place.[19] The college (called National Beiping Arts College) was renamed the Central Academy of Fine Arts in 1950. Three Russian-style, utilitarian structures were added during the following decade, including an office building for the school's administration, a student dormitory and a research institute. After I entered the school, therefore, I slept in the Russian-style dormitory (with five room-mates in three bunk beds); took classes in the Japanese U-Building, where the coat hangers, designed for kids, were four feet from the ground and the urinals were below our knees; and ate in a wooden-framed hall with Li Zongren's Rococo-style plaster mouldings on the ceiling.

Upon entering the Academy I was amazed to learn that the school had more than two hundred faculty members but only one hundred plus students. The reason was that, while the faculty kept swelling, the student body had been shrinking due to irregular admissions caused by frequent political movements. My class of ten in the Department of Art History, in fact, was the only incoming class in 1963; all the studio art departments had stopped taking in new students. The reason soon became apparent: most artists/professors in the school were in trouble. As products of either Western 'capitalist' education or Russian 'revisionist' education, they were now subject to a 'socialist re-education' campaign, which later turned into a prelude to the Cultural Revolution. As a result, I belonged to the Academy's last pre-Cultural Revolution class; the next class would not arrive until ten years later, when Jiang Qing (i.e., Madam Mao) transformed the Academy into a 'school of revolutionary art' called the May Seventh College of Arts (that being the date of a letter that Mao wrote to Lin Biao, in which he demanded that students and intellectuals be re-educated by the revolutionary masses). She appointed herself the president of the new school and selected Sun Zixi, the painter of *In Front of Tiananmen*, as the school's vice-director.

In my memory Sun was a friendly and soft-spoken person, always seen in a slightly worn Mao suit. In the early 1960s he was teaching mainly in the professional high school attached to the Academy, and appeared on the main campus only during assemblies. According to some of my more 'politically sensitive' schoolmates, he was almost an anomaly on the Academy's faculty because of his pure, revolutionary background. They told me that Sun had joined the Communist army when he was still a teenager, and worked in the army's propaganda department throughout the civil war. He demonstrated his artistic talent in that capacity and was recommended to the Central Academy in the mid-1950s. He joined the faculty of the Oil Painting Department after graduating in 1960. I never got to know him personally, partly because of my inferior, bourgeois family background. For the same reason, I felt closer to those teachers who shared my parents' professional profile and class identity. Liu Kaiqu, Dong Xiwen and Zhou Lingzhao fell into this category.

But I didn't know them well either: the gap between students and professors in the Academy had become unbridgeable in the 1960s, when mistrust and suspicion came to govern any human relationship. I got to know them better because of family ties and personal encounters. One of my best friends at the time was Dong Shabei, a son of Dong Xiwen; my parents knew Liu Kaiqu and his wife Chang Shana; and I was there when Zhou Lingzhao was nearly beaten to death by Red Guards at the beginning of the Cultural Revolution. The gap between me and these three professors largely diminished when we were brought into a single place that we called Ox Street (Niu Jie), a ghetto established by the Academy's revolutionary masses for the enemies (and potential enemies) of the people. We became fellow residents of the place for seven months from mid-1968 to early 1969.

I have mentioned this episode in my life in Chapter Two: like all colleges and universities throughout the country, the leadership of the Central Academy of Fine Arts was taken over by a Workers' Mao Zedong Thought Propaganda Team in July 1968. Consequently, the 'ox-demons and snake-spirits' previously held in custody by the Academy's two major Red Guard factions (called the Prairie Fire group and the Revolutionary Alliance/Red Flag group) were united into a single camp.

The camp was located in a narrow lane along the Academy's northern edge, flanked by two rows of single-level rooms. The northern row was left over from the Qing dynasty; the darkened wooden beams still bore a faint decoration of traditional patterns. Until 1966 the five low-ceilinged rooms in this row provided space for students to make sculptures and lithograph prints. The southern row consisted of larger, brighter art studios of a more recent date. I was very familiar with these studios: before the Cultural Revolution my class met there eight hours each week to paint plaster busts or life models as part of our curricular requirements. The area was transformed into a sealed ghetto in July 1968 when gates were installed between the two rows of houses at either end of the lane. It became known as Ox Street because its residents were all 'ox-demons and snake-spirits'.

We were divided into several groups. My group included Dong Xiwen and Liu Kaiqu. Zhou Lingzhao belonged to another group. The camp life was mechanical and repetitive: getting up – cleaning the campus, including all the toilets – studying newspapers and Mao's recent 'supreme instructions' (*zuigao zhishi*) – confessing crimes and doing self-criticism – studying Marxism, Leninism and Mao Zedong thought – pledging loyalty to Mao's portrait – sleeping. Eating took place after the school's revolutionary teachers and students had finished their meals. Three times a day, Little Xu, a Red Guard working in the kitchen, unlocked the gate at the west end of the lane and shouted: 'Oxen! It's your turn now!' Then, slowly, more than a hundred of us walked through the gate, one by one in a long line, to receive food in the dining hall next door and bring it back to eat on Ox Street.

The Street was devoid of casual conversation. (The only exception was a tiny cell occupied by two hepatitis patients, Huang Yongyu and Han Zengxing. I often sneaked in there to chat with them.) Still, Dong Xiwen was unusual for being completely silent except for making confessions and doing self-criticism in group meetings – a mandatory task for all of us living there. From his confessions I learned that he had a bad family background, because his father (or uncle?) was an antique collector and dealer. (This explained to me how my friend Shabei could have some Tang dynasty Buddhist manuscripts in his possession, which he hid in his shoes at the beginning of the Cultural Revolution to avoid the Red Guards' destruction.) Also in these meetings, Dong Xiwen confessed that he became part of a counter-revolutionary, colonial intelligentsia when he went to study painting on a government scholarship in Hanoi, then a French colony. He said this in a monotone. Not even once did he mention *The Founding of the Nation*, as if he were no longer credible as the work's author.

He spent most of his free time writing self-criticism in a nearly perfect Liu script (a formal calligraphic style invented by Liu Gongquan during the Tang dynasty). Although his tool was a cheap ballpoint pen, he wrote each character with utmost concentration, articulating each stroke as if practising calligraphy with a traditional brush. It was impossible to know whether he was demonstrating his sincerity in carrying out self-criticism or using the opportunity to experience the pleasure of writing. He died in 1973 before he reached 60. Shabei told me later that his father kept silent even after he was released from Ox Street. He spent the final days of his life repairing a Song dynasty ceramic vase, which Red Guards had smashed into numerous shards.

Dong Xiwen lived in Dayabao Lane #2 in East Beijing (now demolished). One of the Academy's off-campus faculty dormitories, the compound consisted of a series of traditional houses connected by small courtyards and narrow passageways. His family occupied a row of four or five rooms near the southern entrance of the compound, while Zhou Lingzhao's house was located deeper inside. When I visited Shabei before the Cultural Revolution, I sometimes saw his father and Zhou Lingzhao in the yard, reading books or watering flowers. After the Cultural Revolution started I no longer ran into them, because both were among the Academy's first group of ox-demons subjected to 'class struggles' by the revolutionary masses.

Accidentally I witnessed one of the earliest and most violent of such 'struggles' in the Academy; Zhou Lingzhao was a main target of the attack. In August 1966 the Academy's Red Guards put up a Black Painting Exhibition ('black' means 'reactionary') in a large classroom on the second floor of the U-Building, with an angry preface denouncing the works on display, all made by the Academy's professors, either as 'venomous slander against the revolutionary people' or as 'vicious attacks on our great leader Chairman Mao'. The former category included Dong Xiwen's 1949 painting Liberating Beijing, which was criticized for 'vilifying the People's Liberation Army and Beijing residents'. The latter category included several cartoon portraits of Mao, created by Zhou Lingzhao and Ye Qianyu (a well-known professor in the Academy's Department of Traditional Painting) in the early 1950s.[20] During the period immediately after 1949 it was still possible for artists to draw such humorous images of Mao and publish them in newspapers. But by 1966 these images had become evidence for their 'malicious distortion' of Mao – the worst of all crimes a painter could commit. In the exhibition, these portraits were hung behind curtains, which were drawn only when Red Guards with pure class identities came to visit.

One group of such visitors belonged to the Red Army, a radical Red Guard faction in the professional high school attached to the Academy. Teenage sons and daughters of veteran cadres, members of this group were notorious for their extremely violent behaviour towards anyone whom they considered 'impure' in class origin and/or ideology. It was said that they set up a prison in the basement of their school and jailed 'class enemies' in it. One of the prisoners, a former landowner from the neighbourhood, was severely tortured and left there to die.

In the morning, when I was looking at the Black Painting Exhibition, a dozen members of the Red Army marched in, all dressed in green army uniforms and wearing the Red Guard band on their arms. They flew into a rage when they saw Mao's cartoon portraits. Several of them dashed out to bring in Zhou Lingzhao and Ye Qianyu, who were doing labour outside, to be 'struggled' on the spot. They came back a few minutes later with Zhou, pulling him into the room with a leather belt tied around his neck. They ordered him to kneel in front of the portraits and confess his criminal intention in making them. Zhou was trembling all over and could barely talk. They began to beat him with the heavy metal buckles on their thick leather belts, and to kick him with their army boots. Zhou fell on the ground and cried out in agony, but this brought about even more violent punishment. Until that moment I had never seen people being beaten like this. Shaking uncontrollably, I rushed out of the room and ran back to my dormitory. Unable to tell my room-mates about what was happening in our school, I cried and hit the wall with my fist, leaving bloodstains from my knuckles.

Two years later, Zhou Lingzhao and I became fellow residents of Ox Street. Because we lived in different rooms, however, I saw him mainly during meals. Several ox-demons and snake-spirits were always waiting at the west gate of the Street some twenty to thirty minutes before the gate was opened to let them through to receive food. Under hot sun or in snow they stood there, motionless, holding their bowls or lunch boxes as if these were the only things left in their possession. Zhou Lingzhao was one of them.

I felt I knew Liu Kaiqu better because he and his wife were long-time acquaintances of my parents. His family had visited our family when I was a young boy, and my mother told my sister and me about his illustrious career after one such visit. She said that Liu had studied art in Paris. Upon returning he became the director of the Hangzhou Arts College and a deputy mayor of that famous city, before accepting the invitation to become vice-director of the Central Academy in 1959 (illus. 129). After I entered the Academy, I was told that because he had been a deputy mayor of a major city, his official rank was actually higher than the Academy's chief director Wu Zuoren, and that he had a car exclusively for his use. He was also one of the highest-paid professors in the school.

The Liu Kaiqu I saw on Ox Street was a mere shadow of his former self. His transformation had a precise date, since he turned into a different person overnight after his younger daughter, a top student in the Academy's Department of Sculpture, drowned the previous year. The tragedy took place on 18 July 1967, when the Academy's figurehead Revolutionary Committee organized teachers and students to swim in a Beijing lake to celebrate the anniversary of Mao's swim in the Yangzi River. A whirlwind hit the lake and killed three students, including Liu Kaiqu's daughter. He heard the news while held in a makeshift

129 Liu Kaiqu (centre) and young sculptors discussing the relief carvings for the Monument to the People's Heroes, 1959.

prison under the Prairie Fire's control. Before this event he had suffered, but had not been destroyed, by imprisonment and repeated accusation meetings. His daughter's death finished him: he no longer had any facial expression, and he spent most of the time staring at the void before him with vacant eyes. He had an elder daughter, but polio had left her with a distorted face and paralysed limbs. It was this daughter who came to Ox Street, in callipers, to see him during visiting hours each Sunday.

One Friday Comrade Du, the worker put in charge of Ox Street, called a meeting and announced a decision: to plead guilty and to demonstrate repentance, all the art professors on the Street were to draw self-portraits, doing their best to vilify themselves. The ugliest image would be testimony of the sincerest self-criticism. The portraits would then be posted on a wall before Sunday, the next visiting day for the painters' family members. It was a long agonizing evening for the artists. No one picked up his pencil for two hours. Finally some reluctantly began to draw; others just sat there and looked at blank sheets of paper. Huang Yongyu, always full of clever ideas, secretly suggested to some fellow ox-demons that they could portray each other – a much easier way to produce ugly images to satisfy the requirement. It was then agreed that he and Liu Kaiqu would make portraits for each other. A talented painter, Huang soon produced a cartoon image of Liu, with a pair of pea-like cross eyes in the middle of an enormous, flat face. He then added to the head the coiled body of a cobra.

The next day, this and other portraits were posted on a wall next to the east gate of the Street, the entrance for family visitors. On Sunday, before visiting hours, someone found and reported that Liu Kaiqu's portrait had been changed: his eyes were no longer crossed, but looking straight in front of him with a blank, innocent expression. It was then discovered that he had redrawn the image in the night, before his paralysed daughter could see it.

Counter-Image

China's political situation changed dramatically in the late 1970s: the Cultural Revolution was officially over; the new generation of Chinese leaders turned away from ideological campaigns to economic reforms. More than 100,000 intellectuals and cadres who had been in detention or in political disgrace since 1957 were rehabilitated in 1978. Writers and artists regained professional credibility and a certain measure of confidence to recount their experience in their works. Not surprisingly, their first task was to reflect upon the Cultural Revolution, which had silenced them for a long, painful decade. Different methods were deployed for this purpose. The so-called scar artists (*shanghen meishu jia*) and scar writers (*shanghen wenxue jia*), for example, took it as their mission to expose the dark side of the Cultural Revolution – the violence and lawlessness of the period, the suffering of individuals, the meaningless sacrifices and self-sacrifices, and the general apathy towards the victims.[21] Their means remained realistic representation, however. While voicing strong political criticism and attracting much public attention, they nevertheless operated within the confines of academic art under government patronage.

It is therefore from a different group of paintings and sculptures that one detects an early effort to articulate new artistic concepts and languages beyond realism.[22] Instead of rediscovering 'authentic' history and reality, their authors – avant-garde or experimental artists outside government-sponsored art institutions – appropriated existing images, often the most famous official icons and monuments. In contemporary Chinese art such 'counter images' emerged around 1979 amidst a nationwide reaction against the cult of Mao. By this time, the ritual of making loyalty pledges had become memory. The removal of Mao portraits and monoliths from public spaces further stirred up considerable excitement. The anti-Mao sentiment was pushed to extremes by radical intellectuals; some of them became political activists and even went so far as to challenge publicly the mandate of the Communist Party (as in the Democracy Wall Movement of 1978–9). In literature, the poet Sun Jingxuan likened Mao to an omnipresent spectre, one who 'clutches the country with invisible claws'.[23] In art, the sculptor Wang Keping made a satiric bust of Mao in 1978 and entitled it *Idol* (illus. 130). The image employs the conventional iconography of a Mao icon in order to destroy it. Rigidly frontal, it combines Mao's face with a traditional Buddha statue. With one eye open and one eye half-closed, the Great Leader seems both a benevolent deity and a trickster. His Russian-style Bolshevik cap, too narrow for the plump face, appears as an afterthought. The glossy surface of the sculpture further adds an unpleasant feeling of sleaziness.

As an early example of post-Cultural Revolution 'counter images', *Idol* was created above all as a work of political art. Deriving vocabulary from the art of caricature, Wang Keping's chief purpose was to desecrate Mao by bestowing him with a set of negative, albeit still abstract qualities. Since the mid-1980s, however, series of works by new generations of experimental artists have

demonstrated a different tendency, since their appropriations of official art have become increasingly artistic exercises aimed at experimenting with new methods and strategies in visual representation. This is not to say that these artists have rejected political meaning in their works. On the contrary, any distortion of official icons in China is by nature iconoclastic. But to these artists, iconoclasm becomes meaningful only when it offers possibilities to develop new types of representation – that is, when the original image can be fragmented and its elements reused for new purposes. Such projects, which are all 'deconstructive' in nature, have been conducted during the past fifteen years and have produced some canonical works in contemporary Chinese art. The longevity of this trend implies that in today's China direct engagements with the dominant political culture, including political images and spaces, continue to be a chief strategy for experimental artists to identify their alternative positions and to articulate their artistic languages.[24]

Among these artists, some have refashioned masterpieces of official art into self-conscious 'counter images'. Works by three artists – Wang Guangyi's *Mao Zedong – Black Grid* and *Mao Zedong – Red Grid* (1988), Wang Jinsong's *In Front of Tiananmen* (1991) and Shao Yinong's and Mu Chen's *New China* (2003) – exemplify three different directions in appropriating official representations of Mao and Tiananmen Square. It would be helpful to take a close look at these examples, whose diverse intentions and strategies will then lead us to examine additional works created along each direction.

Instead of caricaturing Mao, as Wang Keping had done a decade before, Wang Guangyi tried to 'rationalize' through revisiting Mao's famous portrait on Tiananmen. Born in Harbin in 1956, Wang Guangyi studied oil painting in the prestigious Zhejiang Academy of Fine Arts (now the Chinese Academy of Fine Arts) in Hangzhou. His career as an experimental artist began when he founded, together with some friends, an avant-garde art society called The North Group (Beifang qunti) in 1986. The society's manifesto denounced the 'blind emotions' prevalent in contemporary Chinese art, and promoted instead rational thinking in pursuing the 'essence of things'. This idea guided Wang Guangyi to create a series of 'post-Classical' paintings in 1986 and 1987, each displaying his formal analyses and abstraction of a canonical image in European art history. His *Mao Zedong – Red Grid* of 1988 continued this direction, but derived its 'subject of objectification' from China's own visual culture (illus. 131).

At first glance each painting in this set seems simply to copy a standard Mao portrait. But to this archetypal image Wang Guangyi has made three subtle revisions to subvert it: he has duplicated the portrait multiple times and placed the copies side by side; he has duplicated the portrait in grey tones; and he has superimposed a uniform grid on the copies, adding the letters o and A at the corners. As a result, the monochrome, black-and-white images appear as shadows of the coloured original; the surface grid and letters – signs of non-pictorial kinds – distance the viewer from the images; and the multiplicity of the copies destroys the singularity of a sacred icon. According to Wang Guangyi, his work aimed 'to serve as a clearing house for the dire straits result-ing from the lack of logic, a consequence of the widespread humanistic zeal in our artistic circle.'[25] What he intended to achieve was therefore to get rid of the ideology associated with the portrait, thereby reinstalling its status as a sheer image. Martina Köppel-Yang has suggested that in developing his visual vocabulary Wang Guangyi was deeply influenced by Ernst Gombrich's *Art and Illusion* (translated into Chinese in 1987),[26] in which the British art historian proposes that the superimposition of a grid on a painting can effectively objec-tify the syntactic elements and perception.[27] It is possible, however, that the grid in Wang's painting also had an indigenous origin. Similar grids were used widely during the Cultural Revolution in making Mao's portrait: the painter first drew a grid on a canvas and then copied the portrait to scale. What Wang Guangyi did, either consciously or unconsciously, was to bring this hidden grid underneath every Mao portrait to the surface. His grid, now serving as an analytical framework, thus restores the portrait's historicity and artificiality, and liberates the viewer from emotional engagement with the image.

Wang Guangyi made this painting for the *China/Avant-garde* exhibition in 1989, which concluded the '85 Art New Wave, a nationwide avant-garde move-ment in the second half of the 1980s. Less than four months after the exhibition, the June Fourth Movement broke out in Tiananmen Square and ended in

bloodshed. Experimental Chinese art in the early and mid-1990s differed sharply from that of the 1980s. If the '85 Art New Wave introduced a host of Western art styles and theories to China and connected them with contemporary Chinese art, experimental artists of the 1990s often responded directly to China's recent history and contemporary situation. Some of their works (discussed in the next section) commemorated the June Fourth Movement and expressed the artists' traumatic experience during the government suppression. Other works continued to desecrate traditional revolutionary symbols while satirizing the rapid commercialization of Chinese society in the 1990s.[28] Wang Jinsong's *In Front of Tiananmen* is a supreme example in this second group (illus. 132).

This oil painting was shown in the *New Generation* exhibition in 1991, one of the first public art exhibitions mounted in Beijing after the June Fourth Movement. Organized by a group of independent curators and artists and held in the Museum of Chinese History next to Tiananmen Square, it attracted much attention from Beijing's artistic circles as well as the general public. Works in the exhibition departed considerably from the socialist realist model; but all the artists still insisted on representing reality. What distinguished this 'new generation' of painters from orthodox socialist realists was their distinct understanding of the spirit of their time. Instead of depicting the heroic deeds of revolutionary masses, they invariably derived their subjects from personal observations of society and developed a penchant for representing urban life. Many of their works showed mundane scenes with a cynical twist: beauticians sporting fake smiles, shoppers lost in department stores, lonely men and women daydreaming in a sleeping car on a train. The tone is cold and raw; the figures are ugly and emotionless. On a deeper level these images redefined the purpose of a realistic painting: it was in the meaninglessness of contemporary life that the artists found the reason to depict it.

It was from this standpoint that Wang Jinsong designed his *In Front of Tiananmen*. Like Wang Guangyi's *Mao Zedong – Black Grid* and *Mao Zedong – Red Grid*, it both copies and subverts a canonical work of official art, this time Sun Zixi's oil painting of the same title (see illus. 128). Departing from Wang Guangyi's rationalism, however, Wang Jinsong makes 'superficiality' the point of his reworking of the socialist masterpiece. His painting retains the general composition of the original work but rejects its socialist realist style. Rendered in unnatural colours and rigid outlines, Tiananmen appears as a fake stage set, and the figures in front of it all wear exaggerated smiles on their mask-like faces. These figures – no longer revolutionary workers, farmers and soldiers but fashionable urban professionals – are much enlarged, so they now take up the entire space before Tiananmen, even blocking Mao's portrait on the gate. I have discussed the significance of this portrait in Sun Zixi's original painting: from the exact centre of the composition, Mao commands the Square and the people in it. This controlling gaze has disappeared from Wang's painting, but its removal does not lead to a naturalistic rendering of the people and the place. Rather, the rejection of the revolutionary idealism results in an ideological void – a new Square populated by a people under the impact of materialism and commercialism.

132 Wang Jinsong, *In Front of Tiananmen*, 1991, oil on canvas.

Twelve years after Wang Jinsong showed this painting in the *New Generation*, Shao Yinong and Mu Chen – husband-and-wife collaborators who had impressed art critics with their striking photographic portrayals of members of their extended families in a long scroll – submitted a set of three images to an exhibition called *Water Knife*. Like many other non-official exhibitions organized in Beijing in September 2003, the timing of this small show coincided with the opening of the official Beijing Biennale in that month. By this time the Chinese government had largely overcome its fear of contemporary art. Some cultural officials even argued that new art forms such as installation and video could be effective means for promoting globalization, a major goal of China's campaign for modernization. Large public museums in Shanghai and Guangzhou had followed the international trend to hold costly biennales and triennials, in which works of experimental Chinese art were often displayed alongside their Western counterparts. The First Beijing Biennale represented a new stage in this process, which Chinese artists and critics have dubbed a 'normalization' or 'legalization' of contemporary art: now it was the central government's turn to organize such a trendy event.

While this process may indeed signify China's coming of age, it also threatens to neutralize the alternative identity of experimental artists, and challenges them to find new ways to reassert their independence. Some alternative artists have thus made their art more radical and difficult for the public to accept. Several underground exhibitions that they organized from 1999 to 2002, for example, featured controversial experiments involving the use of living animals and human corpses to make art, and can be considered counteractions to the official normalization of contemporary art.[29] Other artists have made their works more introspective, reflecting on the state of experimental art, including the vanishing of its alternative identity. This second direction was exemplified by the exhibition *Water Knife* in 2003, the introduction of which begins with this statement: 'Lost, or possibly diluted, in all the information around us, things lose their distinction from one another.' The text then goes on to define the commonality of the six artists in the show, whose works all supposedly responded to this general feeling of dilution and non-differentiation.

The set of photographs by Shao Yinong and Mu Chen internalizes this feeling through conflating iconoclasm and a visual game (illus. 133). On the surface, they continue the avant-garde tradition of subverting official representations – this time three images of National Day celebrations, including Dong Xiwen's *The Founding of the Nation* (see illus. 125), and two propaganda photos showing the parading masses in the Square. But the appropriations lack both Wang Guangyi's rationalism and Wang Jinsong's cynicism. Instead, they are lighthearted, playful and visually pleasing. The original images have dissolved into numerous tiny squares, each tinted with a different hue and each containing a coloured dot in the middle. The viewer can still recognize the famous painting and the original photographs from these geometric mazes, but feel that he is looking at them through patterned glass panels, which readily translate the pictures into semi-abstract configurations of geometric shapes. (Alternatively, each image resembles a mosaic mural made of

188

133 Shao Yinong and Mu Chen, *New China*: a. '*The Founding of the Nation*', b. and c. '*Red Ocean*', 2003, digital photographs.

(a)

(b)

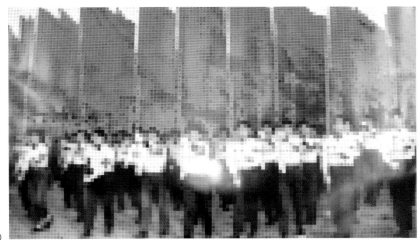

(c)

coloured tiles or a finished jigsaw puzzle.) In any event, these images do not deliver heavy-handed political criticism. Rather, there is a sense of ease in manipulating the official models – once powerful images that have become echoes of the past, and which can be further reduced to nothingness.

Created over three decades from the 1980s to the 2000s, these three works help map out a general field in which experimental Chinese artists have appropriated official representations of the two most important visual symbols of Communist China: Mao and Tiananmen. More specifically, these three works exemplify three basic strategies in producing 'counter images': (1) to rationalize or objectify Mao and Tiananmen; (2) to reframe Mao and Tiananmen with contemporary references and/or the artist's personal experience; and (3) to 'empty' Mao and Tiananmen for perpetuity. It is important to realize, however, that the visual field constituted by these and related works is far richer than a few abstract formulas. In fact, as the following examples will demonstrate, experimental artists have made such persistent efforts to appropriate Mao and Tiananmen precisely because they have found this an effective means to articulate their individual voices and to respond to broad social changes. In this process, they have also communicated and indeed competed with each other to experiment with new forms of visual representation.

Objectifying Mao and Tiananmen

Finding it impossible to follow Christo's and Jeanne-Claude's example by wrapping the most sacred monuments in China, the photographer Liu Wei nevertheless discovered a solution – and an easier one: these monuments were actually wrapped periodically, but such moments had never been documented by the media or shown in art. He thus began to record these moments systematically in 1999. It took him a year to accumulate a series of photographs, which he called *Chang'an Avenue* – the collective location of the monuments.

Three photographs in the set focus on the three buildings on the axis of Tiananmen Square: from south to north, the Chairman Mao Memorial Hall, the Monument to the People's Heroes and Tiananmen itself (illus. 134). In each picture the monument is hidden behind walls of curtains suspended on scaffoldings – the structure is under repair or redecoration. Because of the sacredness of the buildings, such mundane architectural operations have to be concealed from the public scrutiny, until the monuments re-emerge in all their restored brilliance. Because of the importance of these buildings, the scaffolding structures are carefully constructed and even artfully designed (see, for example, the triangular patterns of the scaffolding around Tiananmen), and the curtains covering each monument are neatly arranged to outline the structure's hidden contour. These images are easily overlooked – indeed the passers-by and tourists in the pictures pay no attention to the wrapped monuments. Captured by a camera, however, the images register rupture and absence. It is has been suggested that documentary photographs both objectify and 'subjectify' reality.[30] In Liu Wei's case, his images objectify the monuments because they strip their aura and

134 Liu Wei, *Chang'an Avenue*: a. Chairman Mao Memorial Hall b. Monument to the People's Heroes c. Tiananmen, 1999, black-and-white photographs.

(a)

(b)

(c)

return them to the ordinary. They subjectify the monuments because no viewer of these photographs can see the structures as before. As Christo and Jeanne-Claude have achieved through wrapping famous Western historical buildings, Liu Wei's images rock the common perception of the Square through disrupting the order of a carefully constructed political environment.

In similar ways, Liu Ming and Wu Rijin have explored aspects of Tiananmen that people have never seen or recognized before. The effect of Liu Ming's photograph *The Forbidden City* (1998) is almost surrealistic: Tiananmen, devoid of the usual crowd, appears cut in half against an empty sky (illus. 135). The atmosphere is still and desolate. The focal image is no longer the famous *Mao* portrait, but a lonely basketball stand in the middle of a deserted courtyard. No digital technology is employed here to create a composite photograph, to be sure; Liu Ming simply photographed the monument from its back. The image reminds us that the building actually has two nearly identical sides, which, however, are associated with two disjunctive spaces and have different meaning. This implication is subtly played up in the photograph's title: it is called *The Forbidden City* because only the front side of the building is recognized as Tiananmen – the symbol of New China and the place from where the Chinese leaders review the holiday parades. The back of the building, which possesses no such significance, still connects itself to China's past.

This image can be related to Wu Rijin's oil painting *Work No. 3* (1997), because both subvert Tiananmen's official iconography through manipulating points of view. If Liu Ming photographed Tiananmen from the rear, Wu Rijin continued to depict Tiananmen from the front, but violated the monument's conventional perception by positioning himself inside the Chairman Mao Memorial Hall at the far end of the Square (illus. 136). From this imaginary vantage point, he shows us an image that no visitor to the Square has ever

135 Liu Ming, *The Forbidden City*, 1998, colour photograph.

encountered – the back of Mao's posthumous statue (for the front of the statue, see illus. 96), and forces us to adopt Mao's gaze in beholding the two monuments standing north of the Memorial Hall: the Monument to the People's Heroes and Tiananmen. It then occurs to us that this imaginary view actually has a very realistic meaning: located at the vanishing point of the painting's perspective, Tiananmen is a distant image associated with a backward-looking, 'posthumous' gaze.

But to some other artists, the two sides of Tiananmen, like the front and back of any gate or door, are inseparable and ought to be represented in conjunction or continuation. Between 1995 and 1997 the Beijing artist Yin Xiuzhen spent two years photographing many doors and gates (both called *men* in Chinese) that she remembered walking through since her childhood: doors of her family house, doors of relatives and friends, and doors of public buildings. In each case, she photographed both sides of a door or gate, and mounted the

pair of black-and-white photos on the two sides of a small wood block. Among these images is Tiananmen – the Gate of Heavenly Peace (illus. 137): we see on one side of the block the portrait of *Mao*, which in this instance identifies the passageway underneath it as the main entrance to the Forbidden City. The photo on the reverse side captures the casual image of some tourists who have just emerged from the other end of the passageway. Behind them, through the tunnel-like gate, we see a portion of the Monument to the People's Heroes and then the Chairman Mao Memorial Hall.

Tiananmen has never been represented in a fragmentary manner like this: the monument always appears as a magnificent whole when it is the subject of an official photograph or painting. But because Yin Xiuzhen's project focuses on spaces that are intimate to her, it necessarily debases Tiananmen's identity as a collective monument. To her, the only intimate aspect of Tiananmen – that is, the 'gate' she has walked through – is the passageway. Grouped together with many other doors and gates in an installation, Tiananmen's political significance is further compromised: it is just a gate like the others.

Reframing Tiananmen and Mao

We have seen two paintings that juxtapose Tiananmen (and the *Mao* portrait on it) with figures in the Square (see illus. 128 and 132). This composition has actually become the basis of a well-established subgenre in contemporary Chinese art. Artists employing this composition share a premise: although Tiananmen and the *Mao* portrait remain physically unaltered, the surrounding crowd constantly changes identity and attitude. While this phenomenon is plainly visible in the Square (the tourists taking pictures in front of Tiananmen in the early 2000s bear little resemblance to the Red Guards performing the same act there thirty years ago), experimental artists have most sensitively noticed such shifts and translated the social phenomenon into artistic expressions. The result is a series of images that constantly reframe Tiananmen and the *Mao* portraits in a transforming social environment.

Historically, Wang Jinsong's *In Front of Tiananmen* (see illus. 132) was not the first avant-garde counteraction to Sun Zixi's socialist masterpiece (see illus. 128). A painting that Yang Yiping created in 1987–88, entitled *The Square* (illus. 138), had already considerably eroded the revolutionary idealism essential to Sun's work. A veteran avant-garde artist, Yang was a member of the Stars, the first unofficial art society to emerge in post-Cultural Revolution China, and participated in the group's two early exhibitions in 1979 and 1980. *The Square* marked a new departure in his art, since it initiated a series of works that infused supra-realism (a style he previously favoured) with the historical temporality of old photos. In this sense, calling this painting a 'realistic' representation, as some art critics have done, is misleading. Rather, Yang's subject is his personalized vision of the Square that both unites and contrasts the past and the present. This interpretation explains many puzzling and seemingly contradictory features of the painting: the brownish, nearly monochromic colouration alludes to an aged photograph; but the figures' clothes and hairstyle are all contemporary. These figures are portrayed naturalistically as seen

138 Yang Yiping, *The Square*, 1987–8, oil on canvas.

in a snapshot; but the depiction of the place is deliberately unrealistic: Tiananmen's base is artificially shortened and the stone sculptures in front of the monument are eliminated. Indeed, a major goal of the painter must be to create spatial/temporal disjunction and to contrast Tiananmen with the surrounding people, who seem to belong to a different world and accidentally walk into this place. While Tiananmen's physical prowess is emphasized – it dominates the painting's upper half with its heavy superstructure – the figures in the painting's lower half are in a startling state of disunity. No one in the crowd pays the slightest attention to the monument; and Mao's gaze, so much in control in Sun Zixi's original painting, travels over people's heads with little effect on them.

With this painting as a direct predecessor of Wang Jinsong's *In Front of Tiananmen*, we can reinterpret Wang's work, done three years later, as representing a shift from a past/present juncture to a renewed sense of the present. Zhao Bandi's *Listen to Me* (1992) gives this present orientation a sharper focus: the figures in front of Tiananmen are reduced to two – the artist and his girlfriend (illus. 139). When this painting was shown in Berlin in 1993, a critic remarked that it 'at first glance resembles a tourist snapshot with the well-known motif of the Gate of Heavenly Peace'.[31] This impression is probably generated by the two figures' informal, spontaneous movements: the girlfriend in a long skirt seems to be leaping out of the picture-frame in a dance-like gesture, and the artist is walking out of the picture in the opposite direction. While the meaning of such movements is not apparent, other features of the painting invite us to read them as political metaphors. First, an iron fence with sharp spikes (which does not exist in reality) separates the couple from Tiananmen. Second, Zhao portrays himself wearing only a pair of shorts; his semi-nudity could be considered an offensive gesture in the solemn, ceremonial space. Third, his black parasol shields him from Tiananmen and Mao, not from the sun in the south. Finally, tilting sharply in an unusual diagonal perspective, Tiananmen is destabilized and Mao no longer looks from his portrait into the viewer's eyes. Direct eye contact is instead established between the viewer and the artist's self-portrait.

All these details make it clear that Zhao Bandi's reframing of Tiananmen serves the particular purpose of asserting his individuality against the Communist symbol, an intention also confirmed by the extraordinary size of his self-image (the painting is 2.4 metres tall and the figures are nearly life-size). I have written elsewhere that the early 1990s saw the resurgence of the art of self-portraiture in China.[32] The desire for such images came from an absence: this art disappeared entirely during the Cultural Revolution. In a period when every action and thought had to be directed by a collective ideology, self-portraiture was naturally identified with bourgeois self-indulgence and was thus counter-revolutionary. On the other hand, the art of portraiture was exaggerated in importance by being reduced to the mass production of the image of one man.

A significance of this painting thus lies – as will be suggested in the following section – in bridging earlier pictorial reframing of Tiananmen with later

139 Zhao Bandi, *Listen to Me*, 1992, oil on canvas.

site-specific performances, in which the artists actually staged art projects in the Square. Another significance of the painting is its invocation of absurdity: it asserts individuality not only with reason but also through illogicality and idiosyncrasy, since some aspects of the representation (such as the figures' motion and ambiguous relationship) cannot be explained by logic. Absurdity becomes the single most important element in *June*, a black-and-white photograph first published in 1994 in an underground anthology of avant-garde art and poetry (illus. 140).[33] Signed with the initials W. A., its author is Ai Weiwei, a principal editor of the volume. Like Wang Keping and Yang Yiping, Ai was another original member of the Stars; but his works, including *June*, reflected noticeable influence from Dadaism. Two figures – a female exhibitionist and a disabled man on a motorcar – dominate the foreground of this photograph. The former is conducting an obscene act; the latter watches her in close proximity without being noticed. They are separated from Tiananmen by the usual crowd of visitors to the official monument, whose towering silhouette fills the background. Mao's portrait remains on the monument. Seen over the exhibitionist's shoulder, however, the Great Leader appears as an indiscreet voyeur.

A more recent image that again reframes Tiananmen is found in Shao Yinong's and Mu Chen's photo series *Childhood Memory* (illus. 141). As discussed earlier, their other photo series, *New China*, transforms *The Founding of the Nation* and two propagandist pictures into colourful, semi-abstract mosaics (see illus. 133). Created in 2001, *Childhood Memory* infuses images of political monuments with nostalgia – a longing for a recent past that prevailed over the Chinese cinema, TV and other forms of popular art throughout the

140 Ai Weiwei, *June*, 1994, black-and-white photograph.

141 Shao Yinong and Mu Chen, *Childhood Memory: Tiananmen Square*, 2001, digital photograph.

1990s.[34] *Childhood Memory* imitates an old, hand-tinted black-and-white photo, such as one can find in antique shops and in numerous 'old photo' publications. But it has probably been produced with the help of a computer: not only is it highly unlikely that two naked boys could pose for a photograph in the Square, but their shadows on the ground are unnaturally shaped and the national flag-pole (which in reality stands right before Tiananmen) has been moved to the side. The taller boy wears a traditional hairstyle that is rarely seen today. The pink parasol he holds has a distinctly 'Oriental' flavour, found frequently in old postcards (made originally for foreign customers) as a trademark of fashionable Chinese beauties. Resurrected from the past, these and other visual tropes of 'old times' and 'Orientalness' constitute a language of kitsch. Pushing this language even further, Hung Tung-lu's poster-size laser print juxtaposes Tiananmen with *Chun Li*, a super 'cyber girl' inspired by computer games and Japanese anime (illus. 142). Neither challenging nor reinforcing Tiananmen and Mao, these images – both Shao Yinong's and Mu Chen's world of nostalgia and Hung Tung-lu's virtual paradise – hijack the Communist symbols and turn them into their equal.

Emptying Mao and Tiananmen

Blending, while appropriating, existing images from divergent sources, *Childhood Memory* and *Chun Li* continue the tradition of Political Pop, a style in contemporary Chinese art dating back to the early 1990s.[35] Artists who started this trend turned away from 'heroism, idealism, and the yearning for metaphysical transcendence that characterized the '85 Art New Wave',[36] and derived their appeal instead from making fun of any political or ideological commitment. Multiple factors contributed to this nihilist attitude. One factor was

China's political situation at the time: the official crackdown of the June Fourth
Movement was followed by the banning of unauthorized public gatherings,
including the exhibition and publication of experimental art. Another factor
was psychological: as Chang Tsong-zung has remarked, 'in shock, [these] artists
came to a sudden realization of their impotence in the face of real politics. The
idealism and utopian enthusiasm so typical of new art in the 1980s met its
nemesis in the gun barrels in Tiananmen.'[37] As a consequence, the iconoclastic
tendencies of the 1980s turned into sarcasm, and the disillusioned artists found
a major vehicle in appropriating 'ready-made' political images.

Political Pop thus represented a deepening stage of deconstructing a previous visual culture.[38] Unlike Wang Guangyi's *Mao Zedong – Black Grid* and *Mao Zedong – Red Grid*, its recycling of Mao icons no longer aimed to restore rationalism and objective thinking, but promised new freedom to combine these icons with signs from heterogeneous sources: textile patterns (Yu Youhan, illus. 143), sexual symbols (Li Shan, illus. 144), popular prints (Wang Ziwei, illus. 145), commercial advertisements (Wang Guangyi), computer images (Feng Mengbo), folklore and legend (Liu Dahong), and family portraits (Liu Wei and Zhang Xiaogang).[39] These works were introduced to the West as a 'dissident art' that rebelled against Communist rule. To insiders of contemporary Chinese art, however, the irony of Political Pop was that it was

143 Yu Youhan, *Mao's Image with Patterned Flowers*, 1992, acrylic on canvas.

144 Li Shan,
*Mao: The Rouge
Series No. 24*,
1992, acrylic on
canvas.

itself 'commodified and used to grease the wheels of commerce'.[40] Indeed,
Political Pop was the first contemporary art style from China embraced by
Western collectors and curators, whose enthusiasm helped make some
Political Pop artists millionaires and international celebrities.

But there are artists who, though working in the style of Political Pop, have
consciously rejected commercialization in order to keep their works politically relevant. One of them is Zhang Hongtu, who emigrated to the USA in 1982
and mingled with the struggling artists on New York's Lower East Side. When
he painted a Mao cap onto the Quaker Oats man on an oatmeal carton in 1987,
he accidentally created perhaps the first work of Chinese Political Pop. But he
has refused to affiliate himself with the Political Pop artists in China, partly

145 Wang Ziwei,
*Old Mao and Red
Flags*, 1989,
oil on canvas.

because of the affluent economic status of these artists and partly because of their ambiguous political stance. When the Political Pop artist Yu Youhan was quoted in the *New York Times* as saying 'if we reject Mao, we reject a part of ourselves', Zhang responded sharply: 'So what if we [must] reject part of ouselves?'[41] This approach has made Zhang Hongtu one of the most politically committed Chinese artists abroad. Especially after the June Fourth Movement of 1989, he has consistently used his art to make political statements.[42] Created immediately after the political incident, his *Last Banquet* replaced all the figures in Leonardo da Vinci's famous painting with multiple guises of Mao, with the 'Christ Mao' in the centre speaking into a microphone and the 'Judas Mao' holding the Little Red Book. *Material Mao* is a large group of negative images of Mao that he made between 1991 and 1995. Using various materials, ranging from brick, corn, fur and metal to paper soaked in soy sauce, he made large and small frames to outline the silhouette of Mao's 'standard image' (illus. 146). Another method he used to 'empty' Mao was to satirize and commercialize the great leader simultaneously. The *Mao Dresses*, on which he collaborated with the Hong Kong designer Vivienne Tam, were worn by fashionable

146 Zhang Hongtu, *Material Mao*, clockwise from upper left: 'Lipstick Mao', 'Corn Mao', 'Soy Sauce Mao' and 'Feather Mao', 1994, various materials.

Hong Kong women in 1997. From all these works one detects a deep obsession with Mao – a kind of love-hate relationship that is explained by the artist himself:

> At the beginning of the Cultural Revolution, like everyone of my genera-tion, I completely trusted in Mao. Yet, what Mao did during the Cultural Revolution changed my mind. I saw art and culture being destroyed by the Red Guards. I saw people dividing into different groups, fighting and killing each other, but everyone – killers and victims – declared they were on the side of Mao's revolution. I found that all the young people, includ-ing myself, were all fooled and used by Mao . . . For me, Mao's image was god-like in China. What I have done is pull down this image from the pantheon to reality. Working on Mao is one way to extricate myself from the nightmare; first I felt sinful and fearful, now I feel nothing.[43]

Here Zhang Hongtu reveals his fundamental technique to destroy the Mao myth, which is to turn a sacred icon into 'nothing'. In this sense, the kind of political work that he professes to create is in the same class as *anti-monuments*, not *counter-monuments*. A counter-monument rebels against a traditional monument and this rebellion results in a new monumental form. An anti-monument, on the other hand, negates the very notion of a monu-ment as an embodiment of history and memory. This idea is most clearly realized by the empty silhouette in his *Material Mao* series. In Jonathan Goodman's words, here 'Mao, or rather his absence, becomes the means for an experiment in formal application. Through repetition, the content of Mao's form is rendered meaningless.'[44] This visual strategy is shared by Liu Hung, who now teaches at Mills College in California. Interestingly, her life and art show many parallels with Zhang Hongtu: also trained in a top Chinese art school, she emigrated to the United States in the early 1980s and continued to engage Chinese politics through art. Again like Zhang, she belonged to an earlier generation of artists who first trusted Mao but later rebelled against him. It is not surprising, therefore, that such rebellion often has a strong personal dimension, since the two artists have tried to 'empty' Mao not only from Chinese politics but also from their own system. A one-person exhibition that Liu Hong held in 2000, *Where is Mao?*, included many drawings and prints that faithfully copy Mao's famous historical photos while erasing the man's face in each picture (illus. 147).[45] Significantly, she also reproduced some of her own 'historical' photos in the exhibition catalogue: one of them, taken at the beginning of the Cultural Revolution, shows her standing on a ladder in front of a huge Mao portrait, with paint-brushes and a palette in her hands (illus. 148).

Wang Youshen is also from an older generation of artists, but has remained in his country and critiqued the Chinese political system from within. An anom-aly among Beijing's experimental artists, who have mostly turned freelance, he has been working as an art editor for the official newspaper *Beijing Youth Daily* since 1988, largely because this position gives him a unique perspective

204

from which to reflect upon the nature of public media. The threatening omnipresence of the newspaper has been a constant theme of his installations and performances since the early 1990s. For the landmark exhibition *New Generation*, held in the Museum of Chinese History in 1991 (in which Wang Jinsong showed his *In Front of Tiananmen*), he made a life-size mannequin standing next to a window, absorbed in the act of reading a newspaper. All the surfaces of the figure and his surroundings were covered with an edition of the *Beijing Youth Daily*. Going a step further in 1993, he staged a performance in which he appeared as an anonymous newspaper reader who had merged with a universe of newspapers. Turning his attention from figures to monuments, he covered a portion of the Great Wall with newspapers.

Whereas Wang Youshen has developed these projects to explore the nature of the newspaper as an information technology that has turned against individuals, other works by him have exposed the vulnerability of printed images – and hence the impermanence of the history that they represent and preserve. An installation in this second group displayed photographs that he found in the archives of the *Beijing Youth Daily*, including eroded and scratched pictures representing National Day parades in Tiananmen Square (illus. 149 and 150). The ruinous conditions of the prints cancel the images' representational purpose and dismiss their credibility as historical records of lasting value. In terms of visual representation, this work indicates two directions to obliterate further an official icon for perpetuity, either by fragmenting it or by transforming its materiality. Three recent 'counter images' are created along these directions and can be used to conclude this section.

The first, again by Ai Weiwei, represents an honour guard stationed in front of the Monument to the People's Heroes (illus. 151). Chosen from the

149 Wang
Youshen, *News
Paper*: 'Parade',
2001, photo
installation.

150 Wang Youshen,
News Paper:
'*Tiananmen*', 2001,
photo installation.

151 Ai Weiwei,
Seven Frames,
1998, black-and-
white photo-
graphs.

152 Lu Hao,
*Tiananman Fish
Tank*, 1998,
plexiglass.

entire People's Liberation Army, the honour guards in Tiananmen Square embody and enhance the dignity of the place, and are a frequent subject of official journalism. Ai photographed the guard in sections from head to foot, and printed the images in their original sequence in the negatives. Simply by doing so he is able to destroy the guard's official symbolism: the series of frames forces the viewer to scrutinize the guard as an object, finally discovering an untied shoelace on his right shoe.

The second and third examples, both sculptures, empty Tiananmen and Mao literally. Lu Hao's plexiglass Tiananmen faithfully duplicates the minute architectural details of the monument (illus. 152). But this see-through model has no aura and holds no secret: Tiananmen is not only emptied but has also been turned into a practical goldfish tank. Similarly, Sui Jianguo has made a series of sculptures to represent a hollowed Mao suit (illus. 153, 154). Monumental yet bodiless, the image belongs to a suspended temporality between past and future, in which the Mao suit still exists as a sign but has lost the subject of signification. The transient quality of Sui's Mao suit is enhanced by the photograph in illus. 154a, in which several copies of the statue have been loaded onto a truck and are about to be shipped to an undisclosed place.

153 Sui Jianguo, *Legacy Mantel*, during transportation.

154 Sui Jianguo, *Legacy Mantel*, in the Forbidden City, 1997–2000, painted fibreglass.

The Square Revisited

The paintings and photographs discussed so far are at once intertextual and contextual. On the one hand, these images – whether state projects or experimental works – derive compositions from one other and acquire meaning by referring to one other. On the other hand, they do not constitute a self-contained system of representation because all of them ultimately represent Tiananmen Square – an architectural space external to the images' intertextuality. In other words, although the Square is itself a representation loaded with political and ideological meaning, it exists as the shared 'reality' of various pictorial and photographic representations; and although many of these pictorial and photographic representations appropriate existing images, the artists can never ignore the existence of the 'real' Square, which contextualizes their works within Beijing's political space.

In this way, these self-referential images are also site-referential. Created as independent paintings and photographs, however, they differ from site-specific works, commonly defined as art projects carried out in actual locations.[46] The appearance of avant-garde site-specific projects in Tiananmen Square signified a crucial change in the relationship between artists and the place: until then, even the most radical Chinese artists had responded to the Square only through the mediation of painting or photography, but now some experimental artists decided to interact with this official space directly by staging unofficial art projects *in situ*. Because it is impossible for these artists to construct even temporary installations in this most sacred (and hence most prohibited) place in China, their projects have typically taken the form of performance, in which the artists have used their own bodies to make political statements.

Historically, performance became a regular component of experimental Chinese art in the mid- to late 1980s, after this form of contemporary art was introduced to China and adopted by avant-garde artists. But these artists did not conduct performances in Tiananmen Square until the mid-1990s. This means that we cannot directly attribute these projects to Western influences, but must explain their emergence in terms of the place's changing relationship with contemporary Chinese art and artists. An examination of this relationship reveals a development consisting of three phases, all connected to two important political demonstrations in the Square. First, the April Fifth Movement in 1976 (the mass mourning for Zhou Enlai) gave birth to independent photography in the People's Republic of China: a group of amateur photographers risked their lives to record the demonstration and to preserve the images they took. Three years later they organized an unofficial photo club and mounted their exhibition next to the Square. Second, the *China/Avant-garde* exhibition in February 1989 was a precursor of the June Fourth Movement later the same year. Many participants in the exhibition also took part in the movement; the demonstrations they staged in the Square merged political expression with art performance. Third, the tragedy of the June Fourth Movement became a strong stimulus for 1990s experimental art. Whereas painters and photographers expressed their traumatic experience by juxtaposing their own images with the Square, an increasing number of experimental artists designed performance projects there to commemorate the failed pro-democracy movement. Together with other types of real and simulated performances, these projects finally transformed the Square into 'a space of the avant-garde'.

To those of us who had survived the Cultural Revolution, early 1977 was an exceedingly anxious, tantalizing moment. For the first time in more than a decade we saw hope, yet fear lingered, since Hua Guofeng – the new Party chief who had officially ended the Cultural Revolution a few months earlier – vowed once again to 'unswervingly follow any instruction given by Chairman Mao'. Zhou Enlai was now recognized as a national hero; but the mass mourning for him the previous year was still labelled an anti-government movement. I was therefore astonished to see a group of photographs of this movement in an exhibition at the Museum of Chinese History.

Held in January that year, the exhibition commemorated the anniversary of Zhou's death. Expecting no revelation from this government-sponsored event, two friends and I went to see the show as a tribute to the deceased premier. As we had anticipated, it documented Zhou's life in a conventional biographical format; Mao's words were still quoted in every paragraph of the explanatory texts. But towards the end of the exhibition some twenty black-and-white photos suddenly caught our attention and made our blood boil. Posted on two large panels, these were images taken during the April Fifth Movement. Some photos showed the innumerable mourners covering the entirety of the Square. Others focused on individuals in the Square: a young man standing above the crowd vehemently reading a poem; a child fixing a miniature wreath on a tree branch.

It is difficult to describe the feeling that these photographs aroused in us. The images were still so fresh, not having become memories yet. But they had been repressed and threatened with erasure. (Terror continued for months after the government's crackdown on the movement. Numerous arrests were made; photos and tape recordings of the mass gathering were confiscated; people who refused to surrender these records were threatened with the death penalty.) To encounter these images in a public space, not alone but with other onlookers, was like rediscovering our missing selves and vindicating our shared identity as 'the people'. I heard an older woman sobbing. The gallery guard, a girl, came over quickly and whispered something in her ear, and then gently escorted her to the exit. I suddenly realized that we stood literally next to the Square, the site of the ill-fated mass movement documented in the photographs. But in January 1977 there were no spontaneous gatherings there; through the windows I could see soldiers patrolling the immense ground to prevent any unwanted event.

Later, I learned from Jin Bohong – a former colleague in the Palace Museum's photography department – that these photographs were taken by some young, amateur photographers, who hid the negatives despite the government's threat. Jin told me that some of his friends were secretly collecting these images. He also introduced me to Li Xiaobin, a staff member of the Museum of Chinese History, who was helping to organize the collection. Li was in his twenties and worked in the museum's conservation department. He showed me an album containing photographs that he had taken during the April Fifth Movement, with a handwritten title *Feng bei* (A Heroic Monument) on the cover. He said that he and his friends had already collected more than 10,000 negatives, and that they hoped one day they would be able to publish them. It took two more years for them to realize this goal.[47]

Jin Bohong himself was not an 'April Fifth photographer', as those amateur photographers of the April Fifth Movement came to be known. But he became an active member of the April Photo Society, the first unofficial photography club to appear in post-Cultural Revolution China. By that time (1979) I had returned to the Central Academy of Fine Art to pursue a Master's degree in art history and art criticism. The coursework was nominal in the Academy's newly re-established graduate programme; we were instead attracted by the ferment outside the school – the debates at the Democracy Wall, the noisy gatherings of artists and critics in their tiny apartments, and the informal art shows in parks and on the street. One of my friends described Beijing in 1979 as being at the moment of *jingzhe* in the traditional calendar, when all sorts of animals and insects wake up from hibernation, impatiently making noises to start a new life cycle.

In the art world, the year's most sensational events were two exhibitions organized by the April Photo Society and the Stars Painting Society. Members of both groups were artists unaffiliated with art institutions. Both their exhibitions were highly controversial, attracting large crowds but condemned by the government. Historians have treated these two events very differently, however: the Stars exhibition is discussed in every book on contemporary Chinese art; the photography show is rarely mentioned even in passing. The reason may be that the authors of these books find the latter's apolitical tendency less engaging. But to the numerous Chinese visitors who mobbed this exhibition in April 1979 (I was among them) its attraction lay precisely in its 'art for art's sake' approach, which was anything but 'apolitical' at that moment. Held inside Sun Yat-sen Park next to Tiananmen, it also defined an alternative art space in the heart of Beijing.

The core of the April Photo Society – the sponsor of this exhibition – consisted of two groups or 'salons'. One group met regularly in Wang Zhiping's small apartment on the eastern side of Beijing; most of its members had started their photographic careers by documenting the April Fifth Movement. The other group, nicknamed the Every Friday Salon, gathered on Friday evenings in the dorm of Chi Xiaoning on the western side of the city. Featuring lectures by established photographers, film directors and artists, these gatherings attracted young artists and writers citywide, among whom Wang Keping, Huang Rui, Gu Cheng and A Cheng would soon emerge as avant-garde pioneers of their generation.

I don't remember who took me to a gathering in Wang Zhiping's place. It was a cell-like apartment in a traditional courtyard. The room was too small even for six or seven people to sit around, so many of us stayed in the yard. Everyone was smoking and talking. The time had to be March 1979 because they had decided to call the exhibition Nature, Society and Man, and because the conversation that evening focused on the selection of artists and works for the show. I went to see the exhibition with some schoolmates after it opened on 1 April. Installed inside the Orchid Pavilion in Sun Yat-sen Park, it featured works by some fifty artists, mostly members of the two salons. None of us had anticipated the kind of excitement it created among Beijing residents, who packed the small exhibition hall from morning to evening; enthusiasts visited the show several times, copying down the poems that accompanied the images (illus. 155). It was said that the

155 *Nature, Society and Man*, exhibition organized by the April Photo Society in April 1979, Sun Yat-sen Park, Beijing.

show, which lasted for two weeks, received 2,000 to 3,000 visitors each weekday, and more than 8,000 people on a Sunday.

The exhibition's preface written by Wang Zhiping may sound naïve today: 'The beauty of photography lies not necessarily in "important subject matter" or in official ideology, but should be found in nature's rhythms, in social reality, and in people's emotions and ideas.' But the show's mild humanism and aestheticism were extremely fresh at the time. In fact, only by juxtaposing this exhibition with the Cultural Revolution (and with Tiananmen Square outside the park) can one understand its tremendous appeal to the public: in a country where art had been reduced to political propaganda for an entire decade, any expression of private love or appreciation of abstract beauty was considered a revolutionary act. When this exhibition was criticized by some official critics for its 'bourgeois tendency' and lack of 'Communist spirit', it attracted even more people from all over Beijing, who saw in it an unmistakable sign of the beginning of a cultural renaissance.

From its very beginning, unofficial art in the post-Cultural Revolution period had a shifting boundary. The first *Stars* exhibition in 1979, for example, took place on the street outside the National Art Gallery; its location indicated the artists' alternative identity. But the second *Stars* exhibition the following year was already 'legalized' and accepted into the National Art Gallery, the most privileged official exhibition space in China. Similarly, the first two *Nature, Society and Man* exhibitions could only be held in public parks, but the third one in the series also entered the National Art Gallery in 1981. The changing sites of these exhibitions signified the changing identities of their organizers. Once they became insiders of the art establishment, their original marginal positions were filled by a new generation of unofficial artists, whose emergence around the mid-1980s foreshadowed the arrival of a nationwide movement of experimental art in China.

This movement, known as the '85 Art New Wave, surfaced partly as a reaction to the Sixth National Art Exhibition in 1984, which led to a direct confrontation between the official and unofficial positions. Artists whose works were rejected criticized the exhibition committee for its unfair selection process, and went on to hold their own show entitled *Exhibition of Works Which Failed to Enter the Sixth National Art Exhibition*. In this case the hard-core official position created its antithesis: it destroyed any illusion for compromise and forced even 'neutral' artists to take more decisive steps. Numerous unofficial art groups appeared spontaneously in 1985 and 1986: according to one statistic, more than 80 such groups emerged during these two years scattered across 23 provinces and major cities.[48] The members of these groups were mostly in their twenties; a considerable number of them had just graduated from or were still studying in art schools. Compared with the earlier generation of unofficial artists, they were more knowledgeable about recent developments in Western art, and their opposition to official art was more radical, sometimes verging on iconoclasm. Their works, as well as their speech and writing, often consciously demonstrated an 'avant-garde intent'[49] and aimed to demystify established political icons.

From 1986, local and individual groups of experimental artists began to communicate with one another to organize joint exhibitions and activities.[50] This then paved the way for a nationwide network of experimental artists, a development facilitated by a group of art critics committed to promoting experimental art in China. *China Fine Arts Weekly*, a newspaper published by a group of Beijing art critics to advocate experimental art, organized an important conference in August 1986 on the state of Chinese experimental art, which took place in the southern city of Zhuhai in Guangdong. Participants from various regions reviewed more than a thousand slides of recent works by experimental artists, and proposed to organize a national exhibition of exper-imental art in Beijing.[51] But when the show – the famed *China/Avant-garde* exhibition – finally took place two-and-a-half years later, there was little feeling of celebration; instead it was inspired by the sense of a final struggle. The artists turned the National Art Gallery into a solemn site resembling a tomb: long black carpets, extending from the street to the entrance of the exhibition hall, bore the emblem of the show: a 'No U-turn' traffic sign signalling 'There is no turning back' (illus. 156). This feeling of tragic heroism was closely relat-ed to the political situation of the time: a heightening pro-democracy move-ment was preparing itself for a major confrontation with the Party's hardlin-ers, and no one could predict the outcome of the struggle.

Hoping to shock society, the organizers of the exhibition placed almost all installation and performance pieces on the first floor of the gallery, including a number of works directly attacking Communist ideology and official art policies. Among them, the lengthy titles of Zhang Nian's *Sitting on Eggs – No Theory During This Period in Order to Save the Next Generation* and Huang Yongping's *'History of Chinese Art' and 'History of Modern Western Art' Having Been Put in a Laundry Machine for Two Minutes* are self-explanatory. Gu Xiong performed in front of his installation *Net* in a costume painted to look as through he had just broken through a wire mesh fence and bore the fence's marking on his body. Wu Shanzhuan sold 400lb of fresh prawns at discount

156 *China/Avant-garde* exhibition, National Gallery, Beijing, February 1989.

price, turning the National Art Gallery into a black market. Many 'accidents' during the exhibition, including a premeditated shooting performance and the subsequent police intervention, generated a strong sense of happening and uncertainty.[52] The exhibition was closed down twice in two weeks; each time it reopened only after a prolonged negotiation with the authorities.

The sense of happening inherent to a grassroots movement did not vanish after the exhibition ended. Three months later many participants in the exhibition took part in the June Fourth Movement in Tiananmen Square. There, they continued to argue and negotiate with the authorities but explicitly for a political cause. Additional evidence further clinches an unambiguous relationship between the political demonstrations and the experimental art movement at the time. For example, the 'No u-turn' sign reappeared in the Square but subtly changed its meaning: it was now understood as signalling 'There is no turning back' in the struggle for democracy (illus. 157). Some artist-demonstrators wrapped themselves head to toe in white bandages – a performance they had planned but failed to conduct in the *China/Avant-garde* exhibition. They succeeded in carrying out this project in the Square (illus. 158), but here the performance acquired a prophetic significance: government troops took over the Square a few days later and ended the demonstration with bloodshed.

Some artists living outside China reacted to the massacre swiftly. Liu Hung, for example, created a large mural in September for her show *Trauma* in San Diego, California (illus. 159).[53] In the main section of the painting she superimposed two sets of images on a grim, black background. One set, drawn in white, consists of two medical diagrams of a man, with acupuncture points marked on the figure's front and back. Another set, painted in red, is a map of Beijing centred on the Square, with Tiananmen flanked by the Great Hall of

214

the People and the Museum of Chinese History on either side. The painting's message is clear: the acupuncture points indicate the energy nexuses in the human body; the Square is the centre of Beijing's political body. Drawing the map over the figure, Liu Hung interprets the June Fourth Movement as a conflict between the natural human order and an external political structure, which ended with the repression of the former by the latter.

Two additional images in the mural further link this political metaphor to the artist's personal experience. A large figure to the right portrays a furious officer of the People's Liberation Army – a hero in the 'model opera' *Shajiabang* that Jiang Qing promoted during the Cultural Revolution. Holding a pistol in a dramatic gesture, this is an image that Liu Hung remembered from the time she lived in China and which she associated with Mao's doctrine of 'revolutionary dictatorship'. Right under the pistol Liu Hung painted her self-portrait, a copy of the ID photo in her Chinese passport. Positioned close to the lower edge of the painting, this image functions as Liu's signature and posits the artist as a bearer of the political trauma. We recognize this significance of the portrait from her stern face that seems to conceal pain, and from the red stamp of Beijing's Public Security Bureau imprinted on her body. Not coincidentally, here Liu Hung once again superimposes Beijing's political space, defined by Tiananmen's silhouette at the centre of the stamp, on a human figure – this time herself.

Liu Hung was able to show this mural in America in 1989. In China, however, the official crackdown on the movement was followed by the government's banning of unauthorized public gatherings, including the exhibition and publication of any kind of unofficial art. Experimental artists were forced to go

157 A demonstration held by artists and art critics in Tiananmen Square during the June Fourth Movement, 1989.

158 A performance by an unknown artist during the June Fourth Movement, 1989.

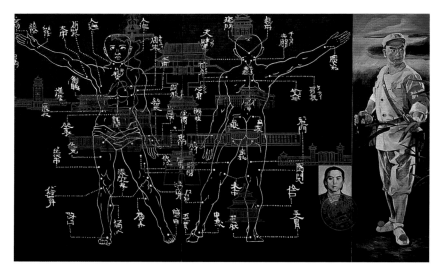

159 Liu Hung,
Trauma, 1989,
acrylic on canvas.

underground, creating works and communicating with one another only in private. When they re-emerged two to three years later, their works showed different responses to the June Fourth Movement. Some artists, as mentioned earlier, turned cynical, rejecting the idealism of the '85 Art New Wave as Utopian fantasy or self-delusion. Other artists took the tragedy of the student demonstrations to heart, and tried to find voices to express their traumatic experience. A direct consequence of this second reaction was a type of self-portrait, in which the artist depicts himself as a bitter, disillusioned subject in Tiananmen's shadow.

An early example of this type of image is Zhao Bandi's *Listen to Me* of 1992 (see illus. 139). I suggested earlier that this painting followed an established tradition in experimental art of reframing Tiananmen with changing figures. By making himself the focus of viewing (through direct eye contact with the spectator) and by depicting himself in a state of action, however, Zhao also introduced a new composition, in which the artist (or his agent) seems to be 'performing' in the Square. Works in this tradition include Zhao Shaoruo's *Tiananmen 1 and 2* (which juxtaposes Tiananmen with the artist's blurry faces and replaces Mao's portrait with Zhao's own image), Wu Xiaojun's *Three Men Lost in the Square* (which resembles a scene in a puppet show), Yang Qing's *A Man Cannot Step Twice into the Same River* (which transforms the Square into a wild landscape and shows the artist sticking his head in a brook in front of Tiananmen) and Sheng Qi's *AIDS. Tiananmen* (illus. 161). This last image is particularly noteworthy because it self-consciously explores the potential of a simulated performance in a composite photograph. Using computer technology to piece together fragmentary images, Sheng Qi has succeeded in creating a composition that instantaneously destabilizes the conventional perception of the place.

AIDS. Tiananmen belongs to a series of images, each featuring the artist, dressed in a bizarre assortment of clothes, in front of a monument or Mao's 'Tiananmen portrait' (illus. 160). In this particular picture, he stands full-height in the foreground like a statue. A piece of red cloth wrapped around his head

160 Sheng Qi, AIDS. *Beijing*: 'AIDS. Mao', 1999, composite photograph.

161 Sheng Qi, AIDS. *Beijing*: 'AIDS. Tiananmen', 1999, composite photograph.

obscures his identity. Wearing a tightly buttoned military jacket and a pair of white gloves, he has no trousers. Above the bare legs, his genitals are concealed in white fabric and tied with a string, held at the other end by a uniformed policeman. The Square in the background is no longer a sparkling field of concrete that inspires order and control, but a construction site filled with dirt and rubble. Scattered railings and discarded construction equipment further make it look like an abandoned battlefield. Beyond this ruin Tiananmen, perfectly maintained, appears as a stage set, artificial and unreal. It is most likely that Sheng Qi made this picture not to deliver a coherent message, but to convey the feeling of disturbance both in his psychology and in his relationship with the external world. The viewer is startled by the picture's visual disharmony and thematic self-contradiction. On the one hand, it expresses the artist's repressed sexuality and self-identity; on the other, Sheng Qi recycles conventional props of revolution (the red cloth, the military uniform and the site) to express his individuality. On the one hand, the work's title and the squalid site link the Square with the incurable disease of AIDS; on the other, the ribbon pinned on the artist's chest identifies him as an AIDS sympathizer. It would have been impossible actually to conduct such a performance in the Square. Instead, Sheng Qi conjures it up in a composite picture, representing himself as a man at once rebellious and vulnerable, a victim as hero.

The relationship between such a simulated performance and an actual performance in Tiananmen Square poses an interesting question in interpreting contemporary Chinese art. An actual performance in the Square acquires its meaning from its interaction with the place and from the artist's effort to overcome the formidable difficulty of carrying out a performance in this particular location. In this sense the project can be called site-specific. Yet, owing to the heavy police surveillance in the Square, even a real performance staged there can never expect a public audience; only through photographic or video records can the project be known to the art community and society at large. For this reason, an artist who decides to perform in the Square often doubles as a photographer or a video artist, with a clear plan to transform his site-specific performance into images that can be reproduced and presented in other locations. As photographs and videos, these images are often crafted, edited or digitally manipulated. Shown in exhibitions and sold in commercial art galleries, they gain value as independent works of art. In other words, these are re-presentations of the original performances, not simply records of the performances.

This does not mean, however, that such photographic or video representations have lost the site-specificity of the performances. Rather, the meaning of the 'site' has changed from a physical location to a pictorial context. As the former, the Square is understood as a tangible reality. The performance enables the artist to establish a physical relationship with the place in order to exceed the limitations of painting and photography. As the latter, the Square is relocated within the limitations of a photograph or video, whereas the performance – now reconfigured as the content or subject matter of a representation – certifies the authenticity of a photographic or video work displayed in an exhibition space.

Some performance artists/photographers are well aware of this difference, and have tried to articulate the dialectical relationship between a site-specific performance and its representations. One of these artists is Li Wei, who has invented a special instrument for both performance and photographic projects. It is a rectangular mirror with a hole cut in the middle. With his head stuck through the hole, he looks like a criminal in pre-modern China sentenced to wear a wooden cangue around the neck. The difference is that Li Wei's cangue is reflective and turns everything in front of him into mirror images. Wearing this mirror-cangue he visits important monuments to 'reverse' them; the photographs he has made to record these performances are taken from a distance, showing a full view of the surroundings (illus. 162a). But he has also produced close-up photographs that omit such contextual information, even the edge of the mirror-cangue. The result is a puzzling optical illusion, in which his disembodied head is suspended in mid-air, against the (reversed) image of a monumental site such as Tiananmen Square (illus. 162b). These close-up images have been selected for photography exhibitions; and the reason is apparent: their quality as independent photographs is enhanced by dismissing any reference to the performances.

A similar experiment has also been attempted by the Tianjin artist Mo Yi. When the June Fourth Movement erupted, Mo Yi immediately sided with the

162 Li Wei, *Mirror 2000*: *left*: 'Reversing the Forbidden City' (performance on Coal Hill) *right*: 'Reversing Tiananmen', 2000–01, colour photographs.

demonstrating students despite his usual disinterest in politics. He told me in an interview: 'I was moved by the situation in Tiananmen Square and enraged by the Party leaders' antagonism towards the students. I felt that I was cheat- ed. I finally lost my faith in the government.'[54] He designed a performance, marching on Tianjin's streets with a funerary banner in hand, mourning his lost hope for democracy (illus. 163). A big crowd gathered around him, cheering and taking pictures. This performance made him a household name in Tianjin, but also one of the 'ten grave criminal cases' handled by the city's Public Security Bureau. He lost his job, was under house arrest for several years, and in 1999 was still living in fear.

On 4 June 1999, on the tenth anniversary of the failed pro-democratic movement, Mo Yi staged another performance, this time in Beijing. For years he had been growing a beard. That morning he shaved off his beard as well as his hair and eyebrows, and then took photographs of himself in Tiananmen Square. It is possible to think that he carried out this self-inflicted punish- ment to activate his traumatic memory of the June Fourth Movement. It is also possible that he designed the performance to trace the source of the trauma – to show that his personal tragedy was rooted in a greater tragedy that had taken place in the Square ten years earlier. He recorded the performance in two photographs, but manipulated them in different ways to create dialogue between the images and the performance as well as between the images them- selves (illus. 164). Although the pictures were taken on 4 June 1999, he printed the date 89-6-4 on them to indicate the historical event that the performance commemorated. The two photographs have similar compositions, but one appears as a documentary record of the performance while the other resembles an art photograph, with the edge tinted blood-red and Mo Yi's self-portrait cut in half.

Sheng Qi, Li Wei and Mo Yi are among many experimental Chinese artists who have created art works related to Tiananmen Square since the early 1990s. The three types of work discussed above – paintings and photographs of the place, images of simulated performances, and on-site performances and their representations – have continued to develop in tandem.[55] For some artists like Gao Zhen, Gao Qiang and Song Dong, their fixation with the Square has led them to conduct projects of all three types over a prolonged period of experimentation. A closer look at these three artists and their works will deepen our understanding of the seminal role this political space plays for contemporary Chinese artists.

The Gao Brothers

Gao Zhen and Gao Qiang grew up in Ji'nan, the capital of Shandong in east China. Their father was a factory clerk and their mother a housewife skilled in making paper-cuts. A tragedy befell the Gao family on 1 October 1968: the Red Guards in the father's factory identified him as a 'hidden enemy of the people' and took him away. Twenty-five days later they informed the family that he had 'committed suicide to escape justice'. But the brothers saw their father's corpse covered with wounds from torture. To Gao Zhen:

Although this happened when I was only eleven to twelve, I can never forget the red terror of the Cultural Revolution. Whenever I think about that period I feel it was like an endless nightmare. That man [i.e., Mao] who victimized millions of lives to satisfy his thirst for power should be cursed forever![56]

The brothers were able to return to school after the Cultural Revolution was over. Gao Zhen studied traditional painting and Gao Qiang pursued the career of a writer. But when the '85 Art New Wave arrived, they became the earliest participants in this avant-garde movement; the extemporaneous performance *Story of a Life* that they conducted in 1985 was probably the first such project in post-Cultural Revolution China. Later, they described this period in their artistic development as a rebellious phase, when they eagerly embraced contemporary Western art in order to break away from their academic training. This phase was followed by a 'period of experimentation', in which they explored various materials and mediums to express their thoughts and feelings. Their piece in the 1989 *China/Avant-garde* exhibition, called *Midnight Mass*, was an enormous installation made of hundreds of inflated balloons and condoms (illus. 165). Set against a black-and-red backdrop, it shocked the audience by both resembling exaggerated and distorted sexual organs and alluding to a *Mao* statue worshipped during the Cultural Revolution.

This work placed the brothers among the most radical Chinese artists in the late 1980s. But to them, the pro-democratic movement that followed the *China/Avant-garde* exhibition was 'art on a much grander scale'. Like Mo Yi in Tianjin, they contributed to the movement (which soon spread from Beijing to the whole country) with a street performance. With four other local artists they planned to release inflated balloons and condoms at strategic locations in Ji'nan, thereby transforming an art project into a political expression. Unable to find hydrogen to realize this plan, they turned the backdrop of *Midnight Mass* in the *China/Avant-garde* exhibition into a horizontal banner, and inscribed it with a sentence from the national anthem: 'Rise up, those who do not want to be slaves!'[57] Wearing turbans with 'freedom' and 'democracy' written on them, they carried this enormous banner through Ji'nan's streets.

The brothers were interrogated by the authorities for their involvement in the June Fourth Movement. Their connection with the political dissident Wei Jingsheng further made them targets of the secret police.[58] This connection had also started during the *China/Avant-garde* exhibition, when they signed a petition asking Deng Xiaoping to honour Wei's civil rights and free him from jail. Five years later, Wei Jingsheng paid the brothers a visit after he was temporarily released, and discussed with them his plan to organize an unofficial art exhibition. As a result, the brothers were put on a blacklist and forbidden to travel abroad for the next nine years. But the prohibition strengthened their desire to create political art, especially when they sensed a popular desire in the early and mid-1990s to 'move beyond' the June Fourth Movement, as they described in an interview: 'Rather than reflecting on the tragedy in a profound way, people preferred to turn their serious pain into minor pain, and to turn

their minor pain into cynical remarks, finally sinking into personal, pitiful arguments.'[59]

Many of the art projects they carried out during this period can be understood in this context. A large series of 'copy machine art' dated to 1992, for example, duplicated sacred political icons while blaspheming them. An informal photo taken that year shows the brothers in their studio (illus. 166). Every surface of the space is covered with sabotaged portraits of Mao, Marx and Deng Xiaoping – images that registered their resentment of the Cultural Revolution and the government repression of the June Fourth Movement. There are also plenty of distorted images of Chinese currency with Tiananmen's silhouette in the middle. The random combination of these two kinds of images alluded to China's state at that moment: while championing economic reforms to promote a market economy, a new generation of Chinese leaders was insisting on 'upholding Marxism and Mao Zedong thought'.

If this 'copy machine art' was still associated with the general trend of Political Pop in the early 1990s, the brothers found a more distinct way to voice their political criticism in the mid-1990s by staging performances in Tiananmen Square. Around this time, the Square also became the dominant

166 Gao Zhen
and Gao Qiang
in their studio,
Ji'nan, Shandong,
1992.

167 Gao Zhen
and Gao Qiang,
*A Mass in the
Square*, per-
formance, 1995.

168 Gao Zhen
and Gao Qiang,
*Looking for ufos
in the Square*,
performance,
1995.

subject of their photographs, which either recorded their performances or turned this official space into its own antithesis. In one performance called *A Mass in the Square* (illus. 167), Gao Zhen walked back and forth in front of Tiananmen holding his arms wide open. His unconventional behaviour and Bohemian appearance alerted two security guards, who followed him closely and became in effect part of the performance. Gao Qiang took a photo of the scene and inscribed it with the question: 'Is performance art forbidden here?' In another performance called *Looking for ufos in the Square* (illus. 168), the brothers simply stood in the middle of the Square and stared into the empty sky. Their purposeless concentration sharply contradicted the (supposedly) purposeful movements of the surrounding crowd.

This second performance was related to the brothers' digital photograph *Flying RMB*, in which the anonymous crowd reappears, unconscious of an enormous coin hovering over them like a huge UFO (illus. 169). Bearing the national emblem with Tiananmen in the centre, the coin stands for the state-sponsored

169 Gao Zhen
and Gao Qiang,
Flying rmb,
c. 1998–9, digital
photograph.

capitalism (dubbed by Deng Xiaoping as 'socialism with Chinese characteristics') that has come to control Chinese people's lives. The contradiction between the government's capitalist practice and socialist self-identity is the theme of another photograph in the series. Conceived as three consecutive frames in a sequence, it represents a coin falling from the sky onto a *Mao* portrait. Though seemingly weightless, this symbol of commercialism turns the already ruined portrait into rubble (illus. 170). But has Mao's spectre really disappeared in China? A third picture in the series provides a more complex answer to this question (illus. 171). Here, a giant *Mao* portrait hovers over the Square in the same manner as the UFO-like coin in *Flying RMB*. The image is hollowed and Mao is now faceless, but the empty portrait still retains its physical power to dominate the Chinese capital. Perhaps more profoundly, to the brothers (and to people who shared their experience), Mao still provides them with a historical frame to represent themselves: through the hollowed portrait we see a naked man lying face down in the snow – an image from one of their performances commemorating their father's tragic death during the Cultural Revolution.

In my view, however, the brothers' most poignant Tiananmen images are two succinct photographs made without the aid of computer manipulation. The first, entitled *An Installation on Tiananmen*, re-presents the familiar *Mao* portrait on the monument from an unfamiliar angle (illus. 172). By simply taking the photograph from under the portrait, they are able to dismiss the aura of this famous icon. From this angle, the spectator is no longer subject to Mao's gaze. The portrait appears as a flat (and unimpressive) painting in a thin frame, and that is all. The second photograph shows a uniformed policeman on Tiananmen overlooking the vast space below (illus. 173). In all its deceptive simplicity, it argues that, although Mao is gone, the Square is still under a dominating gaze from Tiananmen's rostrum.

170, 171 Gao Zhen and Gao Qiang, *Idol at Dusk* (top) and *A Beautiful View of China: The Forbidden City,* c. 1998–9, digital photographs.

172 Gao Zhen and Gao Qiang, *An Installation on Tiananmen*, 1995, colour photograph.

173 Gao Zhen and Gao Qiang, *Watcher on Tiananmen*, 1996, colour photograph.

Song Dong

Song Dong, one of the most original contemporary artists in China, grew up in Beijing and still lives there. Born in 1966, his life began when the Cultural Revolution started. When he was three years old his father, a civil engineer, was accused of being a member of a counter-revolutionary organization, labelled as an enemy of the state, and spent the next eight years in reform-through-labour camps. Until he was twelve Song Dong hardly knew his father, who returned home only occasionally from the camps. Showing early talent in visual art, however, he was accepted into a Youth Palace (one of the city's

174 Song Dong,
A test shot for
the 2003 video
*I Love Beijing's
Tiananmen*.

174 Song Dong, A test shot for the 2003 video *I Love Beijing's Tiananmen*.

extra-curricular centres for the arts) to study painting, despite his unfavourable family background. In elementary school he copied images of Tiananmen and sang revolutionary songs. Now he is planning to make a video to recall such childhood memories. Entitled *I Love Beijing's Tiananmen*, a popular song familiar to every Chinese child, even today, it will feature an old doll from his childhood, which Song Dong identifies as his alter-ego, interacting in various ways with a model of Tiananmen – embracing it, riding on it and holding it up. He has constructed the toy Tiananmen and made some test shots (illus. 174), but in early 2004 he was still working on the storyline.

After graduating from high school in 1985, Song Dong entered the Capital Normal University in Beijing to study oil painting. First he flourished there as a model student: one of his academic-style works was even selected for the National Art Exhibition in 1987, an unusual achievement for a young artist who had not graduated from college. But suddenly he abandoned his academic training and the career path of a successful professional artist. Two circumstances caused this change: the June Fourth Movement in 1989 and the introduction of new contemporary art forms to China in the 1980s and early '90s. Song Dong was elated by the student movement and dumbfounded by its tragic ending. Watching the tanks overrun Beijing's streets, he felt that he had become a new and mature person overnight.[60] As an artist, he found freedom in installation, performance and video; a framed canvas had become too limiting for his newly discovered creativity. He held his first installation/performance exhibition, *One More Lesson: Do You Want to Play with Me?* in 1994 in Beijing. He transformed the exhibition hall into a classroom, in which some students were reading wordless textbooks, while the audience participated freely in the performance. The local authorities cancelled the show the day it opened. But he never returned to painting.

Song Dong's *Breathing*, a moving performance he carried out in front of Tiananmen in 1996, demonstrated his maturity as a politically minded avant-garde artist (illus. 175). It was a cold night at the beginning of 1996. Holiday lights outlined the familiar contour of Tiananmen in the distance; the temperature was minus 7° Celsius. Song Dong lay prone and motionless in the deserted Square, breathing onto the cement pavement for 40 minutes. On the ground before his mouth a thin layer of ice gradually formed, which seemed to increase in thickness and solidity with each breath. When he left the square, the ice was still shimmering like an elusive islet in an ocean of concrete. It disappeared before the next morning, leaving no visible trace.

As this Chapter has shown, by 1996 many experimental Chinese artists had attempted to demystify Tiananmen by rationalizing and blaspheming this most sacred symbol of Communist China (see, for example, illus. 132–42). Shifting his focus from Tiananmen to the Square, however, Song Dong departed from the logic of iconoclasm underlying these works. The meaning of *Breathing* lies in the artist's desperate effort to inject life into that official space where the June Fourth Movement was repressed seven years earlier. There is little doubt that Song Dong designed the performance/photography project to commemorate this failed pro-democratic movement. While his performance in the Square can be considered a personal tribute to the massacred students, the photograph that documents the performance (taken by his wife Yin Xiuzhen following his direction) brings the viewer back to that heated month in 1989, when hundreds of thousands of demonstrators transformed the Square into an exhilarating 'living place', and reminds us that whatever the year, 1996 or 2004, this place remains stiflingly barren.[61]

Song Dong has continued to conduct performances in the Square since 1996 and to record these site-specific projects in photographs and videos. But these works have increasingly focused on broader issues about the relationship between site and representation. The significance of *Breathing* thus also lies in bringing to a close an earlier phase of more explicit political art, and in introducing new, more conceptually orientated experiments. (Not coincidentally,

175 Song Dong, *Breathing*, 1996, performance/ colour photograph.

works by other experimental artists, such as the Gao brothers, also showed similar changes, demonstrating a general shift in contemporary Chinese art around this time.) One group of Song Dong's later works, including *Taking Pictures in Front of Tiananmen* (1998), *Jump* (1999), *Family Members: A Photo Studio* (1998) and *The Motherland Has Made Stage Sets for Me* (1999), reflects on the social conventions of photography in China. The first work is an anthropological study of picture-taking in front of Tiananmen. From a fixed angle, this hour-long video records group after group of people who followed a common pattern of behaviour to record their images at this spot: suddenly becoming serious, they each stiffened their bodies and concealed their personality in front of the camera. The artist's own idiosyncratic behaviour disrupts such social convention in the second work: refusing to stand still like everyone else, Song Dong jumped up and down in front of a camcorder that he had set up in the Square, leaving a series of unstable images in the video (illus. 176).[62]

The other two works in this group shift the focus of exploration from people to the site. *Family Members: A Photo Studio* consists of group portraits of the artist's family in a number of 'typical photo spots' in Beijing. Song Dong then projected these images on walls in a gallery, and invited visitors to stand before the portraits to take their pictures. While the volunteers' features were blurred by the projected images, the sites – Tiananmen Square among them – remained fixed, as the unchanging frame for the portrait-taking (illus. 177). *The Motherland Has Made Stage Sets for Me* further identifies these sites as socio-political constructs: in the video Song Dong pretends to be making a film, documenting the evening scenes on a National Day along Chang'an

176 Song Dong, *Jump*, 1999, video.

230

177 Song Dong, *Family Members: A Photo Studio*, 1998, video installation/ performance.

178 *left* Song Dong, *The Motherland Has Made Stage Sets for Me*, 1999, video.

Avenue and Ping'an Avenue, Beijing's two major avenues. Moving back and forth from ordinary street onlookers in dim light to brilliantly illuminated official buildings reflected in a clapper-slate made of a mirror, the video contrasts these two sets of images and highlights the latter's artificiality (illus. 178).

Pushing this last point further, Song Dong conducted three other performance/video projects – *Smashing Mirrors* (1999), *Crumpling Shanghai* (2000)

179 *right* Song Dong, *Burning Pictures*, 2001–2, video.

180 Song Dong, *Smashing Mirrors*, 1999, video.

and *Burning Pictures* (2001–2) – to reflect specifically upon the fragility of visual representations (illus. 179–80). Among them, *Smashing Mirrors* is unique for its effectiveness as both a site-specific performance and a video work. Song Dong brought a mirror to Tiananmen Square and other strategic locations in Beijing, looked at the place's reflection in the mirror and then smashed it with a heavy hammer. The sound of the violent act startled the passers-by and disrupted the 'normality' of the place. Represented in the video, however, the mirror dominates the picture frame, and the hammer seems to strike directly the image (such as Tiananmen) reflected in the mirror (illus. 180). Only after the mirror has shattered does the viewer realize that the image was an optical illusion. Now the video shows the street scene that the mirror had blocked – but can one be sure that it is not another illusion?

The last time I interviewed Song Dong for this book was in January 2004. The only question I planned to ask was why he was so obsessed with the Square and had made so many works involving it.[63] Knowing his fondness for telling stories and his ability to articulate ideas, I was expecting an explanation that could last for hours. But his answer was surprisingly (though not disappointingly) short: although he has made and shown works around the world, he feels that the Square is his real 'art space' (*yishu kongjian*) – a space that is intimately connected to his experience as an artist and as a person, and a space that can bring out the full meaning of his work. He hopes that one day he can really exhibit his work there. To prove this last point, he showed me a large print with the title *Big Art Action*, which he made for a 'poster' exhibition in 2001 (illus. 181). In the picture, the Square is jammed with disorientated individuals; many are doing nothing while others seem to be waiting for some-

232

181 Song Dong, *Big Art Action*, 2001, poster.

one's arrival. (Song Dong told me that he actually photographed this part of the composite picture in front of the Beijing train station.) Dressed in the uniform of a salesman, Song Dong appears multiple times in the crowd, holding up a board with a question on it: 'Would you like to play with artists?' The exhibition's organizer rejected this work on the grounds that the representation of the Square was 'too ambiguous'. But to Song Dong there is nothing ambiguous about this image: as a public artist he is still looking for his public.

182 Hongmiao's position in relation to Beijing's urban development.

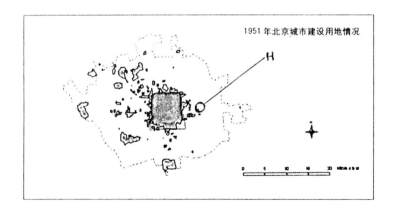

1951年北京城市建设用地情况

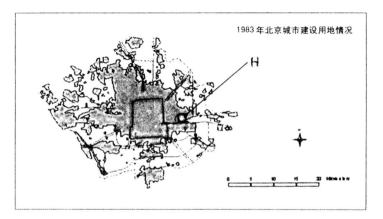

1983年北京城市建设用地情况

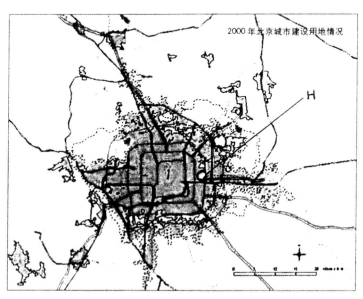

2000年北京城市建设用地情况

Coda: Entering the New Millennium

My sister has an apartment, 6 kilometres east of Beijing's old city wall, that she inherited from my mother. I inherited our family's old courtyard house near the Drum Tower. But because of the house's dilapidated state and primitive amenities, we have stayed in my sister's place whenever we have returned to Beijing since 1998, including for a whole sabbatical year from 1999 to 2000. During that year my wife Judy became serious about traditional Chinese opera and frequented theatres and drama schools; our daughter Lida enrolled in a local elementary school as its first foreign student; and I wrote a chapter of this book and curated an exhibition of experimental Chinese art (which involved transporting a site-specific art project from Beijing to Chicago).[1] After three more years of returning to the apartment annually like migratory birds, we have gained a particular local vantage point to observe and experience Beijing's rapidly changing geography.

Belonging to one of many housing complexes at Hongmiao, the nondescript five-storey building that houses the apartment was constructed in the mid-1980s and was originally owned by the Central Academy of Drama, where my mother worked. When the long-awaited building was eventually completed, apartments of different sizes were allotted to the academy's employees based on rank. My mother received this three-bedroom unit, the largest of all, because she had been rehabilitated and become a distinguished professor again. But my father refused to move there despite its natural gas heating and better insulation; to him moving to Hongmiao (meaning literally Red Temple) would mean an exile from city to countryside. Indeed, in the mid-1980s most Beijingers considered Hongmiao part of the city's rural suburbs, where new, multi-level buildings had just begun to invade local villages and agricultural fields. As for me, I took my first bicycle trip to the place from our house in the old city in 1991, upon my first return to Beijing in a decade; it was a laborious journey through dark and unfamiliar roads, some flooded by sewage.

By the time we moved to Hongmiao for the year in 1999, however, the place had been completely urbanized. Crowded with shops and restaurants, it was now one of Beijing's established neighbourhoods within the city's newest boundary – the largely completed Fourth Ring Road (for Hongmiao's position in relation to Beijing's urban development, see illus. 182). Close to the foreign communities at Maizidian, the location even offered certain cosmopolitan conveniences that the city's more famous districts lacked, including imported

cheese and genuine Italian, German and Japanese food. Hongmiao was finally integrated into Beijing's 'inner city' by 2003, when the Fourth Ring Road was completed and the construction of the Fifth Ring Road had begun. To the south, Chang'an Avenue now runs to Tongxian 30 kilometres away; its utility as Beijing's main east–west road is doubled by a subway running underneath the street. Luxurious high rises are mushrooming along the avenue (illus. 183); the fashion leader in 2004 is an immense complex of yellow, blue and red structures not far from Hongmiao, called 'Xiandaicheng' (Modern City) in Chinese and 'Soho' in English. Older institution-owned apartment buildings have been privatized, so my sister now owns her apartment, which she was able to buy well below market price. We have all abandoned our bicycles: distances are long and taxis are abundant and affordable. We travel to Peking University and the Summer Palace via the Fourth Ring Road, and to the Forbidden City and the Liulichang antique district through Chang'an Avenue. Although traffic congestion has become a headache, a bicycle is cumbersome and even dangerous in a car-filled city.

This experience of living in Hongmiao has made us sensitive to Beijing's shifting boundaries and changing cityscape. At the same time, I have been collecting and studying Beijing's successive urban plans for this book, and these documents (which became available after the mid-1980s) connect our experience with the city's overall development.[2] To make a long analysis short, living in a place like Hongmiao we relate ourselves to the city at large through three structural links – links that are 'structural' because they indicate fundamental spatial systems underlying both Beijing's development and our perception of the city. The first link is the 'ring-road' system. Surrounding traditional Beijing with a growing number of concentric circles, these roads constantly redefine the city's periphery while providing access to a newly established local centre like Hongmiao. These roads also draw boundaries within Beijing. Three completed ring roads now divide new Beijing into four zones with different property values and social status: (1) the old town within the Second Ring Road, (2) the belt between the Second and Third Ring Roads, (3) the area between the Third and Fourth Ring Roads, and (4) the space beyond the Fourth Ring Road. Multi-levelled intersections (called *lijiaoqiao* or 'vertical traffic bridges') that regularly punctuate the roads are given names just as Beijing's vanished city gates were; and indeed these *lijiaoqiao* have taken over the gates' role to become the most recognizable place markers of new Beijing.[3]

The design of the ring roads is related to the second link or spatial system — the 'poly-nuclear' urban form of new Beijing (illus. 184).[4] The purpose of this form is to establish subsidiary residential centres around the old city; the neighbourhood at Hongmiao emerged as a result of this master plan. In time, the gap between these sub-centres would be filled, and they would be assimilated into continuous zones between ring roads. Even so, their positions in Beijing would still be determined by their relationship with the city's core area within the Second Ring Road, which, built on the site of the destroyed city walls, outlines traditional Beijing. In 2004 this core area as Beijing's centre has a twofold meaning: it is still the seat of government and holds the most important political activities, while an ongoing campaign boosts Beijing's identity as a historical city with a 500-year history. A belated conservation plan was made in 1999 to protect 'twenty-five historical neighborhoods', shown in illus. 185 as

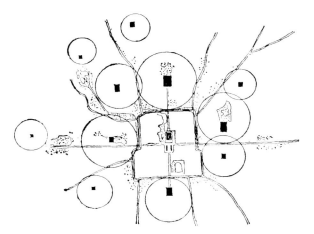

184 Poly-nuclear development strategy, Beijing.

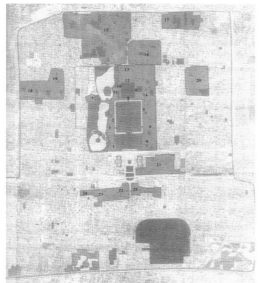

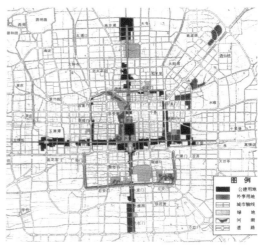

disconnected blocks superimposed on a ghostly map of now-vanished traditional Beijing. Together with the Forbidden City and some imperial parks,
these neighbourhoods will be what old Beijing leaves to the future.[5]

Beijing's north–south and east–west axes constitute the third spatial system
underlying Beijing's development and the perception of the city. I have discussed
in this book how Chang'an Avenue gradually became Beijing's new axis in the
twentieth century. Associated with the recent emphasis on the city's historical
identity, however, an effort has been made to restore and develop the traditional north–south axis.[6] An early sign of this effort was a 1992 ten-year master plan
for Beijing's development, which forecast many public buildings constructed
along this axis (illus. 186). But this plan became obsolete after China won the
competition to hold the 2008 Olympic Games. It is now planned that a new
town centred on two buildings, envisioned to be the tallest in the world, will
extend the north end of Beijing's central axis to a point beyond the Fourth Ring
Road (illus. 187). As for the south end of the axis, the municipal government has
decided to reconstruct Yongdingmen, the southern gate of old Beijing destroyed
during the Great Leap Forward in the 1950s (illus. 188).

These three structural links or spatial systems – the ring roads, the poly-
nuclear pattern and the axes – belong to a larger spatial system on account of
how they overlap. Their shared centre in the administrative/historical area of
the old city is most precisely mapped out by the intersection of the two axes in
Tiananmen Square (illus. 189). This should not come as a surprise. As stated at
the opening of this book, the single most important moment in Beijing's modern development came after this city became the capital of the newly established People's Republic of China. The location of the government had to be
decided immediately. While some conservation-minded architects proposed a

187 Proposed Olympic village for the 2008 Olympic Games in Beijing.

separate administrative centre west of traditional Beijing, others argued that the imperial city itself had to be transformed into a socialist capital centred on a reconstructed Tiananmen Square. Endorsed by Mao, this second plan prevailed and has controlled Beijing's urban planning to this day. The concentric ring roads, the subsidiary residential centres surrounding the old city, and the two expanding axes are all concrete manifestations of this decision made more than half a century ago. As such, these spatial systems offer both practical solutions to the city's needs and ideological support to the political authority. Urban planners often conceive these systems as a means to decentralize Beijing;[7] the other side of the coin is that these systems also reinforce Tiananmen Square's position as the unchallenged centre of the capital.

188 A computer rendering of reconstructed Yongdingmen.

189 The centre
of new Beijing
defined by the
two axes and
the ring roads.

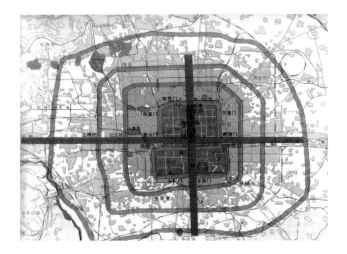

This leads us back to the Square and to its changes in recent years. The most remarkable thing, however, is that this place has actually changed very little in comparison with the rapid transformation of the rest of Beijing. As noted above, no permanent structure has been added to the Square since the completion of the Chairman Mao Memorial Hall in 1977; all the architectural projects in the locale have served mainly maintenance purposes. Such absence of change is itself highly significant for two reasons: first, it means that the Square still maintains its physical integrity and ideological coherence. Continuing as the site of National Day celebrations, its connection with China's statehood is reconfirmed every year with full ceremonial. Second, it also means that the Square has become merely a 'conceptual centre' of the city and the country – a place insulated from the outside world where real events take place. These real events are all associated with change – changes in the environment and in people's living conditions and lifestyle. In fact, enormous changes can be seen next to the Square: to the east, glittering five-star hotels and fashionable shopping malls have taken over the whole stretch from Wangfujing to Dongdan; to the west, the ultra-modern pearl-shaped National Theatre is rising from the ground. Compared to these new neighbours, the plain, brownish Square seems almost quaint. Its 30-to-40-year-old monuments no longer impress people as architectural marvels achieved by a spiritually invigorated people; instead they arouse nostalgia in those who witnessed their creation.

To Jiang Zemin, who succeeded Deng Xiaoping in 1989 to become China's supreme leader, keeping the Square in its original form must have signified his commitment to Communist ideals as well as his disassociation from Mao's era. Plenty of evidence reveals this double-edged tactic. For example, to celebrate the country's fiftieth anniversary, he orchestrated the most extravagant National Day parade in the Square to clinch his rule as 'the third milestone' in the country's history after Mao and Deng Xiaoping. To welcome the new millennium the following year, he constructed the mammoth Millennium Altar. But instead of locating this monument in Tiananmen Square, he placed it in

Beijing's new urban space between the Second and Third Ring Roads.[8] Jiang's architectural legacy will also include the National Theatre, now being constructed next to the Great Hall of the People on Chang'an Avenue. After an intense international competition, which went three rounds and lasted a year and a half, the top leadership finally made a decision in July 1999. The design that Jiang approved was by the French architect Paul Andreu, who proposed building a shiny egg of glass and titanium, encircled by a large pool and entered through an underwater tunnel (illus. 190). In selecting this design the great difference between his vision for a 'socialist monument' and Mao's became unmistakable. By completing an architectural project first proposed in 1958, and by constructing an ultra-modern structure next to the Great Hall of the People,[9] he once again connected himself to the Mao era while simultaneously disassociating himself from it.

Jiang Zemin's attitude toward Mao's legacy calls into question my earlier observation: Is it really true that the Square did not change during the Jiang era from 1998 to 2003, or did it change in ways that have escaped our attention? Looking beyond permanent monuments, we notice a form of symbolic representation that has become a routine feature of the Square since the early 1990s. These are temporary installations constructed to celebrate the founding of the country and other important occasions. Their themes and images have changed year after year: an installation can take the form of a mythological dragon or phoenix, a famous historical site such as the Great Wall, a traditional lantern enlarged several hundred times, or a mountain of giant vegetables and fruit that symbolizes a good harvest (illus. 191). Often designed as a group to transform the Square into a theme park, these bright, colourful images convey a general sense of auspiciousness, not specific political agendas. Made of wood, paper, silk, plants and flowers, they appeal to popular taste with their intricate craftsmanship and gaudy appearance. Thousands and thousands of people go to see them every year, to be delighted by their ingenious designs and the ironic contrast between their larger-than-life images and perishable materials. Newspaper reports detail the cost and labour put into these playful images: 200,000 potted flowers were used to construct nine installations for the 1994 National Day celebration, including a golden dragon made of 10,000 pots of yellow chrysanthemums.[10] It is interesting to wonder why flowers are used so extensively in

190 Paul Andreu's design for the National Theatre, Beijing.

191 'Soft monu-
ments' installed
in Tiananmen
Square for the
National Day
celebration in
2001.

making such images. The answer must be that this 'material' most effectively reinforces the meaning of the installations as auspicious but ephemeral representations associated with a holiday occasion.

No historian has attached any importance to these temporary visual spectacles, which, however, have actually introduced a new mode of political expression in the Square and demand explanation. I call these installations 'soft monuments'. The word 'soft' pertains to both their impermanent form and fluid content: although constructed in this most important political space on the most important political occasions, they have little substance in either a physical or ideological sense. Unlike a 'hard monument' from the previous era that commemorated history and demanded faith, a 'soft monument' of the 1990s and early 2000s is deliberately short-lived and goal-specific; its brief but extravagant appearance reflects a more practical and fragmented notion of time. Paul Virilio's formulation of two types of monumentality in the contemporary world helps to explain the differences between the 'hard' and 'soft' monuments in today's Tiananmen Square. According to him, the first kind, architectonic monuments in the classical tradition, is precisely located and constructed from concrete physical elements. In contrast, the second kind is immaterial, and its representations 'are the vectors of a momentary, instantaneous expression'. The first is linked with a 'grand narrative of theoretical causality'; the second is associated with a 'petty narrative of practical opportunity'.[11]

Virilio's evidence for the second kind of monumentality consists mainly of disembodied electrical signals that dissolve solid volume. We can relate such elusive forms to the 'soft monuments' in the Square because they too are likewise momentary expressions of a 'petty narrative of practical opportunity'. This understanding enables us to see today's Tiananmen Square anew, and to discover other visual inventions that have helped transform the place's visual culture over the past ten years. These inventions include a network of water jets hidden under the square's pavement and in the moat before Tiananmen, which come to life only on grand occasions such as National Day celebrations. Operated by complex computer programs, they can create fountains in 30 different patterns and can even spray water to form auspicious phrases in

Chinese characters (illus. 192). Other inventions are designed for holiday evenings. Whereas new kinds of firework (each with an auspicious title) have been continuously created for National Day celebrations, 22 laser projectors send bright beams into the sky, forming colourful patterns and slogans in the void above the Square – exactly the kind of disembodied images that Virilio has described as a contemporary form of monumentality.

It would be a mistake, however, to attribute these new visual forms in the Square to a general postmodern global culture. In fact, inspirations for most of these forms come from traditional Chinese popular culture; advanced technologies are employed to reinforce the bustling, exciting atmosphere (called *renao*) typical of a Chinese holiday gathering. The history of 'soft monuments' can actually be traced to the last dynasty, when hundreds of temporary buildings and sculptures were designed and constructed in Beijing for the birthday of an emperor or empress (see illus. 112). The resurrection of this tradition served new political needs in the People's Republic of China: it is possible that the first group of 'soft monuments' was related to the June Fourth Movement. The occasion for their creation, the Pan-Asian Games in 1991, gave the Chinese government the first chance since 1989 to show the world its mandate and benevolence. The Square was transformed: multi-coloured flowers brightened its concrete surface; giant smiling pandas stood on turntables, waving flower bouquets to welcome athletes and visitors from different countries (illus. 193).

The construction of such installations became a routine practice in the following years. In time, the purpose for their creation became more broadly defined, often described in newspaper reports simply as creating ambience for a holiday occasion and making people happy. These descriptions disclose a government agenda subtly to depoliticize the Square: instead of empowering the Chinese people to carry out political or military campaigns against domestic and foreign enemies, images in the Square now express citizens' happiness and unification. Consequently, slogans and paintings calling for class struggle and global revolution have virtually disappeared. Instead, part of the Square was turned into lawns in 1999 to soften its harsh contour; the Museum of Revolutionary History was absorbed into the new National Gallery in 2003;

and the National Theatre will be unveiled in 2005. This does not mean, however, that surveillance in the Square has loosened at all: security guards are prepared to arrest Falungong demonstrators at any moment.

This government-sponsored depoliticization of the Square provides us with a context to revisit the unofficial art projects discussed in the last Chapter. The timing of these projects, all of which have been created since the early 1990s, is not coincidental: these are actually the artists' responses to the government campaign, which they feel conceals the nature of this political space and erases the memories of the June Fourth Movement and the Cultural Revolution. A sense of urgency towards such erasure also explains the appearance of avant-garde performances in the Square around the mid-1990s, conducted *in situ* to express the artists' experience during the Cultural Revolution and to commemorate the June Fourth Movement. This is why Song Dong tried to inject life into the Square's unfeeling surface in his *Breathing* (see illus. 175). Opposed to all kinds of monuments, including 'soft monuments', a performance like this amounts to an *anti-monument*: it rejects any form of monumental expression and gains its significance by creating a space for individual remembrance and imagination.

References

INTRODUCTION

1 Beijing's history can be traced to the Western Zhou period (c. 1050–256 BC), but the city inherited by the Communists in 1949 was constructed by the Ming emperor Yongle on the site of the Yuan capital Dadu. The basic construction work was completed during the fifteen years from 1406 to 1420. The outer city, however, was added in 1553, more than a century after the construction of the imperial city and the inner city. For a concise introduction to Beijing's history, see Hou Renzhi and Deng Hui, *Beijing cheng de qiyuan he bianqian* [The origin and transformation of the city of Beijing] (Beijing, 1997). While Hou and Deng's discussion focuses on Beijing's construction and planning throughout Chinese history, Susan Naquin's *Peking: Temples and City Life, 1400–1900* (Berkeley, CA, 2000) provides a detailed account of Beijing's cultural scenes and urban life during the Ming and Qing dynasties. A third perspective is represented by Jeffery F. Meyer's *The Dragons of Tiananmen: Beijing as a Sacred City* (Columbia, SC, 1991), which focuses on Beijing's symbolic structure.

2 For these campaigns and their results, see Madelaine Yue Dong, *Republican Beijing: The City and its Histories* (Berkeley, CA, 2003).

3 David Strand offers a vivid description of pre-1949 Beijing in his *Rickshaw Beijing: City People and Politics in the 1920s* (Berkeley, CA, 1989). As he shows, although efforts were made in the late Qing and Republican era to modernize the city, early twentieth-century Beijing 'remained a city stubbornly defined by walls, wall enclosures, and gates' (p. 1). Although major roads were first paved with macadam and then with asphalt and concrete, the sides of the roads were often left unpaved to allow wheeled country carts to travel through (p. 3). For an insightful account of the urban reconstruction taking place in Beijing after 1928, the year when the Republican government moved its seat to Nanjing, see Madeleine Yue Dong, 'Defining Beijing: Urban Reconstruction and National Identity, 1928–1936', in Joseph W. Esherick, ed., *Remaking the Chinese City: Modernity and National Identity, 1900–1950* (Honolulu, 2000), pp. 121–38.

4 Among the architects directly involved in Beijing's urban planning in the early 1950s, Liang Sicheng, Chen Zhanxiang and Hua Lanhong studied in the USA, Britain and France, respectively.

5 The most comprehensive study of this debate is Wang Jun's *Cheng ji* [The story of a city] (Beijing, 2003).

6 Friedrich Engels, *Dialectics of Nature*, trans. Clemens Dutt, in *Karl Marx, Frederick Engels: Collected Works* (New York, 1975–), vol. XXV, pp. 540–41.

7 Chen Gan, *Chen Gan wenji: Jinghua daisi lu* [Collected writings of Chen Gan: Finished and unfinished thoughts on Beijing] (Beijing, 1996), cited in Wang Jun, *Cheng ji*, pp. 233–4. Chen Gan repeated the same idea on other occasions. In one place he wrote: 'In fact, as soon as the decision was made to hold the country's founding ceremony in Tiananmen Square, the idea of preserving Beijing's old city in its original shape was rejected' (ibid., p. 40).

8 Wang Jun, *Cheng ji*, p. 101.

9 Mao's remarks on several occasions reveal his negative view toward Beijing's conservation. For example, once on Tiananmen's rostrum he said that in the future he would like to see this place surrounded by tall chimneys – symbols of industrialization. In meetings he also ridiculed Liang Sicheng's sentimentality toward old Beijing (ibid., p. 177).

10 Wu Liangyong, *Rehabilitating the Old City of Beijing* (Vancouver, 1999), p. 19.

11 Chen Zhanxiang, 'Yi Liang Sicheng jiaoshou' [Remembering Professor Liang Sicheng], in *Liang Sicheng xianshen danchen bashiwu zhounian jinian wenji* [Papers presented to Mr Liang Sicheng on his 85th birthday] (Beijing, 1996). Under pressure, Liang Sicheng and his colleagues modified their original plan, agreeing to locate the administrative centre near Tiananmen Square, but, because he insisted on preserving traditional Beijing, even the modified plan was rejected. See Wang Jun, *Cheng ji*, pp. 117–18.

12 Wang Jun, *Cheng ji*, p. 18.

13 Some of these books include: Xue Fengxuan, *Beijing: You chuantong guodu dao shehuizhuyi shoudu* [Beijing: From an imperial capital to a socialist capital] (Hong Kong, 1996); Zhang Jinggan, *Beijing guihua jianshe wushinian* [Fifty years of Beijing's urban planning and construction] (Beijing, 2001), a slightly revised version of the same author's *Beijing guihua jianshe zongheng tan* [A general survey of Beijing's urban planning and construction] (Beijing, 1997); Dong Guangqi, *Beijing guihua zhanlue sikao* [A strategic consideration of Beijing's urban planning] (Beijing, 1998); Wu Liangyong, *Rehabilitating the Old City of Beijing*; Fang Ke, *Dangdai Beijing jiucheng gengxin* [Contemporary redevelopment in the Inner City of Beijing] (Beijing, 2000); and Wang Jun, *Cheng ji*. The

most up-to-date scholarship on Beijing's planning and transformation in the pre-modern and Republican periods is represented by Jianfei Zhu's *Chinese Spatial Strategies: Imperial Beijing, 1420–1911* (London and New York, 2004) and Dong's *Republican Beijing*, respectively. There are also books that compare the experience of Beijing with other Chinese cities in the twentieth century: Joseph W. Esherick, ed., *Remaking the Chinese City: Modernity and National Identity, 1900–1950* (Honolulu, 2000); Alfred Schinz, *Cities in China*, Urbanization of the Earth, vol. 7, ed. Wolf Tietze (Berlin and Stuttgart, 1989); Kai Vöckler and Dirk Luckow, eds, *Peking Shanghai Shenzhen: Cities of the 21st Century* (Frankfurt, 2000).

14 Jianfei Zhu writes in his exhaustive study of Beijing's spatial structure during the late imperial period: 'There is no open and collective spatial field where a society can congregate in a central area. An open space, with its fluidity and continuity and its tendency to gather and to form a centrality, is missing in imperial Beijing' (*Chinese Spatial Strategies*, p. 46).

15 For different notions of public space, see David M. Henkin, *City Reading: Written Words and Public Spaces in Antebellum New York* (New York, 1998), pp. 8–11.

16 One way to understand such interdependence between collective protests and personal experiences is to interpret these protests as 'political theaters', as Joseph W. Esherick and Jeffery N. Wasserstrom have suggested in their influential essay, 'Acting Out Democracy: Political Theater in Modern China', in Wasserstrom and Elizabeth J. Perry, eds, *Popular Protest and Political Culture in Modern China: Learning from Tiananmen* (Boulder, CO, 1991), pp. 28–66. In a political movement like the 1989 student demonstrations in Tiananmen Square, 'Once the public stage has been captured, the street actors are all the more free to write their own script' (p. 34). Also see Richard Schechner, 'The Street Is the Stage', *The Future of Ritual: Writings on Culture and Performance* (London and New York, 1993), pp. 45–93.

17 Whereas personal experience must contribute to one's approach toward one's research subject, a historical study can help to retrieve memories. The psychologist Frederic C. Bartlett argued in 1932 that autobiographical memory is fundamentally reconstructive and interpretative, because representations in memory always confine facts within certain schemata or reflective generalizations of past events. This theory has been substantiated by recent scholars such as William F. Brewer, Martin A. Conway and Bruce M. Ross. See F. C. Bartlett, *Remembering: A Study in Experimental and Social Psychology* (Cambridge, 1932), pp. 204–12; Martin A. Conway, *Autobiographical Memory: An Introduction* (Milton Keynes, 1990), p. 101; Bruce M. Ross, 'Relation of Implicit Theories to the Construction of Personal Histories', *Psychological Review*, 96 (1989), pp. 371–416.

18 Some psychologists distinguish 'self-narratives' from autobiographical memories, which are mundane and less relevant to one's self-conception. According to them, self-narratives 'consist of a set of temporally and thematically organized salient experiences and concerns that constitute one's identity or self-concept'. See John A. Robinson and Leslie R. Taylor, 'Autobiographical Memory and Self-Narratives: A Tale of Two Stories', in Charles P. Thompson *et al.*, eds, *Autobiographical Memory: Theoretical and Applied Perspectives* (Mahwah, NJ, 1998), pp. 125–44 [p. 126].

19 In terms of memory formation, M. K. Johnson suggests that autobiographical memory typically consists of three basic sub-systems – the sensory, perceptual and reflective – characterized by varying degrees of concreteness and abstraction. The sensory memory contains information about elementary aspects of perception, such as the physical attributes of an object and direction of a movement. The perceptual memory represents a higher level of perceptual information, such as the conscious experience of an array of objects or a place. The reflective memory represents information about internally generated events such as thinking, imagining and planning. Memories in the last sub-system incorporate 'our attempts to control what happens to us and our commentary on the events that do happen to us'; and thus entail historical reflection and reasoning. M. K. Johnson, 'The Origin of Memories', in P. C. Kendall, ed., *Advances in Cognitive-Behavioural Research and Therapy* (New York, 1985), pp. 1–27 [p. 17]. Also see Bruce M. Ross, *Remembering the Personal Past: Descriptions of Autobiographical Memory* (New York and Oxford, 1991), pp. 159–60.

As for historical research, it develops in an opposite direction from broad historiographic assumptions to specific historical reconstructions with growing tangibility. Sensory and perceptual information provided by memoirs constitutes a particularly important category of evidence for research of visual forms, because it helps to make a historical reconstruction an actually experienced event rather than a mechanical account of factual details. Scholars have emphasized over and over the importance of autobiographical memories in storing and stimulating mental images. William F. Brewer, for example, argues that the remembering of such memories is essentially experienced as having mental images of the memory content. 'What is Recollective Memory?', in David C. Rubin, ed., *Remembering our Past: Studies in Autobiographical Memory* (Cambridge, 1996), pp. 19–66. Brewer's theory is re-examined by Steen F. Larson in 'What Is It Like to Remember?: On Phenomenal Qualities of Memory', in Thompson *et al.*, eds, *Autobiographical Memory*, pp. 163–87.

20 According to James W. Pennebaker, 'significant historical events form stronger collective memories'. Pennebaker, Dario Paez and Bernard Rimé, eds, *Collective Memory of Political Events: Social Psychological Perspectives* (Mahwah, NJ, 1997), p. 6.

21 Maurice Halbwachs, *On Collective Memory* (Chicago, 1992). For Vygotsky's ideas, see David Bakhurst, 'Social Memory in Soviet Thought', in David Middleton and Derek Edwards, eds, *Collective Remembering* (London, 1990).

22 Information about this performance comes from 'Zheng Lianjie xingdong yishu: *Jiazu suiyue*' [Zheng Jianjie's performance art project: *Family History*]. Unpublished text provided by the artist.

23 These reconstructed memories necessarily fall into the category of episodic memories, which 'refer to situations in which a person remembers an experienced event which contains spatio-temporal knowledge': Endel Tulving, 'Episodic and Semantic Memory', in Tulving and W. Donaldson, eds, *Organization of Memory* (New York, 1972). In another place, Tulving identifies 'episodic memories' with 'autobiographical memories': 'How Many

Memory Systems are there?', *American Psychologist*, 40 (1985), pp. 385–98. Compromised of such spatio-temporally defined memories, the autobiographical narratives in this book echo the historical narrative both structurally and thematically: like the historical narrative, they are also context-bound, refer to specific times and places, and are closely associated with both self-identity and public environment.

24 For example, my description and interpretation of the 1989 pro-democratic demonstrations in Tiananmen Square is clearly influenced by my personal experience back in China. For a review of different 'stories' of the event, see Jeffrey N. Wasserstrom, 'Afterword: History, Myth and the Tales of Tiananmen', in Wasserstrom and Perry, eds, *Popular Protest and Political Culture in Modern China*, pp. 244–80.

ONE

1 Quoted by Rene Wellek in his *History of Modern Criticism* (New Haven, 1955), vol. I, p. 211.

2 Sir Claude MacDonald, commander of the army, reasoned that this march was necessary: 'lest the Chinese, with their infinite capacity for misrepresentation, should infer that some supernatural power had intervened, so that the Allied forces had been affected by fear of the consequences of invading the sacred precincts.' Peter Fleming, *The Siege at Beijing* (Hong Kong, Oxford and New York, 1986), p. 245.

3 In an insightful essay, Linda Hershkovitz argues that Tiananmen Square is the product of two distinct but intertwined spatial traditions. While its monuments have embodied the orthodox, hegemonic political power, its 'symbolic geography' also incorporates a tradition of dissent or rebellion through its association with unorthodox political protests and demonstrations. 'Tiananmen Square and the Politics of Place', *Political Geography*, XII/5 (September 1993), pp. 395–420.

4 Tiananmen was constructed in 1430 (the eighteenth year of the Hongwu reign).

5 A description of the Thousand-step Porches (Qianbu lang) is given in *Qing gong shi xu* [Sequel to a history of Qing palaces]: 'There are the Thousand-step Porches inside the Gate of the Great Qing. Facing east or west, each of the two porches contains 110 bays, and includes an additional 34 bays after it turns to face north. Each porch has a single cornice and connected ridges.' Cited in Lu Bingjie, *Tiananmen* (Shanghai, 1999), p. 153. As Lu notes in his book, the inclusion of these two rows of buildings into this space was based on a convention that can be traced back to the Song dynasty.

6 These occasions included: the annual journey of the emperor to the Altar of Heaven and the Altar of Earth to hold state sacrifices; state ceremonies accompanying important military operations; the wedding ceremony of an emperor when he received his empress from the south gate of the Forbidden City; the issuing of imperial edicts when an emperor ascended or abdicated the throne.

7 At the beginning of the Ming dynasty, this exam was held south of the Golden Water Bridge (Jinshui qiao) in front of Tiananmen (called Chengtianmen at the time). Its location was changed later to the throne hall, Hall of Supreme Harmony (Taihe dian). During the Qing, this exam was given in the Hall of Protecting Harmony (Baohe dian), which was one of the Three Principal Audience Halls (San dadian) in the Forbidden City.

8 Zhao Luo and Shi Shuqing, *Tiananmen* (Beijing, 1957), p. 25.

9 Ibid.

10 A concise discussion of this theory can be found in Fung Yu-lan, *A Short History of Chinese Philosophy* (New York, 1948), pp. 129–42.

11 The Chinese emperor who devoted himself most diligently to this theory is Wang Mang (r. AD 8–25). For an introduction to the ritual architecture that he created for this purpose, see Wu Hung, *Monumentality in Ancient Chinese Art and Architecture* (Stanford, CA, 1995), pp. 176–87.

12 For a discussion of administrative centres in Qing dynasty Beijing, see Zīanfei Zhu, *Chinese Spatial Strategies: Imperial Beijing, 1420–1911* (London and New York, 2004), pp. 135–9.

13 Zhao Luo and Shi Shuqing, *Tiananmen*, p. 22.

14 Following China's globalization and commercialization in recent years, new types of *guangchang* have emerged in major cities as commercial and entertainment centres. One such example is the Oriental Square, east of Tiananmen.

15 In Ann Anagnost's words, 'The Party authorizes itself to "represent", in the sense of "speaking for" the people as a unitary social body. Any dissent with the Party's will must therefore come from "outside the people".' 'Socialist Ethics and the Legal System', in Jeffery N. Wasserstrom and Elizabeth J. Perry, eds, *Popular Protest and Political Culture in Modern China*, pp. 177–205; quotation from p. 198.

16 Quoted in Wu Liangyong, 'Tiananmen Guangchang de guihua he sheji' [The plan and design of Tiananmen Square], in *Jianzhushi lunwenji* [Essays on architectural history] (Beijing, 1979), vol. II, p. 26.

17 Wu Liangyong, 'Renmin Yingxiong Jinianbei de chuangzuo chengjiu' [The architectural achievement of the Monument to the People's Heroes], *Jianzhu xuebao* [Architectural journal] (1978), no. 2, pp. 4–5.

18 Ibid., p. 19.

19 Some architects, especially Liang Sicheng and Lin Huiyin, strongly opposed the destruction of these two gates and other old structures. For a detailed description of their struggle, see Wang Jun, *Cheng jie* [The story of a city] (Beijing, 2003), pp. 163–90.

20 This piece of stone was obtained in Shandong province for this particular purpose. Its original weight was 280 tons, which was then reduced to 103 tons after rough processing. By every possible means of transportation this stone was shipped to Beijing, where it was further refined to make a 60-ton slab.

21 Wu Liangyong, 'Renmin Yingxiong Jinianbei de chuangzuo chengjiu', p. 8.

22 The upper layer of the terrace has a floor plan 32 metres square. The lower layer has a rectangular floor plan, 50.5 metres east–west and 61.5 metres north–south.

23 This pine forest was destroyed in 1977 to make room for the Chairman Mao Memorial Hall.

24 These reports include: Wu Liangyong's 1978 and 1979 papers cited above; Zhao Dongri, 'Tiananmen Guangchang' [Tiananmen Square], *Jianzhu xuebao* (1959), nos 9–10, pp. 18–22; Dong Guangqi, 'Tiananmen Guangchang de gaijian yu kuojian' [The reconstruction and expansion of

Tiananmen Square], *Beijing wenshi cailiao* [Data concerning the history of Beijing] (1994), no. 49; Tao Zongzhen, 'Tiananmen Guangchang guihua jianshe de huigu yu qianzhan' [Looking forward and backward at Tiananmen Square's planning and construction], *Nanfang jianzhu* (1999), p. 4. In the following discussion only quotations from these writings will be referenced.

25 Simon Leys, *Chinese Shadows* (New York, 1977), pp. 53–4.

26 Wu Liangyong, 'Renmin Yingxiong Jinianbei de chuangzuo chengjiu'. As the author specifically noted, his article represents the official approach.

27 Ibid., p. 4.

28 For this series of events, see Shu Jun, *Tiananmen guangchang lishi dang'an* [Historical archives related to Tiananmen] (Beijing, 1998), pp. 104–5.

29 Wu Liangyong, 'Renmin Yingxiong Jinianbei de chuangzuo chengjiu', p. 5.

30 Ibid., p. 6.

31 See Shu Jun, *Tiananmen guangchang lishi dang'an*, pp. 107–8.

32 Zhou Dingfang, 'Renmin Yingxiong Jinianbei' [The Monument to the People's Heroes), in *Jinri Beijing* [Beijing Today] (date unknown), p. 949.

33 Pierre Nora, 'Between Memory and History', *Representations*, XXIX (Spring 1989), p. 19.

34 For descriptions and discussions of this mass movement, see David S. F. Goodman, *Beijing Street Voices: The Poetry and Politics of China's Democracy Movement* (London, 1981); Jürgen Domes, *The Government and Politics of the PRC: a Time of Transition* (Boulder, CO, 1985).

35 Anne F. Thurston, *Enemies of the People* (New York, 1987), pp. 5–6.

36 Ibid., p. 21. In this poem the first emperor of the Qin alludes to Mao Zedong.

37 Even the Museum of Chinese History was closed during the Cultural Revolution.

38 During Deng Xiaoping's reign this structure became a collective memorial hall for deceased Party leaders, including Zhou Enlai, Zhu De and Liu Shaoqi.

39 Pierre Nora, 'Between Memory and History', p. 23.

40 Michel de Certeau calls this spatial strategy a *tactic*: 'A space of tactic is the space of the other. Thus it must play on and with a terrain imposed on it and organized by the law of a foreign power . . . [It] is a manoeuvre "within the enemy's field of vision" . . . and within enemy territory . . . In short, a tactic is an art of the weak.' *The Practice of Everyday Life* (Berkeley, CA, 1984), pp. 36–7. For an excellent discussion of this strategy in relation to Tiananmen Square, see Hershkovitz, 'Tiananmen Square and the Politics of Place', pp. 396–400.

41 In addition to the mass movements in 1976 and 1989, many other unofficial and anti-government gatherings have been centred on the Monument. The photographer Li Xiaobin has documented some of these gatherings and described his experience in an interview. See Li Xiaobin and Ding Dong, 'Yong jingtou jilu lishi' [Recording history with a camera], *Laozhaopian* [Old photos], 31, pp. 105–22.

42 During the demonstrations there were rumours that the Communist leaders were watching the demonstrators from the top of the Great Hall and Tiananmen, and that soldiers were sent to these buildings through secret tunnels.

43 An important political event between these two movements

was a protest organized by Shanghai students in late 1986 and early 1987. For information, see Jeffrey N. Wasserstrom, *Student Protests in Twentieth-Century China: The View from Shanghai* (Stanford, CA, 1991), pp. 304–8. In terms of chronology, this Shanghai protest was more directly related to the June Fourth movement.

44 Such links between earlier and later protests can also be understood in terms of 'scripts', which, in Esherick and Wasserstrom's words, 'gave them [i.e., protesters) a shared sense of how to behave during a given action, when and where to march, how to express their demands, and so forth.' 'Acting Out Democracy', in Wasserstrom and Perry, eds, *Popular Protest and Political Culture in Modern China*, pp. 32–3.

45 The most authoritative report on the making of this monument is Hsing-yuan Tsao's 'The Birth of the *Goddess of Democracy*', in Wasserstrom and Perry, eds, *Popular Protest and Political Culture in Modern China*, 2nd edn, pp. 140–47. Tsao witnessed the construction of the statue in the Square and also interviewed several artists.

46 The following events are recorded in Wu Muren, *et al.*, *1989 Zhonggong Minyun jishi* [A factual record of the 1989 Chinese democratic movement] (New York, 1989), vol. I, pp. 12–13.

47 For a discussion of the concept of 'democracy' in this and other post-Cultural Revolution student movements, see Esherick and Wasserstrom, 'Acting Out Democracy', pp. 30–32.

48 'Students declared', we read in a report, 'that they will continue to occupy the Square and that even the threat of death cannot make them leave', in ibid., I, p. 27.

49 Tsao, 'Birth of the *Goddess of Democracy*', p. 141.

50 Ibid., p. 142. A conflicting report is given in the *New Yorker*, 23 October 1989, p. 43. A female student posed for the *Goddess* and some pictures of the *Statue of Liberty* were consulted. My sources confirm Tsao's account. In terms of the sculptural style of the female imagery, Tsao notes that it was strongly influenced by 'the Russian school of revolutionary realism, and specifically the style of the woman sculptor Vera Mukhina, whose monumental statue of *A Worker and Collective Farm Woman*, placed originally atop the Soviet Pavilion at the 1937 Paris World's Fair, is still much admired in China.' 'Birth of the *Goddess* of Democracy', p. 142. Additional information about the Goddess can be found in Liang Tieshan, 'Minzhu niushen yongzai woxinzhong' [The Goddess of Democracy will always live in my heart], *Zhongguo zhichun* [China's Spring] (1989), p. 8.

51 According to Hsing-yuan Tsao, 'The place on the Square where the statue was to be erected had been chosen carefully. It was on the great axis, heavy with both cosmological and political symbolism, that extended from the main entrance of the Forbidden City, with the huge portrait of Mao Zedong over it, through the Monument to the People's Heroes that had become the command headquarters of the student movement. The statue was to be set up just across the broad avenue from Mao, so that it would confront him face-to-face.' 'Birth of the *Goddess of Democracy*', p. 144.

52 John Gittings's report from Beijing, *The Guardian*, 31 May 1989, p. 10.

53 Tsao, 'Birth of the *Goddess of Democracy*', p. 145.

54 Wu Ye, 'What does the statue of the *Goddess of Democracy*, which appeared in Tiananmen Square indicate?', *Renmin ribao* [People's daily], overseas edition, 1 June 1989; a translation of the article is provided in *National Affairs*, FBIS-CHI-89-104, p. 28.

55 Liang Tieshan, 'Minzhu Nüshen yongzai woxinzhong', p. 76.

56 According to Hsing-yuan Tsao, the statue was transported to the Square in four horizontal sections. They were placed one on top of another *in situ*. Plaster was poured into the hollow core to lock the sections onto a vertical iron pole in the middle. 'The statue was deliberately made so that once assembled it could not be taken apart again but would have to be destroyed all at once.' 'Birth of the *Goddess of Democracy*', p. 144.

TWO

1 See definitions and examples given in Luo Zhufeng, *et al.*, *Zhongwen dacidian* [A comprehensive dictionary of Chinese], 12 vols (Beijing, 1993), XII, pp. 378–9.

2 Richard Brilliant, *Portraiture* (London, 1991), p. 9.

3 Roman Jakobson, 'Two Aspects of Language and Two Types of Aphasic Disturbances', in R. Jakobson and Morris Hale, *Fundamentals of Language* (The Hague, 1956), pp. 109–14. Also see, Paul Friedrich, 'Polytropy', in James W. Fernandez, ed., *Beyond Metaphor: The Theory of Tropes in Anthropology* (Stanford, CA, 1991), pp. 17–55, especially p. 44.

4 Yang Rong, 'Chongzao youzhuo guoqu jiyi de xinjianzhu' [Creating new architecture with memories of the past], *Jianzhushi* [Architect], 78 (October 1997), pp. 39–45, especially p. 43. The first architectural historian to study the 'shop front' seriously was Liang Sicheng. The examples he collected in the 1930s are published in his *Zhongguo jianzhu yishu tuji* [Visual materials on the art of Chinese architecture] (Tianjin, 1999), vol. I, pp. 97–146.

5 *Zhou li* (Rite of Zhou), 'Xiaguan'. See Ruan Yuan, ed., *Shisanjing zhushu* [Annotated Thirteen Classics] (Beijing, 1980), vol. I, p. 865. A similar expression is found in *Yi jing* [The book of changes], 'Shuo gua', ibid., vol. I, p. 94.

6 For an introduction to the imperial palace as Tiananmen's architectural context, see Zianfei Zhu, *Chinese Spatial Strategies: Imperial Beijing, 1420–1911* (London and New York, 2004), pp. 99–103.

7 The last major reconstruction of Tiananmen took place from 1968 to 1970. The gate-tower after this reconstruction is 34.7 metres high, 83 centimetres taller than the original one. See Jia Yingting, ed., *Tiananmen* (Beijing, 1998), p. 119.

8 The Outer City of Beijing, which enclosed the area south of the Inner City, was built during the sixteenth century. The original plan was to construct a city wall that would surround the entire Inner City. The plan was never completely realized, but it showed the intention to expand Beijing based on the ancient model.

9 Before the Ming, Beijing had been the capital of the state of Yan (403–221 BC), the Liao (AD 916–1125), the Jin (1115–1234) and the Yuan (1279–1368), but Tiananmen was first built during the Ming dynasty in 1420.

10 For the origin and the political symbolism of this ancient design, see Wu Hung, 'From Temple to Tomb: Ancient Chinese Art and Religion in Transition', *Early China*, XIII (1988), pp. 78–116. For general principles in ancient Chinese city planning, see Paul Wheatley, *The Pivot of the Four Quarters* (Chicago, 1971), pp. 3–221; Jeffrey F. Meyer, *The Dragons of Tiananmen: Beijing as a Sacred City* (Columbia, SC, 1991), pp. 8–78.

11 These walls actually created endless 'extrinsic spaces', which, in Rudolf Arnheim's words, 'control the relation between independent object systems and provide them with standards of reference for their perceptual features'. *New Essays on the Psychology of Art* (Berkeley, CA 1986), p. 83. For applications of this architectural device in early Chinese city planning, see Wu Hung, 'From Temple to Tomb', pp. 80–86.

12 *Han Feizi* (third century BC), section 5, 'The way of the ruler'; based on Burton Watson's translation in *Basic Writings of Mo Tzu, Hsün Tzu, and Han Fei Tzu* (New York, 1963), 'Han Fei Tzu', pp. 17–18.

13 Cited in William Willetts, *Chinese Art* (New York, 1958), pp. 678–9.

14 This is at least one Qing author's opinion. See Yu Minzhong, *Rixia jiuwen kao* [Examining 'Old stories heard everyday'] (Beijing, 1983); cited in Jia Yingting, ed., *Tiananmen*, p. 5.

15 See M. S. Samuels and C. M. Samuels, 'Beijing and the Power of Place in Modern China', in John A. Agnew and James S. Duncan, eds, *The Power of Place: Bringing Together Geographical and Sociological Imaginations* (Boston, MA, 1989), pp. 202–27.

16 This ritual is recorded in *Erxia jiuwen kao*. A good summary is given in Jia Tingying, ed., *Tiananmen*, pp. 7–8. For a discussion of this and other rituals, see Meyer, *Dragons of Tiananmen*, pp. 46–62.

17 Jianfei Zhu has analysed the structural relationship between Tiananmen and other ceremonial spaces *inside* the Forbidden City during this type of ceremony. See *Chinese Spatial Strategies*, pp. 207–11. My focus here is the relationship between Tiananmen and the space immediately outside it.

18 Xihuangcheng, or the west wall of the Imperial City, was demolished in 1917. The east gate of the Imperial City, Donganmen, was destroyed in 1924. After continuous demolition from 1924 to 1927, only the wall between the Ancestral Temple and Bei Xinhua Street still existed. See Department of History at Peking University, History of Beijing Writing Group, *A History of Beijing*, expanded edn (Beijing, 1999), pp. 446–7.

19 See Madeline Yue Dong, *Republican Beijing: The City and its Histories* (Berkeley, CA, 2003) pp. 82–4; Shi Mingzheng, 'From Imperial Gardens to Public Parks: The Transformation of Urban Space in Early Twentieth-Century Beijing', *Modern China*, XXIV/3 (July 1998), pp. 219–54.

20 For a detailed account of these events, see Wu Shizhou, *Zijincheng de liming* [The dawn of the Forbidden City] (Beijing, 1998).

21 In Hou Renzhi's words, the subsequent promotion of Tiananmen to an independent political monument 'relegated the location of the old Forbidden City to "back yard" status. That ancient symbol of imperial primacy thus lost its exalted position relative to the rest of the city.' 'The Transformation of the Old City of Beijing', in Michael P. Conzen, ed., *World Patterns of Modern Urban Change* Department of Geography Research Paper no. 217–18 (Chicago, 1986), pp. 217–39; quotation from p. 234.

22 For a concise discussion of student protests up to the Cultural Revolution, see John Israel, 'Reflections on the Modern Chinese Student Movement', *Daedalus*, XCVII/1 (Winter 1968). More extensive discussions of the topic include: David Strand, *Rickshaw Beijing: City People and Politics in the 1920s* (Berkeley, CA, 1989), pp. 167–97; John Israel, *The Chinese Student Movement, 1927–1937* (Stanford, CA, 1959); Jeffrey N. Wasserstrom, *Student Protests in Twentieth-Century China: The View from Shanghai* (Stanford, CA, 1991). By focusing on Shanghai, the last book provides an alternative perspective in observing and analysing Chinese student movements from the early twentieth century to the June Fourth Movement.

23 For descriptions and discussions of this famous event, see Ts'e-tung Chow (Zhou Zezong), *The May Fourth Movement: Intellectual Revolution in Modern China* (Cambridge, MA, 1964); Jonathan Spence, *The Gate of Heavenly Peace: The Chinese and their Revolution, 1895–1989* (Harmondsworth, 1982); Immenuel C. Y. Hsu, *The Rise of Modern China* (New York, 1983).

24 The May Thirtieth demonstrations started from Shanghai and spread to Beijing. For protests organized in these two places, see Wasserstrom, *Student Protests in Twentieth-Century China*, pp. 95–124; Strand, *Rickshaw Beijing*, pp. 182–91; and Richard Rigby, *The May 30th Movement* (Canberra, 1980).

25 Although my discussion here focuses on Tiananmen Square, it is important to realize that the student protests held there were integral components of larger, national political events in the first half of the twentieth century. Large-scale student demonstrations also took place in Shanghai, Nanjing and other cities. Shanghai was a centre of political protests from the early twentieth century. Nanjing increased its political significance after becoming the capital of Republican China in 1928. For information about student protests outside Beijing, see Israel, *The Chinese Student Movement* and Wasserstrom, *Student Protests in Twentieth-Century China*.

26 Wen Fu, *Tiananmen jianzheng lu* [History as witnessed by Tiananmen] (Beijing, 1998), vol. I, pp. 354–61.

27 For the concept of 'democratic revolution of the new type', see discussion on pp. 28–31.

28 Before 1905 the road was paved with loess. The paving material was changed to fragmented stone in 1905, and to tar concrete in 1955. In 1958 the section of the road before Tiananmen (391.9 m long) was repaved with granite blocks.

29 For the installation of the tram, see Strand, *Rickshaw Beijing*, pp. 121–41; Shi Mingzheng, *Zuoxiang jindaihua de Beijing cheng: Chengshi jianshe yu shehui biange*, pp. 269–80. Dong, *Republican Beijing* [The city of Beijing moves towards modernization: City construction and social change] (Beijing, 1995), pp. 66–71. During the Japanese occupation, Chang'an Avenue was planned to connect an industrial district in Beijing's east suburbs and a 'new urban district' in the west suburbs. For this purpose, in 1939 two city gates, named Chang'anmen (present-day Fuxingmen) and Qimingmen (present-day Jianguomen) were opened in the city walls to allow the avenue through. See Zhang Jinggan, *Beijing guihua jianshe zonghengtan* [A general survey of Beijing's urban planning and construction] (Beijing, 1997), p. 173.

30 The old and new sections of the road, each 15 metres wide, were separated by tram lines. The old structures demolished in 1950 included the two free-standing brick gates (conventionally called Sanzuomen) outside the Left and Right Chang'an Gates, as well as two wooden archways called Lüzhong and Daohe. See Zhang Jinggan, *Beijing guihua jianshe zonghengtan*, p. 174.

31 Jia Yingting, ed., *Tiananmen*, p. 119.

32 Ibid., p. 120.

33 Although this design was proposed by a team led by Liang Sicheng, Liang put the image of Tiananmen in the centre only after Zhou Enlai's insistence. See Wang Jun, *Cheng ji* [The story of a city] (Beijing, 2003), pp. 39–40.

34 'Zhonghua renmin gongheguo guohui tu'an ji dui sheji tu'an de shuoming' [The design of the insignia of the People's Republic of China with an explanation]. Cited in Yu Jiang, *Kaiguo dadian liuxiaoshi* [The six hours of the grand founding ceremony of the People's Republic of China] (Shenyang, 1999), pp. 277–8.

35 A term used in the following sense: 'Emblems are those nonverbal acts which have a direct verbal translation, or dictionary definition . . . [which] is well known by all members of a group, class or culture.' Paul Ekman and Wallace V. Friesen, 'The Repertoire of Nonverbal Behavior: Categories, Origins, Usage, and Coding', *Semiotica* (1969), p. 1.

36 For a case study of this type of imperial portrait, see Wu Hung, 'Emperor's Masquerade: "Costume Portraits" of Yongzheng and Qianlong', *Orientations*, XXVI/7 (July–August 1995), pp. 25–41.

37 For this practice during the Ming and Qing dynasties, see Jan Stuart and Evelyn S. Rawski, *Worshipping the Ancestors: Chinese Commemorative Portraits* (Washington, DC, 2001), pp. 45–6.

38 For example, Shanghai's Youzheng Press first published imperial portraits in 1904. A sentence in the advertisement reads: 'The purpose of this publication is to allow the people of the Qing empire to see these sagely visages, just as every family in Western countries have the portraits of their rulers on their walls.' Two years later, the same press published *Zhongwai erbai mingren zhaoxiang tuce* [A complete collection of the photographic portraits of 200 famous people in China and abroad], which includes images of Cizi, Guangxu and top ministers in the Qing government. See *Shi bao* [The Times], 12 June 1904 and 23 November 1906. Portraits of the Chinese emperor were also featured on postcards with captions written in English. See Chen Shouxiang, *et al.*, *Jiumeng chongjing: Fan Li, Bei Ning cang Qing dai mingxinpian xuanji, 1* [Startled again by old dreams: a selection of Qing postcards collected by Fan Li and Bei Ning, i] (Nan'ning, 1998), figs 5, 7.

39 For example, during her meeting with the crown prince of Germany in 1904, Cixi asked the visitor to give her portrait to his mother, the empress of Germany. The portrait was carried in a yellow sedan to the Ministry of Foreign Affairs before it was brought to Europe. See Hu Zhichuan and Ma Yunzeng, eds, *Zhongguo sheying shi, 1840–1937* [A history of Chinese photography, 1840–1937] (Beijing, 1987), pp. 64–5. Cixi also presented a large oil painting by the American artist Katharine Carl at the St Louis Exposition. Another of her old portraits, painted by Hubert Vos, was exhibited at the Paris Salon in 1906.

40 This was the case in the St Louis Exposition appearance of

Cixi's portrait.

41 For a detailed account and discussion of Sun's funeral, see Henrietta Harrison, *The Making of the Republican Citizen: Political Ceremonies and Symbols in China, 1911–1929* (New York, 2000), especially pp. 133–72.

42 The American scholar and photographer Sidney D. Gamble photographed the complete process of this service. One of the images, showing the portrait in the hearse, is published in *Turbulent Years: China Before and After the May 4th Movement*, The Sidney D. Gamble Foundation for China Studies (Beijing, 1999), p. 26, no. 483/2787. Central Park was later renamed Zhongshan (Yat-sen) Park to commemorate Sun Yat-sen; its central building was turned into Sun's memorial shrine with a portrait of Sun in the middle. Sun's mausoleum in Nanjing was completed in 1929, and his body was sent from Beijing to the new capital on a special train. A huge portrait of Sun's head was installed on the front of the locomotive. See Harold A. van Dorn, *Twenty Years of the Chinese Republic: Two Decades of Progress* (London, 1933), facing p. 50; Harrison, *The Making of the Republican Citizen*, pp. 214–17. It is also important to note that after Sun died, his portrait defined the focus of any public meeting space. Chen Yifu, an important political figure at the time, instructed in 1926: 'Whenever any group holds a meeting they must first perform three bows to the party and national flags and to the portrait of the Party Leader [Sun Yat-sen], and then read the Party Leader's will, and perhaps also keep a three-minute silence.' *Huiyi changshi* [General knowledge for meetings] (Shanghai, 1926), p. 121; translation from Harrison, *The Making of the Republican Citizen*, p. 187.

43 I want to thank Mr Lai Delin, who brought this image to my attention. According to one report, this portrait was in blue and white, the colours of Nationalist China. See Lewis C. Arlington and William Lewisohn, *In Search of Old Peking* (New York, 1967).

44 The Republican Army under Hou Jingru entered Beijing on 18 December 1945.

45 This seems to support Joseph W. Esherick's contention that the 'Guomindang rule was as much the precursor of the Chinese revolution as its political enemy', and that '1949 was a watershed, not an unbridgeable chasm'. 'Ten Theses on the Chinese Revolution', in Jeffrey N. Wasserstrom, ed., *Twentieth-Century China: New Aproaches* (London and New York, 2003), pp. 37–65, quotations from pp. 40–41.

46 The number of people who attended this event is based on a rough estimate. But available evidence makes it clear that a large number of people participated in this gathering. For example, 114,250 people signed up at Zhonghuamen (formerly Daqingmen). It is reported that at least 20,000 participants did not sign up. See Wen Fu, *Tiananmen jianzheng lu*, vol. II, p. 424.

47 It should be noted that published accounts about the different versions of Mao's portraits on Tiananmen contain many mistakes. One such account is in Jia Yinting, ed., *Tiananmen*, p. 90. It identifies three different versions of Mao's portrait: (1) the one used on 1 October 1949, (2) a 'three-quarter' portrait during 1950–67, and (3) a 'front' portrait from 1968 to the present. My study has found at least five versions.

48 Shu Jun, *Tiananmen guangchang lishi dang'an* p. 43; Wen Fu, *Tiananmen jianzheng lu* [Historical archives related to Tienanman] (Beijing, 1998), III, p. 1014. But the painter is identified differently in Jia Yingting, ed., *Tiananmen*, p. 92. According to Jia's book, the 1949 portrait was painted by Zuo Hui, a member of the Revolutionary Army. This account is mistaken: Zuo Hui was one of the painters responsible for painting the next two *Mao* portraits in 1950.

49 General Nie Rongzhen made this request. See Shu Jun, *Tiananmen Guangchang lishi dang'an*, p. 43.

50 Ibid., p. 44.

51 Wu Hung, *The Wu Liang Shrine: The Ideology of Early Chinese Pictorial Art* (Stanford, CA, 1989), pp. 132–4.

52 Although accounts of these painters often emphasize their personal role in creating the 'Tiananmen portrait', such descriptions cannot be entirely trusted. For example, we are told that in painting the portrait Ge Xiaoguang 'had to consult several dozen photographs of Mao taken from various angles, as well as various painted images of Mao'. Qiu Xiaoyu, 'Xiangzheng' [Symbols], *Beijing wanbao* [Beijing evening newspaper] (19 September 1999), A2. But such reports are vague and do not specify in what way the painter 'consulted' different images. The reliability of these reports is further challenged by the fact that a given version of the 'Tiananmen portrait' always closely copies a 'standard image' of Mao published on the front page of *People's Daily*, the Party's newspaper.

53 Some reports give the dates 1953 to 1963. But Zhang's portrait of *Mao* was already hung on Tiananmen on the National Day in 1952. See *Renmin huabao* [People's pictorial] (1952), no. 10, n.p.

54 For Wang Guodong, see Shu Jun, *Tiananmen Guangchang lishi dang'an*, pp. 44–5; Seth Faison, 'Prolific Chinese Painter Is Anonymous No More', *New York Times* (20 September 1999). But Faison mistakenly gives the painter's name as Wang Qizhi, and also reports, again mistakenly, that Wang 'painted the Mao portrait for 27 years'.

55 For Ge Xiaoguang, see Qiu Xiaoyu, 'Xiangzheng'.

56 The term 'standard portrait' (*biaozhunxiang*) was used during the Cultural Revolution for Mao's formal image hung on Tiananmen and in every public space.

57 Faison, 'Prolific Chinese Painter'.

58 Ibid.

59 Shu Jun, *Tiananmen guangchang lishi dang'an*, p. 44.

60 Ibid., p. 46.

61 Cited in Jia Yinting, ed., *Tiananmen*, p. 92.

62 Wen Fu, *Tiananmen jianzheng lu*, vol. III, p. 1024; see also pp. 1017–18.

THREE

1 Mao Zedong [Mao Tse-Tung], 'On Coalition Government, April 24, 1945', *Selected Works of Mao Tse-Tung* (Beijing, 1965), vol. III, p. 257. This was the speech that Mao delivered at the opening of the Seventh National Congress of the Communist Party of China.

2 For an interesting discussion of political representation of the people, see Gayatri Spivak, 'Can the Subaltern Speak?', in Cary Nelson and Lawrence Grossberg, eds, *Marxism and the Interpretation of Cultures* (Urbana, IL, 1988), p. 275 and *passim*.

3 Tony Bennett has noted that this classification proposed by Foucault may be too rigid to explain other contemporary

phenomena such as the amusement park, which 'occupied a point somewhere between the opposing values Foucault attributes to the museum and the traveling fair'. *The Birth of the Museum: History, Theory, Politics* (London and New York, 1995), pp. 3–4. Similarly, later in this book I will discuss a type of temporary 'soft monument' that has been routinely constructed in Tiananmen Square since the early 1990s.

4 Michel Foucault, 'Of Other Spaces', *Diacritics* (Spring 1986), p. 26.

5 Mao Zedong [Mao Tse-tung], 'On the People's Democratic Dictatorship', in *Selected Works of Mao Tse-tung*, (Beijing, 1965), vol. IV, pp. 417–22. See Maurice Meisner, *Mao's China and After: A History of the People's Republic* (New York, 1986), pp. 67–9.

6 The Constitution passed in 1975 also states: 'The working class exercises leadership over the state through its vanguard, the Communist Party of China.' See Meisner, *Mao's China and After*, p. 417.

7 Bennett, *Birth of the Museum*, p. 6.

8 Michel Foucault, *The Order of Things: An Archaeology of the Human Sciences* (London, 1970), p. 312. My discussion here is also indebted to observations made by Bennett in *The Birth of the Museum*, pp. 6–9.

9 Ann Anaghost, 'The Political Body', *Stanford Humanities Review*, II/1 (1991), pp. 86–102; quotation from p. 86.

10 This type of demonstration can be considered a natural growth of parades as self-representations of the people. As Claude Lefort has suggested, 'the constitution of the People-as-One requires the incessant production of enemies' as 'the other of the outside.' *The Political Forms of Modern Society: Bureaucracy, Democracy, Totalitarianism* (Cambridge, MA, 1986), p. 298.

11 The stone railings were made during the reign of Emperor Qianlong of the Qing to replace earlier wood railings.

12 *Rixia jiuwen kao* records an edict issued in the first year of the Shunzhi emperor in the early Qing, which declared that Tiananmen was the formal entrance to the Imperial City.

13 Jiang Yikui, *Chang'an kehua* [Conversations of a visitor to the capital], quoted in Shu Jun, *Tiananmen guangcheng lishi dang'an* [Historial archives related to Tiananmen] (Beijing, 1998), p. 12.

14 Jia Yingting, ed., *Tiananmen* (Beijing, 1998), p. 23.

15 See *The I Ching, or Book of Changes*, trans. Richard Wilhelm and rendered into English by Cary F. Baynes, *et al.* (Princeton, NJ, 1959), p. 119.

16 About the construction of the stand and the photographic equipment used to take such pictures, see Yuan Ling, 'Tiananmen qingdian paishe ji' [A record of taking pictures of celebration ceremonies on Tiananmen], in *Tiananmen qian* [In front of Tiananmen] (Beijing, 1999), pp. 19–20.

17 Lu Yuan, 'Qingnian fuwubu yu qingnian' [A Youth Service Centre and young people], *Renmin huabao*, 1/1 (July 1950), n.p.

18 The last time Mao reviewed a National Day parade was in 1970.

19 Wen Fu, *Tiananmen jianzheng lu* [History as witnessed by Tiananmen] (Beijing, 1988), vol. II, pp. 726–7.

20 Ibid., p. 727.

21 Although the planners first proposed stationing 100,000 people in the Square, eventually close to 110,000 people participated in making the pattern.

22 This type of display was further developed in the following years. For example, in the 1967 National Day celebration, nearly 100,000 people in the square formed changing pictures and slogans.

23 The building, designed by the Central Academy of Architecture and Design under Russian experts, displays a spire 44.3 metres high. Construction started in October 1953 and was completed in September 1954. For more information, see Gong Deshun, *et al.*, *Zhongguo xiandai jianzhu shigang* [An outline of the history of modern Chinese architecture], (Tianjin, 1989), pp. 47–8.

24 See Jonathan D. Spence, *The Search for Modern China* (New York, 1990), p. 543.

25 For a general introduction to the Great Leap Forward and its ideological background, see ibid., pp. 574–83.

26 The Ten Great Buildings are identified differently in various publications. In some reports, the Workers' Stadium replaces the National Art Gallery. In other reports, the two sections of the Museum of Chinese History – the Museum of (Traditional) Chinese History and the Museum of Revolutionary History – are counted as two 'great buildings'. In fact, the Ten Great Buildings in the original plan differ markedly from the Ten Great Buildings that were actually built. The original plan included the Soviet Union Exhibition Hall and proposed to build a National Theatre, a Museum of Science and Technology, and a 'movie palace'. While the Soviet Union Exhibition Hall had been constructed before 1958, the other three were never built. The National Art Gallery was completed in 1962, three years after the country's tenth anniversary. As a result, the term 'Ten Great Buildings' loosely denotes a group of monuments built around the country's tenth anniversary.

27 According to the original plan, the proposed National Theatre and Museum of Science and Technology would also be constructed along Chang'an Avenue.

28 As a piece of evidence, an official introduction to the Great Hall of the People interprets its façade in these words: 'The twelve columns on the façade, made of light grey marble and standing on red marble bases, symbolize a stable superstructure built upon a red [i.e., revolutionary] foundation.' Design Team of the Great Hall of the People, 'Renmin Dahuitang' [The Great Hall of the People], *Jianzhu xuebao* (1959), no. 9, p. 26.

29 Although the Soviet Union Exhibition Hall was constructed in 1953–4, it was included in the 1958 master plan as one of the Ten Great buildings. The symmetry between this structure and the Museum of Agriculture is therefore deliberate. See Wang Jun, *Cheng ji* [The story of a city] (Beijing, 2003), p. 264, n. 4.

30 Zhang Bo, 'Renmin Dahuitang xiujian shimo' [An account of the construction of the Great Hall of the People], in *Wo de jianzhu chuangzuo daolu* [The path of my architectural career] (Beijing, 1994), p. 143.

31 Shu Jun, *Tiananmen guangchang lishi dang'an*, pp. 155–6.

32 Zhang Bo describes these challenges and solutions in great detail in his 'Renmin Dahuitang xiujian shimo'.

33 These six institutions include Tongji University in Shanghai, the Nanjing Academy of Engineering, Tianjin University, Huanan University in Guangzhou, Beijing Architecture Institute and the Beijing Bureau of City Planning. See ibid., pp. 143–4.

34 Zhao Dongri, 'Cong Renmin Dahuitang de sheji fang'an

pingxuan lai tan xin jianzhu fengge de chengzhang' [The development of new architectural style as seen in the selection of the architectural design of the Great Hall of the People], *Jianzhu xuebao* (1960), no. 2, p. 13.

35 Arthur Waley, trans., *The Book of Songs* (New York, 1960), p. 259. Waley translates *Ling tai* as 'Magic Tower' and *Ling yuan* as 'Magic Park'. 'Spiritual Terrace' and 'Spiritual Park' are closer to the terms' original meaning.

36 For a discussion of the discourses on Bright Hall during this historical period, see Wu Hung, *Monumentality in Early Chinese Art and Architecture* (Stanford, CA, 1995), pp. 176–84.

37 Cai Yong, 'Mingtang yueling lun' [A discussion of Bright Hall and the monthly regulations], in *Cai zhonglang wenji* [Collected writings of Cai Yong] (Shanghai, 1931), *juan* 10, pp. 1a–6b.

38 The memorial reads: 'At present the Duke Protector of Han [i.e., Wang Mang] has arisen among royal relatives and assisted Your Majesty for a period of four years. His accomplishments and virtue have been brilliant. The Duke, in the eighth month at the beginning of the waxing moon, on the *gengzi* day, received documents from the court authorizing the conscription of labour and the construction of the monuments. On the next day, scholars and citizens held a great assembly, and 100,000 persons gathered together. They worked zealously for twenty days, and the great work was completed.' Ban Gu, *Han shu* [History of Former Han] (Beijing, 1962), p. 4069; trans. based on Clyde B. Sargent, trans., *Wang Mang* (Shanghai, 1947), p. 128.

39 For a reconstruction and discussion of this political process, see Wu Hung, *Monumentality in Early Chinese Art and Architecture*, pp. 184–7.

40 This episode is told in almost every report on the construction of these two monuments, though the quotations of Zhou's instructions show minor discrepancies.

41 Masterminded by Yu Weichao, then a director of the museum, this reform abolished most illustrations and explanatory texts in the exhibition of traditional Chinese history.

42 Bennett, *Birth of the Museum*, p. 147.

43 Patrick Wright, 'A Blue Plaque for the Labour Movement? Some Political Meanings of the "National Past"', *Formations of Nation and People* (London, 1984), p. 52.

44 Bennett, *Birth of the Museum*, p. 181.

45 Li Shejian, ed., *Renmin Dahuitang* [The Great Hall of the People], no publisher, date or page number given. The publication has both Chinese and English texts. Except for some minor grammatical corrections, the passage cited here basically preserves the original English caption.

46 For an English translation alongside the original Chinese text, see James Legge, trans., *The Chinese Classics*, III, 'The Shoo King' (Oxford, 1871), pp. 92–151.

47 Translation based on James Legge, ibid., V, 'The Ch'un Ts'ew, with the Tso Chuen', pp. 292–3. For a discussion of this legend, see Wu Hung, *Monumentality in Early Chinese Art and Architecture*, pp. 1–15.

48 Cited in Shu Jun, *Tiananmen guangchang lishi dang'an*, p. 176. For a detailed discussion of the creation of this painting and its stylistic significance, see Julia F. Andrews, *Painters and Politics in the People's Republic of China, 1949–1979* (Berkeley and Los Angeles, 1994), pp. 229–36.

49 It is said that Guo Moruo, the FLAC chairman, suggested

painting the sun to symbolize the ten years of Communist rule. See Shu Jun, *Tiananmen guangchang lishi dang'an*, p. 176; Andrews, *Painters and Politics*, p. 231.

50 Zhao Lidong, 'Cong Renmin Dahuitang de sheji fang'an pingxuan lai tan xinjianzhu fengge de chengzhang', p. 17.

51 Design Team of the Great Hall of the People, 'Renmin Dahuitang', p. 29.

52 Several official reports are collected in a special issue of *Jianzhu xuebao* (1977), no. 4. The most comprehensive one, however, was not published until 2003. Written by Gao Yilan and entitled 'Mao Zhuxi jiniantang sheji guocheng zongjie' [A summary of the design process of the Chairman Mao Memorial Hall], it provides a detailed account of designs proposed at the project's different stages. *Jianzhu shi* [History of architecture] (2003), no. 1, pp. 1–25. Also see Gao Yilan, 'Mao zhuxi jiniantang fang'an sheji de youguan lishi ziliao de shuoming' [Some explanations regarding historical evidence for the design of the Chairman Mao Memorial Hall], *Jianzhu shi* (2003), no. 2, pp. 203–4. Discussions of the monument by Western scholars include Reginald Yin-wang and Annette Kwok, 'Le mausolée du president Mao', *L'Architecture d'Aujourd'hui*, no. 210 (February 1979), pp. 51–3; Eleni Constantine, 'Mao's Mausoleum Echoes JFK Center', *Progressive Architecture*, no. 60 (May 1979), pp. 30–32; Frederic Wakeman Jr, 'Revolutionary Rites: The Remains of Chiang Kai-Shek and Mao Tse-tung', *Representations*, no. 10 (Spring 1985), pp. 146–93; Ellen Laing, *The Winking Owl* (Berkeley, Los Angeles and London, 1988), pp. 90–97; Lother Ledderose, 'Die Gedenkhalle für Mao Zedong', in Jan Assmann and Tonio Hölscher, *Kultur und Gedächtnis* (Frankfurt, 1988), pp. 311–39.

53 For a succinct discussion of Hua Guofeng's political profile, see Meisner, *Mao's China and After*, pp. 448–51.

54 Ibid., p. 449.

55 Hua Guofeng laid the foundation stone of the Memorial Hall on 24 November 1976. The Hall was completed on 24 May 1977.

56 Laing, *The Winking Owl*, p. 92.

FOUR

1 It is significant to note that, although the exhibition of traditional Chinese History has been revised since the Cultural Revolution, the exhibition format of 'revolutionary history' after 1840 has remained basically unchanged.

2 Two large architectural projects in the Square during this period aimed to renovate and strengthen the Great Hall of the People and the Museum of Chinese History; they took several years to accomplish.

3 I say 'symbolically' because Macao was remaining under Portuguese administration at this point.

4 The Hall of Supreme Harmony is 35.05 metres high, but the Drum Tower and Bell Tower are 45.14 and 46.96 metres high, respectively. The only structure on Beijing's central axis that rises above these two towers is the pavilion on the Coal Hill; but the height of the pavilion itself is limited.

5 According to a different report, there were 25 drums, including a large one and 24 smaller ones; the latter symbolized the twenty-four divisions of a year. See Luo Zhewen, 'Beijing Zhonglou, Gulou' [Beijing's Drum Tower

and Bell Tower], in *Jinghua shengdi Shishahai* [Shishahai: a famous spot in Beijing], The Research Association of Shishahai in Beijing (Beijing, 1993), pp. 139–49.

6 As I will discuss later in this Chapter, one official document written by the Qianlong emperor does refers to the sound of the bell. But the language used in the text is flowery and stereotyped. Instead of conveying a listener's real experience, it bestows a finite political symbolism on the sound of the bell. This document is inscribed on a stone stele, which the emperor erected to commemorate the rebuilding of the Bell Tower during his reign.

7 Jin Lin, 'Beijing Zhonggulou wenwu zaiji' [Miscellaneous records of things related to the Drum Tower and the Bell Tower], in Editorial Committee, *Wenshi ziliao xuanbian* [Selected archival materials on modern Chinese history], no. 36, p. 213.

8 One early source of this story is the late Qing publication *Yanjing fanggu lu* [Searching for ancient sites in Beijing] by Zhang Jiangcai, collected in *Jing Jin fengtu congshu* [Books on local customs of Beijing and Tianjin] (Taipei, 1969), p. 79. This story has been told and retold many times, and has been elaborated into modern versions of 'folk literature' (*minjian wenxue*). For one such modern version, see Jin Shoushen, ed., *Beijing de chuanshuo* [Legends of Beijing] (Beijing, 1957), pp. 40–44.

9 The building was destroyed by fire even before the Yuan dynasty perished and rebuilt by Emperor Chengzong in 1297. It was reconstructed during both the early Ming and the early Qing, and extensively repaired in 1800, 1894 and 1984.

10 Starting from Beijing's east wall in a clockwise direction, these gates are: Dongzhimen, Chaoyangmen, Chongwenmen, Zhengyangmen (Qianmen), Xuanwumen, Fuchengmen, Xizhimen, Deshengmen and Andingmen. It is reported that, except for Chongwenmen, which had a bell in its gate-tower, all other gates used a chime-like instrument called a *dian* to ring the hours. See Hu Yuyuan, ed., *Yandu tangu* [Talking about the old days of Beijing] (Beijing, 1996), pp. 40, 75.

11 This is recorded in *Qinding Daqing huidian* [Imperially sanctioned legal codes]. But according to some writers, after the Qianlong period the two towers sounded only in the morning and evening. See Zhu Yingli and Zeng Yixuan, *Beijing zhonggulou* [Beijing's Drum Tower and Bell Tower] (Beijing, 2003), p. 57.

12 Wu Hung, 'Monumentality of Time: Giant Clocks, the Drum Tower, the Clock Tower', in Robert S. Nelson and Margaret Olin, eds, *Monuments and Memory: Made and Unmade* (Chicago, 2003), pp. 108–20.

13 George Macartney, *An Embassy to China; Being the Journal Kept by Lord Macartney during his Embassy to the Emperor Ch'ien-lung, 1793–1794*, ed. J. L. Cramer Byng (Hamden, CT, 1963), p. 158. Other members of the mission, including Sir George Leonard Staunton, John Barrow and Aeneas Anderson, made similar reports. See Alison Dray-Novey, 'Spatial Order and Police in Imperial Beijing', *Journal of Asian Studies*, LII/4 (1993), p. 894.

14 See Jin Lin, 'Beijing Zhonggulou wenwu zaiji', p. 213.

15 David S. Landes, *Revolution in Time: Clocks and the Making of the Modern World* (Cambridge, MA, 1983), p. 69.

16 For the relationship between this system and the security of a city, see Etienne Balazs, *Chinese Civilization and Bureaucracy*, trans. and ed. H. M. Wright (New Haven, 1964), pp. 68–70.

17 This stele still stands in front of the Bell Tower in Beijing.

18 See James Legge, trans., *The Chinese Classics*, III: 'The Shoo King' (Oxford, 1871), pp. 15–27. The passage cited here is translated in Joseph Needham, *Science and Civilization in China*, (London and New York, 1959), vol. III, p. 188. Although traditional Confucians attributed this text to Yao himself, modern scholars believe that it was probably written around the fifth or sixth centuries BC.

19 In one place he writes: 'For an agricultural economy, astronomical knowledge as regulator of the calendar was of prime importance. He who could give a calendar to the people would become their leader.' *Science and Civilization in China*, vol. III, p. 189.

20 Hellmut Wilhelm, *Chinas Geschichte: zehn einführende Vorträge* (Beijing, 1942), p. 16.

21 One definition of a schedule is 'a tabular statement of times of projected operations, recurring events, arriving and departing trains, etc., a timetable.' *Webster's New Collegiate Dictionary* (Springfield, MA, 1958), p. 681.

22 Cited in Carlo Cipolla, *Clocks and Culture, 1300–1700* (New York, 1967), p. 86.

23 Catherine Pagani has discussed the interest in clocks in China both inside and outside the court. According to her, by the eighteenth century Western-style clocks had become a primary possession of the elite. In the eighteenth-century novel *Honglou meng* [The Dream of the Red Chamber], 'self-ringing clocks' signified the status of an elite household. While the novel describes the time-keeping function of such clocks in daily life, in many other cases they served purely symbolic roles. Three young imperial princes who admired European mechanical clocks, therefore, 'candidly owned that they did not comprehend the purposes of them'. *'Eastern Magnificence & European Ingenuity': Clocks of Late Imperial China* (Ann Arbor, MI, 2001), pp. 91–6.

24 This painting is now housed in Beijing's Palace Museum.

25 A witness of the 1860 looting reported: 'A large majority of them [i.e., soldiers in the invasion army] were "grown children" who were "mainly tempted in the midst of all this unbelievable accumulation of wealth" by the extraordinary variety and number of mechanical toys and clocks, so that the whole area was "one continuous symphony" with monkeys beating cymbals, rabbits rolling drums, birds singing, toy soldiers playing cornets and bagpipes, clocks chiming, and some four thousand musical boxes simultaneously tinkling their several tunes, and every now and then all this noise was "drowned out by the easily amused soldiers roaring with laughter"'. Cited in Landes, *Revolution in Time*, p. 43. James L. Hevia provides the most up-to-date discussion of this and subsequent looting in Beijing in *English Lessons: The Pedagogy of Imperialism in Nineteenth-Century China* (Durham, NC, 2003).

26 It is unclear which foreign nationality was responsible for this destruction. Contemporary Chinese authors blame either Russian or Japanese soldiers for this crime. Since evidence is given in neither case, such claims may instead reflect the changing relationship between China and these foreign countries.

27 This was accomplished in 1924 and 1925 by Xue Dubi, the mayor of Beijing at the time. See Jin Lin, 'Beijing Zhonggulou fenwu zaiji', p. 214. For a short but informative

history of the two towers after 1924, see Zhu Yingli and Zeng Yixuan, *Beijing zhonggulou*, pp. 22–9.

28 Pierre Nora, ed., *Realms of Memory: The Construction of the French Past*, trans. Arthur Goldhammer, 3 vols (New York, 1996-8), I, p. 3.

29 The meaning of the Drum Tower as a war ruin and a nationalist monument, however, largely vanished after the establishment of the People's Republic of China. For about three decades from the 1950s to the '80s, the lower level of the tower was used as the site of a Workers' Cultural Palace. It began to draw wider attention in the 1990s when its upper level was reopened to the public. Since then, the building has been renovated, a new set of drums has been made, and the lower level has been turned into a gift shop.

30 Wu Youru [Wu Jiayou], *Wu Youru huabao* [Pictorial treasures by Wu Youru], 4 vols (Beijing, 1998), II, 11.23.

31 Yang Congqing, *Beijing xingshi dalue* [A general description of Beijing], 1737; repr. in *Jing Jin fengtu congshu*, vol VII, p. 13.

32 Shanghai's situation was somewhat different, since textual sources do describe the public effect of the sound issued from modern clock towers. See Liu Shanling, *Xiyang faming zai Zhongguo* [Western inventions in China] (Hong Kong, 2001), p. 211.

33 David Harvey, *The Condition of Postmodernity* (Cambridge, MA, and Oxford, 1990), p. 264.

34 Robert M. Adams, *Paths of Fire: An Anthropologist's Inquiry into Western Technology* (Princeton, NJ, 1996), p. 23.

35 For the changes in space and time conceptions in the modern and postmodern eras, see Harvey, *The Condition of Postmodernity*, pp. 201–326.

36 See Paul Virilio, *The Lost Dimension*, trans. Daniel Moshenberg (New York, 1991), pp. 21–2. A more recent analysis of postmodern conceptions of time and space can be found in Manuel Castells, *The Information Age: Economy, Society and Culture*, I: *The Rise of the Network Society* (Cambridge, MA, and Oxford, 1996), Chapters 6 and 7.

37 Landes, *Revolution in Time*, p. 350.

38 Helga Nowotny, *Time: The Modern and Postmodern Experience*, trans. Neville Plaice (Cambridge, 1994), p. 132.

39 During the Cultural Revolution, any connection with Hong Kong, regardless of its nature, could cause grave danger to a Mainland resident.

40 Private communication with the author.

41 Michael Yahuda, *Hong Kong: China's Challenge* (London and New York, 1996), especially pp. 61–82.

42 Sze-yuen Chung, a long-time Hong Kong politician and a member of both Hong Kong's Legislative Council (1965–78) and Beijing's Preliminary Working Committee (1993–), also reviewed the most important political events surrounding the transfer of Hong Kong's sovereignty. 'What Has Gone Wrong during the Transition?', in Wang Gungwu and Wong Siu-lun, eds, *Hong Kong's Transition: A Decade after the Deal* (Hong Kong, 1995), pp. 1–18.

43 This social group is sometimes categorized as a 'Hong Kong man': 'Quick thinking, flexible, tough for survival, excitement-craving, sophisticated in material tastes, and self-made in a strenuously competitive world. He operated in the context of a most uncertain future, control over which was in the hands of others, and for this as well as for historical reasons lived "life in the short term".' Hugh D. R. Baker,

'Life in the Cities: The Emergence of Hong Kong Man', *China Quarterly*, no. 95 (December 1983), pp. 469–79. For main attributes of Hong Kongers in the 1980s, see Lau Siu-kai and Kuan Hsin-chi, *The Ethos of the Hong Kong Chinese* (Hong Kong, 1988).

44 See Yahuda, *Hong Kong*, pp. 50–51.

45 Lau Siu-kai, *et al.*, eds, *Indicators of Social Development: Hong Kong 1988* (Hong Kong, 1991), pp. 177–8; see Lau and Kuan, *The Ethos of the Hong Kong Chinese*, pp. 178–87.

46 Yahuda, *Hong Kong*, p. 52.

47 See Norman J. Miners, *The Government and Politics of Hong Kong* (Hong Kong, 5th edn, 1994), Chapters 13 and 14.

48 Deng Xiaoping, *Selected Works of Deng Xiaoping*, III: *1982–1992* (Beijing, 1994), pp. 219–20. For the context of Deng's speech, see Yahuda, *Hong Kong*, pp. 114–15.

49 Yahuda, *Hong Kong*, p. 17.

50 For example, the Hong Kong art critic Oscar Ho Hing-kay wrote in 1993: 'Time is running out: people in Hong Kong need to find their cultural heritage and to reassure their sense of identity, for in four years' time they might have lost it.' 'In Search of an Identity', *Art Asia Pacific*, 1/1 (1993), p. 14.

51 As David Harvey has pointed out, the reduction of regional identity is implicitly associated with the notion of social progress, which 'entails the conquest of space, the tearing down of all spatial barriers, and the ultimate "annihilation of space through time"'. *The Condition of Postmodernity*, p. 205.

FIVE

1 Hal Foster's term. For a parallel movement in contemporary Western art, see his discussion in *The Return of the Real* (Cambridge, MA, 1996), pp. 127–204.

2 At least two versions of the painting are known, one in Beijing's Palace Museum and the other in the Suzhou Museum. A poor reproduction of the first painting is in Cao Juren, *Jiuri jinghua* [Beijing in olden days], (Hong Kong, 1971), p. 48. The second painting is reproduced in Lu Bingjie, *Tiananmen* (Shanghai, 1999), p. 46.

3 According to Gu Jiegang, this information is provided in the inscription on the Palace Museum version. See Gu's colophon on the Suzhou Museum version.

4 This scene can also be read as part of a pictorial narrative: a gentleman has just arrived in the capital and is greeted by officials in front of the south gate of the city. The same gentleman is portrayed in the painting for a second time: he has become a prominent official and stands next to Tiananmen.

5 The whereabouts of only nine scrolls are known. Five of them (1, 9, 10, 11, 12) are in the collection of Beijing's Palace Museum. For reproductions, see The Palace Museum, *Gugong Bowuyuan cang Qingdai gongting huihua* [Qing dynasty court painting in the collection of the Palace Museum] (Beijing, 1992), pls 16–20. For a detailed study of this work, see Nie Chongzheng, 'Tan "Kangxi nanxun tu" juan [On the scrolls of *Kangxi's southern expedition*], *Gongting yishu de guanghui: Qingdai gongting huihua luncong* [The splendour of court art: Studies on Qing dynasty court painting] (Taipei, 1996), pp. 75–91.

6 Each scroll is 67.8 cm wide; most handscroll paintings are only 30–40 cm wide.

7　See The Palace Museum, *Gugong Bowuyuan cang Qingdai gongting huihua*, p. 63.

8　As recorded in the *Zhou li* [Rites of Zhou], a Confucian classic that served as a blueprint for all later imperial rituals: 'When great sacrifices and funerals are carried out, special gates and barriers are set up, and the space before palaces and temples are emptied.' *Zhou li. Tianguan. Hunren.*

9　For a stylistic analysis of the painting, see Julia F. Andrews, *Painters and Politics in the People's Republic of China, 1949–1979* (Berkeley and Los Angeles, 1994), p. 86.

10　Dong expressed his view on this matter most explicitly in an essay entitled 'Cong Zhongguo huihua de biaoxian fang-fa tandao youhua Zhongguo feng' [The representational method in traditional Chinese painting and the Chinese style of oil painting], *Meishu* [Fine arts], 1957.1, reprinted in *Meishu*, 2003. 7, no. 427, pp. 55–8. Also see Dong Xiwan, 'Huihua de secai wenti' [Problems concerning the colours of oil painting], *Meishu*, 1957. 1, reprinted in *Meishu*, 2003. 7, no. 427, pp. 59–63.

11　See Jing Yun and Ren Yi, 'Tansuo Zhongguo tese youhua de xianxingzhe – jinian Dong Xiwen xiansheng shishi 30 zhounian' [An early explorer of Chinese-style oil painting – in commemoration of the 30th anniversary of Mr Dong Xiwen's death], *Meishu*, 2003. 7, no. 427, p. 34.

12　This last manipulation is acknowledged by Jing Yun and Ren Yi in 'Tansuo Zhongguo tese youhua de xianxingzhe', ibid.

13　For a detailed narrative of the revisions of the painting, see Andrews, *Painters and Politics*, pp. 82–5.

14　Ibid., p. 85.

15　The main agenda of this art, according to these critics, was to represent reality for the socialist cause. Invented in Soviet Union during the Stalinist period, socialist realism became the guiding principle in official Chinese art in the 1950s and '60s. See ibid., p. 119.

16　Zhou Yang, 'Wei chuangzao gengduo de youxiu de wenxue yishu zuopin er fendou' [Struggle to create even more excellent works of literature and art], talk given to the Second National Congress of Literary and Art Workers, 24 September 1953, *Wenyibao* [Journal of literature and art], ser. no. 96 (1953), no. 19, pp. 7–16, quotation from p. 14, cited in ibid., p. 119; translation slightly altered based on the original text.

17　Claude Lefort, *The Political Forms of Modern Society: Bureaucracy, Democracy, Totalitarianism* (Cambridge, MA, 1986), pp. 292–306.

18　The school was not actually founded that year. What happened in 1946 was that Xu Beihong took over the leadership of an old school called National Beiping Arts College (Guoli Beiping Yishu Zhuanke Xuexiao). The Central Academy considers that it grew out of Xu's school and thus takes 1946 as its founding moment.

19　I haven't found evidence to substantiate this story. Rather, Xu Beihong paid his first wife, Jiang Biwei, one million yuan plus one hundred paintings when he divorced her in December 1945.

20　Another work in this category is Luo Gongliu's *Mao Zeodong at Jinggang Mountains.*

21　For discussions of this movement, see Andrews, *Painters and Politics*, pp. 393–6; Geremie Barmé and Bennett Lee, trans., *The Wounded – New Stories of the Cultural Revolution, 77–78* (Hong Kong, 1979).

22　For a definition of 'experimental art' and 'experimental artists' in contemporary Chinese art, see Wu Hung, *Transience: Chinese Experimental Art at the End of the Twentieth Century* (Chicago, 1999), pp. 12–24.

23　Sun Jingxun, 'A Specter Prowls Our Land', in Geremie R. Barmé and John Minford, eds, *Seeds of Fire: Chinese Voices of Conscience*, 2nd edn (New York, 1988), pp. 121–9.

24　Many of these artistic images were related to a 'Mao Craze', which emerged in the late 1980s and developed into myriad forms in the 1990s. For an introduction to this popular phenomenon and a rich selection of examples, see Geremie R. Barmé, *Shades of Mao: The Posthumous Cult of the Great Leader* (Armonk, NY, 1996).

25　Cited in Lü Peng and Yi Dan, *Zhongguo xiandai yishu shi, 1979–1989* [A history of contemporary Chinese art, 1979–1989] (Changsha, 1992), p. 167.

26　Gongbulixi [Ernst H. Gombrich], *Yishu yu cuojue* [Art and illusion], trans. Fan Jinzhong (Hangzhou, 1987).

27　In Gombrich's words, 'But if we superimpose a regular grid on the painting, we become aware of those objective relationships within the picture that our reading ignores.' Ernst H. Gombrich, *Art and Illusion: A Study in the Psychology of Pictorial Representation* (New York, 1961), p. 304. Köppel-Yang further suggests that, in fact, Wang Guangyi may have been inspired directly by a figure Gombrich had used to illustrate theory: a montage by him of Constable's *Wivenhoe Park* with superimposed white grid. Ibid., fig. 249. Martina Köppel-Yang, 'Discourse and Artistic Practice in Contemporary Chinese Art after the Cultural Revolution', *Art in China: Collections and Concepts: International Symposium, Bonn, 21–23 November 2003.*

28　This can be said to be an important characteristic of Political Pop, a major style of contemporary Chinese art in the early 1990s. For excellent discussions of this style, see Li Xianting, 'Major Trends in the Development of Contemporary Chinese Art', *China's New Art, Post-1989*, exh. cat., Hanart T Z Gallery, Hong Kong (Hong Kong, 1993), pp. x–xxii; idem, 'The Imprisoned Heart: Consuming Mao', in Barmé, *Shades of Mao*, pp. 215–20.

29　For an introduction and discussion of some of these exhibitions, see Wu Hung, *Exhibiting Experimental Art in China* (Chicago, 2000), pp. 42–4, 165–208.

30　See, for example, Michael Kimmelman's discussion of a group of photographs made during the Second World War. 'Photographs That Cry Out For Meaning', *New York Times*, 6 December 2003, A17, 19.

31　Jochen North, Wolfger Pöhlmann and Kai Reschke, eds, *China Avant-Garde: Counter-Currents in Art and Culture* (Berlin and Hong Kong, 1993), p. 195.

32　See Wu Hung, *Exhibiting Experimental Art in China*, pp. 108–15.

33　Ai Weiwei, Zeng Xiaojun and Xu Bing, eds, *Heipi shu* [An untitled book with a black cover] (Beijing, 1994) [private publication].

34　For discussions of nostalgia as a cultural craze in 1990s' China, Hong Kong and Taiwan, see Xiaobing Tang, *Chinese Modern: The Heroic and the Quotadian* (Durham, NC, 2000); David Der-wei Wang, 'Imaginary Nostalgia: Shen Congwen, Song Zelai, Mo Yan, and Li Yongping', in Ellen Widmer and David Der-wei Wang, eds, *From May Fourth to June Fourth: Fiction and Film in Twentieth-Century China*

(Cambridge, MA, 1993); Rey Chow, *Ethics after Idealism* (Bloomington, IN, 1998), pp. 133–48.

35 For a concise discussion of this artistic trend, see Li Xianting, 'The Imprisoned Heart: Consuming Mao', in Barmé, *Shades of Mao*, pp. 215–20.

36 Li Xianting, 'Major Trends in the Development of Contemporary Chinese Art', p. xx.

37 Chang Tsong-zung, 'Into the Nineties', in *China's New Art, Post-1989*, pp. i–vii; quotation from p. i.

38 I have discussed elsewhere the relationship between Political Pop and the 'Mao craze' in Chinese popular culture in the early 1990s. This cultural movement transformed the Mao Cult into contemporary expressions of political criticism, popular fantasy and consumer desire. See Wu Hung, *Transience*, pp. 51–2.

39 Many of these works are reproduced in *China's New Art, Post-1989*.

40 Ibid., p. 45.

41 Lydia Yee, 'An Interview with Zhang Hongtu', *Zhang Hongtu: Material Mao*, exh. cat., Bronx Museum of Arts, New York (New York, 1995), pp. 1–7; quotation from p. 5. For a discussion of the relationship between Zhang Hongtu and Political Pop, see Barmé, *Shades of Mao*, p. 46.

42 For further information about Zhang Hongtu's work and ideas, see *Works by Zhang Hongtu*, exh. cat., HKUST Center for the Arts, Hong Kong (Hong Kong, 1998); Jonathan Hay, 'Zhang Hongtu / Hongtu Zhang: An Interview', in John Hay, ed., *Boundaries in China* (London, 1994), pp. 280–98. For a series of T-shirt designs he made before Hong Kong's handover to China, see Wu Hung, '"Hong Kong . 1997" – T-shirt Designs by Zhang Hongtu', *Public Culture*, ix/3 (Spring 1997), pp. 417–21.

43 Lydia Yee, 'An Interview with Zhang Hongtu', pp. 2–3.

44 Jonathan Goodman, "Zhang Hongtu at the Bronx Museum of the Arts', *Asia-Pacific Sculpture News* (Winter 1996), p. 58.

45 This exhibition was held at the Art Center of Chulalongkorn University in Bangkok, Thailand, in June 2000.

46 Some art historians have discussed the changing definition of the 'site' of site-specific art. Miwon Kwon, for example, characterizes a major change as that 'in advanced art practices of the past thirty years the operative definition of the site has been transformed from a physical location – grounded, fixed, actual – to a discursive vector – ungrounded, fluid, virtual.' *One Place after Another: Site-Specific Art and Locational Identity* (Cambridge, MA, 2002), pp. 29–30. A similar idea is expressed by James Meyer in 'The Functional Site', *Documents*, no. 7 (Fall 1996), pp. 20–29. While parallel changes can be found in contemporary Chinese art and will be discussed later in this section, I prefer to begin this discussion from the most basic definition of the site as an actual place.

47 The volume came out under the title *Renmin de daonian* [People's mourning] (Beijing, 1979). Published after the rehabilitation of the April Fifth Movement, however, this volume was no longer a private undertaking as the editors had planned, but became an official project endorsed by China's top leaders.

48 The most detailed account of this art movement is provided in Gao Minglu's *Zhongguo dangdai meishu shi, 1985–86* [Contemporary art of China, 1985–86] (Shanghai, 1991).

49 See Gao Minglu, 'Bawu meishu yundong de 'qianwei' yishi' [The 'avant-garde' consciousness in the '85 art movement], *Xiongshi meishu*, no. 297 (November 1995), pp. 16–21.

50 In September 1986, for example, a number of groups in Nanjing organized a joint activity called 'Baking under the sun' (Shai taiyang). More than a hundred young painters, sculptors and performing artists gathered in the Xuanwu Lake Park to show their recent works and to stage performances. The slogans of the activity included 'The sun is the only energy source which cannot be polluted; the sun is just about to break through the clouds.' The next month, many artists travelled to Nanjing from other cities, and in 5 October more than 1,000 of them appeared in the park. This kind of spontaneous gathering also happened in other cities in the second half of the 1980s.

51 This exhibition was first planned to be held in July 1987. This plan was interrupted by the 'Against Capitalist Liberalization' campaign mobilized by the Party that year. But when the political campaign subsided, organizers of the 86 conference returned to the drawing board and envisioned an even larger national exhibition of experimental art. A planning conference was held in October 1988 at Huangshan. The proposed location of the show was changed from the Museum of Agriculture to the National Art Gallery. Most of the seventeen members on the preparatory committee of the exhibition were young art critics, with Gao Minglu as the chief coordinator.

52 For an introduction to these works, see Lü Peng and Yi Dan, *Zhongguo xiandai yishushi, 1979–1989*, pp. 327–49.

53 The show was held in Sushi Gallery, San Diego, in September 1989. For a review essay, see Leah Ollman, 'Paintings, Text Speak of the "Trauma" in China's Body Politics', *Los Angeles Times*, 15 September 1989.

54 Interview with Mo Yi by the author, 15 May 1998.

55 It is worth noting that experimental Chinese filmmakers also developed an intense interest in the Square in the 1990s. Representative works include Wu Wenguang's *Tiananmen* (1991), Zhang Yuan and Duan Jinchuan's *The Square* (1994) and Jia Zhangke's *One Day in Beijing* (1994). But these are all documentary works and differ markedly in style and intention from the conceptual art projects discussed here.

56 Yu Xiang, 'Gaoshi xiongdi fangtan lu' [An interview with the Gao brothers], 10–13 July 2003; manuscript provided by the artists.

57 Information provided by Gao Zhen and Gao Qiang to the author in a private communication.

58 Wei Jingsheng wrote a 'big-character poster' in 1978, calling for political reforms in China. He was arrested in early 1979 and brought to trial six months later. Charged with 'counter-revolutionary crimes of a serious nature', he was convicted and sentenced to a prison term of fifteen years. For more information, see Scott Simmie and Bob Nixon, *Tiananmen Square* (Vancouver, 1989), pp. 35–7.

59 Zhang Zhaohui, 'Redefining the Spirit of the Avant-garde in Today's China – Interview with the Gao Brothers', www.CL2000.com/modernart/interview/wen010.shtml.

60 Song Dong recalled his experience during the June Fourth Movement in an interview with the author on 14 May 1998.

61 *Breathing* is a two-part performance/photography project. Part Two took place on the frozen Back Sea – a large pond in the old quarter of Beijing. For a description

and discussion of the project, see Wu Hung, *Transience*, pp. 54–9.

62 To enhance the sense of instability in the video, Song Dong set the camcorder on a slow speed.

63 In addition to the works introduced in this section, Song Dong collaborated with the architect Zhang Yonghe in 1997 to 'dislocate' the Square's central axis to Austria. He has also featured the place repeatedly in his ongoing performance/photography project *Handscroll Series: I have Been Here As a Traveller.*

CODA

1 Entitled *Canceled: Exhibiting Experimental Art in China*, this exhibition was held in the Smart Museum of Art at the University of Chicago from November 2000 to January 2001. For a book-length catalogue, see Wu Hung, *Exhibiting Experimental Art in China* (Chicago, 2000).

2 Two main sources of these plans are: Editorial Committee, *Jianguo yilai de Beijing chengshi jianshe* [Beijing's urban construction after the establishment of the People's Republic of China] (Beijing, 1985); Zhang Jinggan, Chen Hongzhang and Xu Yixie, eds, *Jianguo yilai de Beijing chengshi jianshe ziliao* [Documents regarding Beijing's urban construction after the establishment of the People's Republic of China], i: *Chengshi guihua* [Urban planning] (Beijing, 1995).

3 I want to thank Lai Delin, who made this point in one of our conversations about Beijing's city planning.

4 Proposed by an urban development team at Tsing-hua University, based on an older master plan, this strategy was accepted in principle by the municipal authorities in the early 1980s and practised in the following years. See Wu Liangyong, *Rehabilitating the Old City of Beijing* (Vancouver, 1999), pp. 28–9.

5 The protected areas within the traditional city walls were expanded to 30 neighbourhoods in 2002, amounting to 21 per cent of the total area of the old city.

6 For a brief report on this decision and the debates related to it, see Chen Lingchu, 'Zhongjin baohu zhongzhouxian' [Spending big money to protect the central axis], *Wenwu tiandi*, 2000. 8, pp. 5–7.

7 See, for example, Wu Liangyong, *Rehabilitating the Old City of Beijing*, pp. 28–9.

8 It is interesting to note that a statue of Deng Xiaoping was erected in 2000 in Shenzhen at the twentieth anniversary of the city, and Jiang Zeming presided over the unveiling ceremony. As Carolyn Cartier has remarked: 'Shenzhen is Deng Xiaoping's city, envisioned by him and, at precarious economic moments, promoted and defended by him.' 'Transnational Urbanism in the Reform-era Chinese City: Landscapes from Shenzhen', *Urban Studies*, xxxix/9 (2002), pp. 1513–32; quotation from pp. 1513–14. Unlike Tiananmen Square, this statue and Shenzhen are associated with Deng and Jiang and stand for the post-Mao era.

9 The National Theatre was originally planned in 1958 as one of the Ten Great Buildings to be constructed before the country's tenth anniversary. But this plan was never realized.

10 Jia Yingting, ed., *Tiananmen* (Beijing, 1998), pp. 133–4.

11 Paul Virilio, *The Lost Dimension*, trans. Daniel Moshenberg (New York, 1991), p. 22.

Bibliography

WESTERN SOURCES

Adams, Robert M., *Paths of Fire: An Anthropologist's Inquiry into Western Technology* (Princeton, NJ, 1996)

Anaghost, Ann, 'The Political Body', *Stanford Humanities Review*, II/1 (1991), pp. 86–102

——, 'Socialist Ethics and the Legal System', in *Popular Protest and Political Culture in Modern China: Learning from Tiananmen*, ed. Jeffrey N. Wasserstrom and Elizabeth J. Perry (Boulder, CO, 1991), pp. 177–205

Andrews, Julia F., *Painters and Politics in the People's Republic of China, 1949–1979* (Berkeley and Los Angeles, 1994)

Arlington, Lewis C., and William Lewisohn, *In Search of Old Peking* (New York, 1967)

Arnheim, Rudolf, *New Essays on the Psychology of Art* (Berkeley, CA, 1986)

Baker, Hugh D. R., 'Life in the Cities: The Emergence of Hong Kong Man', *China Quarterly*, 95 (December 1983), pp. 469–79

Bakhurst, David, 'Social Memory in Soviet Thought', in *Collective Remembering*, ed. David Middleton and Derek Edwards (London, 1990)

Balazs, Etienne, *Chinese Civilization and Bureaucracy*, trans. and ed. H. M. Wright (New Haven, CT, 1964), pp. 68–70

Barmé, Geremie R., *Shades of Mao: The Posthumous Cult of the Great Leader* (Armonk, NY, 1996)

——, and Bennett Lee, trans., *The Wounded: New Stories of the Cultural Revolution, 77–78* (Hong Kong, 1979)

——, and John Minford, eds, *Seeds of Fire: Chinese Voices of Conscience* (2nd edn, New York, 1988)

Bartlett, Frederic C., *Remembering: A Study in Experimental and Social Psychology* (Cambridge, 1932)

Bennett, Tony, *The Birth of the Museum: History, Theory, Politics* (London and New York, 1995)

Brewer, William F., 'What is Recollective Memory?', in *Remembering Our Past: Studies in Autobiographical Memory*, ed. David C. Rubin (Cambridge, 1996), pp. 19–66

Brilliant, Richard, *Portraiture* (London, 1991)

Calhoun, Craig, *Neither Gods nor Emperors: Students and the Struggle for Democracy in China* (Berkeley, CA, 1994)

Cartier, Carolyn, 'Transnational Urbanism in the Reform-era Chinese City: Landscapes from Shenzhen', *Urban Studies*, XXXIX/9 (2002), pp. 1513–32

Castells, Manuel, *The Information Age: Economy, Society and Culture*, I: *The Rise of the Network Society* (Cambridge, MA, and Oxford, 1996)

Chang, Tsong-zung, 'Into the Nineties', in *China's New Art, Post-1989*, exh. cat., Hanart T Z Gallery, Hong Kong (Hong Kong, 1993), pp. i–vii

Cheater, A. P., 'Death Ritual as Political Trickster in the People's Republic of China', *Australian Journal of Chinese Affairs*, 26 (July 1991), pp. 67–97

China's New Art, Post-1989, exh. cat., Hanart T Z Gallery, Hong Kong (Hong Kong, 1993)

Chow, Rey, *Ethics after Idealism* (Bloomington, IN, 1998)

Chow, Ts'e-tung [Zhou Cezong], *The May Fourth Movement: Intellectual Revolution in Modern China* (Cambridge, MA, 1964).

Chung, Sze-yuen, 'What Has Gone Wrong during the Transition?', in *Hong Kong's Transition: A Decade after the Deal*, ed. Wang Gungwu and Wong Siu-lun (Hong Kong, 1995), pp. 1–18

Cipolla, Carlo, *Clocks and Culture, 1300–1700* (New York, 1967)

Constantine, Eleni, 'Mao's Mausoleum Echoes JFK Center', *Progressive Architecture*, 60 (May 1979), pp. 30–32

Conway, Martin A., *Autobiographical Memory: An Introduction* (Milton Keynes, 1990)

De Certeau, M., *The Practice of Everyday Life* (Berkeley, CA, 1984)

Deng, Xiaoping, *Selected Works of Deng Xiaoping*, III: *1982–1992* (Beijing, 1994)

Domes, Jürgen, *The Government and Politics of the PRC: A Time of Transition* (Boulder, CO, 1985)

Dong, Madeleine Yue, 'Defining Beijing: Urban Reconstruction and National Identity, 1928–1936', in *Remaking the Chinese City: Modernity and National Identity, 1900–1950*, ed. Joseph W. Esherick (Honolulu, 2000), pp. 121–38

——, *Republican Beijing: The City and its Histories* (Berkeley, CA, 2003)

Dray-Novey, Alison, 'Spatial Order and Police in Imperial Beijing', *Journal of Asian Studies*, LII/4 (1993), pp. 885–922

Ekman, Paul, and Wallace V. Friesen, 'The Repertoire of Nonverbal Behavior: Categories, Origins, Usage, and Coding', *Semiotica*, I (1969), pp. 49–98

Engels, Friedrich, *Dialectics of Nature*; trans. Clements Dutt, in *Karl Marx, Frederick Engels: Collected Works* (New York, 1975–), XXV, pp. 540–41

Esherick, Joseph W., and Jeffrey N. Wasserstrom, 'Acting Out

Democracy: Political Theater in Modern China', in *Popular Protest and Political Culture in Modern China: Learning from Tiananmen*, ed. Jeffrey N. Wasserstrom and Elizabeth J. Perry (Boulder, CO, 1991), pp. 28–66

Esherick, Joseph W., 'Ten Theses on the Chinese Revolution', in *Twentieth-Century China: New Approaches*, ed. Jeffrey N. Wasserstrom (London and New York, 2003), pp. 37–65

——, ed., *Remaking the Chinese City: Modernity and National Identity, 1900–1950* (Honolulu, 2000)

Faison, Seth, 'Prolific Chinese Painter Is Anonymous No More', *New York Times* (20 September 1999)

Fleming, Peter, *The Siege at Beijing* (Hong Kong, Oxford and New York, 1986)

Foster, Hal, *The Return of the Real* (Cambridge, MA, 1996)

Foucault, Michel, 'Of Other Spaces', *Diacritics* (Spring 1986)

——, *The Order of Things: An Archaeology of the Human Sciences* (London, 1970)

Friedrich, Paul, 'Polytropy', in *Beyond Metaphor: The Theory of Tropes in Anthropology*, ed. James W. Fernandez (Stanford, CA, 1991), pp. 17–55

Fung, Yu-lan, *A Short History of Chinese Philosophy* (New York, 1948), pp. 129–42

Gombrich, Ernst H., *Art and Illusion: A Study in the Psychology of Pictorial Representation* (New York, 1961)

Goodman, David S. F., *Beijing Street Voices: The Poetry and Politics of China's Democracy Movement* (London, 1981)

Goodman, Jonathan, 'Zhang Hongtu at the Bronx Museum of the Arts', *Asia-Pacific Sculpture News* (Winter 1996), p. 58

Halbwachs, Maurice, *On Collective Memory* (Chicago, 1992)

Harrison, Henrietta, *The Making of the Republican Citizen: Political Ceremonies and Symbols in China, 1911–1929* (New York, 2000)

Harvey, David, *The Condition of Postmodernity* (Cambridge, MA, and Oxford, 1990)

Hay, Jonathan, 'Zhang Hongtu/Hongtu Zhang: An Interview', in *Boundaries in China*, ed. John Hay (London, 1994), pp. 280–98

Henkin, David M., *City Reading: Written Words and Public Spaces in Antebellum New York* (New York, 1998)

Hershkovitz, Linda, 'Tiananmen Square and the Politics of Place', *Political Geography*, XII/5 (September 1993), pp. 395–420

Hevia, James L., *English Lessons: The Pedagogy of Imperialism in Nineteenth-Century China* (Durham, NC, 2003)

Ho, Oscar, 'In Search of an Identity', *Art AsiaPacific*, 1/1 (1993), pp. 12–14

Hou, Renzhi, 'The Transformation of the Old City of Beijing', in *World Patterns of Modern Urban Change*, ed. Michael P. Conzen (Chicago, 1986), Department of Geography Research Paper no. 217–18, pp. 217–39

Hsu, Immenuel C. Y., *The Rise of Modern China* (New York, 1983)

The I Ching; or, Book of Changes, trans. Richard Wilhelm and rendered into English by Cary F. Baynes *et al.* (Princeton, NJ, 1959)

Israel, John, *The Chinese Student Movement, 1927–1937* (Stanford, CA, 1959)

Jakobson, Roman, 'Two Aspects of Language and Two Types of Aphasic Disturbances', in R. Jakobson and Morris Hale, *Fundamentals of Language* (The Hague, 1956), pp. 109–14

Johnson, M. K., 'The Origin of Memories', in *Advances in Cognitive-Behavioural Research and Therapy*, ed. P. C.

Kendall (New York, 1985), pp. 1–27

Jones, Lindsay, *The Hermeneutics of Sacred Architecture: Experience, Interpretation, Comparison*, I: *Monumental Occasions* (Cambridge, MA, 2000)

Kimmelman, Michael, 'Photographs That Cry Out For Meaning', *New York Times* (6 December 2003), A17, 19

Köppel-Yang, Martina, 'Discourse and Artistic Practice in Contemporary Chinese Art after the Cultural Revolution', *Art in China: Collections and Concepts: International Symposium, Bonn, 21–23 November 2003*

Kwon, Miwon, *One Place after Another: Site-Specific Art and Locational Identity* (Cambridge, MA, 2002), pp. 29–30

Laing, Ellen, *The Winking Owl* (Berkeley, Los Angeles and London, 1988)

Landes, David S., *Revolution in Time: Clocks and the Making of the Modern World* (Cambridge, MA, 1983)

Larson, Steen F., 'What Is It Like to Remember? – On Phenomenal Qualities of Memory', in *Autobiographical Memory: Theoretical and Applied Perspectives*, ed. Charles P. Thompson *et al.* (Mahwah, NJ, 1998), pp. 163–87

Lau, Siu-kai and Kuan Hsin-chi, *The Ethos of the Hong Kong Chinese* (Hong Kong, 1988)

Lau, Siu-kai *et al.*, eds, *Indicators of Social Development: Hong Kong 1988* (Hong Kong, 1991)

Ledderose, Lother, 'Die Gedenkhalle für Mao Zedong', in Jan Assmann and Tonio Hölscher, *Kultur und Gedächtnis* (Frankfurt, 1988), pp. 311–39

Lefebvre, Henri, *The Production of Space*, trans. D. Nicholson-Smith (Oxford, 1991)

Lefort, Claude, *The Political Forms of Modern Society: Bureaucracy, Democracy, Totalitarianism* (Cambridge, MA, 1986)

Legge, James, trans., *The Chinese Classics*, 5 vols (Oxford, 1871)

Leys, Simon, *Chinese Shadows* (New York, 1977)

Li, Xianting, 'Major Trends in the Development of Contemporary Chinese Art', in *China's New Art, Post-1989*, exh. cat., Hanart T Z Gallery, Hong Kong (Hong Kong, 1993), pp. x–xxii

——, 'The Imprisoned Heart: Consuming Mao', in Geremie R. Barmé, *Shades of Mao: The Posthumous Cult of the Great Leader* (Armonk, NY, 1996), pp. 215–20

Macartney, George, *An Embassy to China; Being the Journal Kept by Lord Macartney during his Embassy to the Emperor Ch'ien-lung, 1793–1794*, ed. J. L. Cramer Byng (Hamden, CT, 1963)

Mao, Zedong [Mao Tse-Tung], *Selected Works of Mao Tse-Tung*, 4 vols (Beijing, 1965–7)

Meisner, Maurice, *Mao's China and After: A History of the People's Republic* (New York, 1986)

Meyer, James, 'The Functional Site', *Documents*, 7 (Fall 1996), pp. 20–29

Meyer, Jeffery F., *The Dragons of Tiananmen: Beijing as a Sacred City* (Columbia, SC, 1991).

Miners, Norman J., *The Government and Politics of Hong Kong* (Hong Kong, 5/1994)

Mitchell, W. J. T., ed., *Art and the Public Sphere* (Chicago, 1990)

Munn, Nancy D., 'The Cultural Anthropology of Time: A Critical Essay', *Annual Reviews in Anthropology*, XXI (1992), pp. 93-123

Naquin, Susan, *Peking: Temples and City Life, 1400–1900* (Berkeley, CA, 2000)

Needham, Joseph, *Science and Civilization in China*, vol. III

(London and New York, 1959)

Nora, Pierre, 'Between Memory and History', *Representations*, 29 (Spring 1989)

——, ed., *Realms of Memory: The Construction of the French Past*, trans. Arthur Goldhammer, 3 vols (New York, 1996–8)

North, Jochen, Wolfger Pöhlmann, and Kai Reschke, eds, *China Avant-Garde: Counter-Currents in Art and Culture* (Berlin and Hong Kong, 1993)

Nowotny, Helga, *Time: The Modern and Postmodern Experience*, trans. Neville Plaice (Cambridge, 1994)

Ollman, Leah, 'Paintings, Text Speak of the "Trauma" in China's Body Politics', *Los Angeles Times* (15 September 1989)

Pagani, Catherine, *'Eastern Magnificence & European Ingenuity': Clocks of Late Imperial China* (Ann Arbor, MI, 2001)

Pennebaker, James W., Dario Paez Pennebaker and Bernard Rimé, eds, *Collective Memory of Political Events: Social Psychological Perspectives* (Mahwah, NJ, 1997)

Rigby, Richard, *The May 30th Movement* (Canberra, 1980)

Robinson, John A., and Leslie R. Taylor, 'Autobiographical Memory and Self-Narratives: A Tale of Two Stories', in *Autobiographical Memory: Theoretical and Applied Perspectives*, ed. Charles P. Thompson *et al.* (Mahwah, NJ, 1998), pp. 125–44

Ross, Bruce M., 'Relation of Implicit Theories to the Construction of Personal Histories', *Psychological Review*, XCVI (1989), pp. 371–416

——, *Remembering the Personal Past: Descriptions of Autobiographical Memory* (New York and Oxford, 1991), pp. 159–60

Ross, Kristin, *The Emergence of Social Space: Rimbaud and the Paris Commune* (Minneapolis, MN, 1988)

Rubin, David C., ed., *Remembering Our Past: Studies in Autobiographical Memory* (Cambridge, 1996)

Ryan, Mary, 'The American Parade: Representations of the Nineteenth-Century Social Order', in *The New Cultural History*, ed. Lynn Hunt (Berkeley, CA, 1989), pp. 131–53

Samuels, M. S., and C. M. Samuels, 'Beijing and the Power of Place in Modern China', in *The Power of Place: Bringing Together Geographical and Sociological Imaginations*, ed. John A. Agnew and James S. Duncan (Boston, MA, 1989), pp. 202–27

Sargent, Clyde B., trans., *Wang Mang* (Shanghai, 1947)

Schechner, Richard, 'The Street Is the Stage', in *The Future of Ritual: Writings on Culture and Performance* (London and New York, 1993), pp. 45–93

Schinz, Alfred, *Cities in China*, Urbanization of the Earth, 7, ed. Wolf Tietze (Berlin and Stuttgart, 1989)

Shi, Mingzheng, 'From Imperial Gardens to Public Parks: The Transformation of Urban Space in Early Twentieth-Century Beijing', *Modern China*, XXIV/3 (July 1988), pp. 219–54

Simmie, Scott, and Bob Nixon, *Tiananmen Square* (Vancouver, 1989)

Sirén, Osvald, *The Walls and Gates of Peking* (New York, 1924)

Spence, Jonathan D., *The Gate of Heavenly Peace: The Chinese and their Revolution, 1895–1989* (Harmondsworth, 1982)

——, *The Search for Modern China* (New York, 1990)

Spencer, Thomas M., *The St Louis Veiled Prophet Celebration: Power on Parade, 1877–1995* (Columbia, MO, 2000)

Spivak, Gayatri, 'Can the Subaltern Speak?', in *Marxism and the Interpretation of Cultures*, ed. Car Nelson and Lawrence Grossberg (Urbana, IL, 1988)

Strand, David, *Rickshaw Beijing: City People and Politics in the 1920s* (Berkeley, CA, 1989)

Stuart, Jan, and Evelyn S. Rawski, *Worshiping the Ancestors: Chinese Commemorative Portraits* (Washington, DC, 2001)

Sun, Jingxun, 'A Specter Prowls our Land', in *Seeds of Fire: Chinese Voices of Conscience*, ed. Geremie R. Barmé and John Minford, 2nd edn (New York, 1988), pp. 121–9

Tang, Xiaobing, *Chinese Modern: The Heroic and the Quotidian* (Durham, NC, 2000)

Thurston, Anne F., *Enemies of the People* (New York, 1987)

Tsao, Hsing-yuan, 'The Birth of the Goddess of Democracy', in *Popular Protest and Political Culture in Modern China*, ed. Jeffrey N. Wasserstrom and Elizabeth J. Perry, 2nd edn, (Boulder, CO, 1994), pp. 140–47

Tulving, Endel, 'Episodic and Semantic Memory', in *Organization of Memory*, ed. Endel Tulving and Wayne Donaldson (New York, 1972)

——, 'How Many Memory Systems Are There?', *American Psychologist*, XL (1985), pp. 385–98.

Turbulent Years: China Before and After the May 4th Movement, The Sidney D. Gamble Foundation for China Studies (Beijing, 1999)

van Dorn, Harold A, *Twenty Years of the Chinese Republic: Two Decades of Progress* (London, 1933)

Virilio, Paul, *The Lost Dimension*, trans. Daniel Moshenberg (New York, 1991)

Vöckler, Kai, and Dirk Luckow, eds, *Peking Shanghai Shenzhen: Cities of the 21st Century* (Frankfurt, 2000)

Wagner, Rodulf, 'Reading the Chairman Mao Memorial Hall in Peking: The Tribulations of the Implied Pilgrim', in *Pilgrims and Sacred Sites in China*, ed. Susan Naquin and Chun-fang Yu (Berkeley, CA, 1992)

Wakeman Jr, Frederic, 'Revolutionary Rites: The Remains of Chiang Kai-Shek and Mao Tse-tung', *Representations*, 10 (Spring 1985), pp. 146–93

——, 'Mao's Remains', in *Death Ritual in Late Imperial and Modern China*, ed. James Watson and Evelyn Rawski (Berkeley, CA, 1988)

Waley, Arthur, trans., *The Book of Songs* (New York, 1960)

Wang, David Der-wei, 'Imaginary Nostalgia: Shen Congwen, Song Zelai, Mo Yan, and Li Yongping', in *From May Fourth to June Fourth: Fiction and Film in Twentieth-Century China*, ed. Ellen Widmer and David Der-wei Wang (Cambridge, MA, 1993).

Wasserstrom, Jeffrey N., *Student Protests in Twentieth-Century China: The View from Shanghai* (Stanford, CA, 1991)

——, ed., *Twentieth-Century China: New Approaches* (London and New York, 2003)

Wasserstrom, Jeffrey N. and Elizabeth J. Perry, eds, *Popular Protest and Political Culture in Modern China: Learning from Tiananmen* (Boulder, CO, 1991)

——, *Popular Protest and Political Culture in Modern China* 2nd edn (Boulder, CO, 1994) [this edition differs significantly from the original volume]

Watson, Burton, trans., *Basic Writings of Mo Tzu, Hsün Tzu, and Han Fei Tzu* (New York, 1963)

Webster's New Collegiate Dictionary (Springfield, MA, 1958)

Wellek, Rene, *History of Modern Criticism* (New Haven, CT, 1955)

Wheatley, Paul, *The Pivot of the Four Quarters* (Chicago, 1971)

Wilhelm, Hellmut, *Chinas Geschichte; zehn einführende*

Vorträge (Beijing, 1942)

Willetts, William, *Chinese Art* (New York, 1958)

Wright, Patrick, 'A Blue Plaque for the Labour Movement? Some Political Meanings of the "National Past"', in *Formations of Nation and People* (London, 1984)

Wu, Hung, 'From Temple to Tomb: Ancient Chinese Art and Religion in Transition', *Early China*, XIII (1988), pp. 78–116

——, *The Wu Liang Shrine: The Ideology of Early Chinese Pictorial Art* (Stanford, CA, 1989)

——, 'Tiananmen Square: A Political History of Monuments', *Representations*, 35 (Summer 1991), pp. 84–117

——, *Monumentality in Ancient Chinese Art and Architecture* (Stanford, CA, 1995)

——, 'Emperor's Masquerade: "Costume Portraits" of Yongzheng and Qianlong', *Orientations*, XXVI/7 (1995), pp. 25–41

——, 'The Hong Kong Clock – Public Time-Telling and Political Time/Space', *Public Culture*, IX/3 (Spring 1997), pp. 329–54

——, '"Hong Kong . 1997" – T-shirt Designs by Zhang Hongtu', *Public Culture*, IX/3 (Spring 1997), pp. 417–21

——, *Transience: Chinese Experimental Art at the End of the Twentieth Century*, exh. cat., Smart Museum of Art, Chicago (Chicago, 1999)

——, *Exhibiting Experimental Art in China* (Chicago, 2000)

——, 'Monumentality of Time: Giant Clocks, the Drum Tower, the Clock Tower', in *Monuments and Memory: Made and Unmade*, ed. Robert S. Nelson and Margaret Olin (Chicago, 2003), pp. 107–32

Wu, Hung, and Ackbar Abbas, eds, 'Hong Kong 1997: The Place and the Formula', *Public Culture*, IX/3 (Spring 1997) [special issue]

Wu, Liuangyong, *Rehabilitating the Old City of Beijing* (Vancouver, 1999)

Wu, Ye, 'What does the statue of the Goddess of Democracy, which appeared in Tiananmen Square, indicate?', *Renmin ribao* [People's daily], overseas edition (1 June 1989); a translation of the article is in *National Affairs*, FBIS-CHI-89-104, p. 28

Yahuda, Michael, *Hong Kong: China's Challenge* (London and New York, 1996)

Yee, Lydia, 'An Interview with Zhang Hongtu', in *Zhang Hongtu: Material Mao*, exh. cat., Bronx Museum of Arts, New York (New York, 1995), pp. 1–7

Yin-wang, Reginald, and Annette Kwok, 'Le mausolée du président Mao', *L'Architecture d'Aujourd'hui*, 210 (February 1979), pp. 51–3

Zhang, Hongtu, *Works by Zhang Hongtu*, exh. cat., HKUST Center for the Arts, Hong Kong (Hong Kong, 1998)

Zhang, Yuehong, 'Tiananmen Square: The Rhetorical Power of a Woman and a Man', *Anthropology and Humanism*, XX/1 (June 1995), pp. 29–46

Zhu, Jianfei, *Chinese Spatial Strategies: Imperial Beijing, 1420–1911* (London and New York, 2004)

CHINESE SOURCES

Ai Weiwei, Zeng Xiaojun and Xu Bing, eds, *Heipi shu* [An puntitled book with a black cover] (Beijing, 1994) [private publication]

Ban Gu, *Han shu* [History of Former Han] (Beijing, 1962)

Beijing guihua jianshe [Beijing's urban planning and construction]

Cai Yong, 'Mingtang yueling lun' [A discussion of Bright Hall and the monthly regulations], in *Cai zhonglang wenji* [Collected writings of Cai Yong] (Shanghai, 1931)

Cao Juren, *Jiuri jinghua* [Beijing in old days] (Hong Kong, 1971)

Cao Ying and Yu Chao, *Fengyu Tiananmen* [Storm over Tiananmen] (Beijing, 1993)

Chen Gan, *Chen Gan wenji: Jinghua daisi lu* [Collected writings of Chen Gan: Finished and unfinished thoughts on Beijing] (Beijing, 1996)

Chen Lingchu, 'Zhongjin baohu zhongzhouxian' [Spending big money to protect the central axis], *Wenwu tiandi*, 8 (2000), pp. 5–7

Chen Shouxiang *et al.*, *Jiumeng chongjing: Fan Li, Bei Ning cang Qing dai mingxinpian xuanji* [Startled again by old dreams: A selection of Qing postcards collected by Fan Li and Bei Ning], I (Nan'ning, 1998)

Chen Xianyi and Chen Ruiyao, eds, *Wangshi – 1949 xiezhen* [Past events: Photographs from 1949] (Nanchang, 1999)

Chen Yifu, *Huiyi changshi* [General knowledge for meetings] (Shanghai, 1926)

Deng Xiaoping, *Deng Xiaoping xuanji, 1982–1992* [Selected works of Deng Xiaoping, 1982–1992] (Beijing, 1994)

Department of History at Peking University, History of Beijing Writing Group, *A History of Beijing*, expanded edition (Beijing, 1999)

Design Team of the Great Hall of the People, 'Renmin Dahuitang' [The Great Hall of the People], *Jianzhu xuebao*, 9 (1959), pp. 23–30

Dong Guangqi, 'Tiananmen Guangchang de gaijian yu kuojian' [The reconstruction and expansion of Tiananmen Square], *Beijing wenshi cailiao* [Data concerning the history of Beijing], no. 49 (1994)

——, *Beijing guihua zhanlue sikao* [A strategic consideration of Beijing's urban planning] (Beijing, 1998)

Dong Xiwen, 'Huihua de secai wenti' [Problems concerning the colours of oil painting], *Meishu* [Fine Arts], 1 (1957), reprinted in *Meishu*, 7 (2003), no. 427, pp. 59–63

——, 'Cong Zhongguo huihua de biaoxian fangfa tandao youhua Zhongguo feng' [The representational method in traditional Chinese painting and the Chinese style of oil painting], *Meishu*, 1 (1957), reprinted in *Meishu*, 7 (2003), no. 427, pp. 55–8

Editorial Committee, *Jianguo yilai de Beijing chengshi jianshe* [Beijing's urban construction after the establishment of the People's Republic of China] (Beijing, 1985)

——, *Liang Sicheng xiansheng baisui danchen jinian wenji* [Papers in commemoration of Mr Liang Sicheng's 100 birthday] (Beijing, 2001)

——, *Zhongguo jindaijianzhu zonglan: Beijing pian* [A comprehensive survey of modern architecture in China: Beijing] (Beijing, 1993)

Fang Ke, *Dangdai Beijing jiucheng gengxin* [Contemporary redevelopment in the Inner City of Beijing] (Beijing, 2000)

Gao Minglu, *Zhongguo dangdai meishu shi, 1985–86* [Contemporary art of China, 1985–86] (Shanghai, 1991)

——, 'Bawu meishu yundong, 1985–86 "qianwei" yishi' [The 'avant-garde' consciousness in the '85 art movement], *Xiongshi meishu*, 297 (November 1995), pp. 16–21

Gao Yilan, 'Mao Zhuxi jiniantang sheji guocheng zongjie' [A summary of the design process of the Chairman Mao Memorial Hall], *Jianzhu shi* [History of architecture], 1 (2003), pp. 1–25

——, 'Mao zhuxi jiniantang fang'an sheji de youguan lishi ziliao de shuoming' [Some explanations regarding historical evidence for the design of Chairman Mao Memorial Hall], *Jianzhu shi*, 2 (2003), pp. 203–4

Gao Yilan and Wang Mengmeng, 'Liang Sicheng de gucheng baohu ji chengshi guihua sixiang yanjiu' [A study of Liang Sicheng's ideas regarding the preservation of ancient cities and urban planning], *Shijie jianzhu* [World architecture], nos 1–5 (1991)

Gongbulixi [E. H. Gombrich], *Yishu yu cuojue* [Art and illusion], trans. Fan Jinzhong (Hangzhou, 1987)

Gong Deshun *et al.*, *Zhongguo xiandai jianzhu shigang* [An outline of the history of modern Chinese architecture] (Tianjin, 1989)

Hou Renzhi and Deng Hui, *Beijing cheng de qiyuan he bianqian* [The origin and transformation of the city of Beijing] (Beijing, 1997)

Hu Zhichuan and Ma Yunzeng, eds, *Zhongguo sheying shi, 1840–1937* [A history of Chinese photography, 1840–1937] (Beijing, 1987)

Jia Yingting, ed., *Tiananmen* (Beijing, 1998)

Jiang Yikui, *Chang'an kehua* [Conversations of a visitor to the capital] (Beijing, 1980)

Jianzhu xuebao [Architectural journal]

Jin Lin, 'Beijing Zhonggulou wenwu zaji' [Miscellaneous records of things related to the Drum Tower and the Bell Tower], in Editorial Committee, *Wenshi ziliao xuanbian* [Selected archival materials on modern Chinese history], no. 36

Jin Shoushen, ed., *Beijing de chuanshuo* [Legends of Beijing] (Beijing, 1957)

Jing Yun and Ren Yi, 'Tansuo Zhongguo tese youhua de xianxingzhe – jinian Dong Xiwen xiansheng shishi 30 zhounian' [An early explorer of Chinese-style oil painting – in commemoration of the 30th anniversary of Mr Dong Xiwen's death], *Meishu*, 7 (2003), no. 427

Li Shejian, ed., *Renmin Dahuitang* [The Great Hall of the People] (n.p, n.d.)

Li Xiaobin and Ding Dong, 'Yong jingtou jilu lishi' [Recording history with a camera], *Laozhaopian* [Old photos], no. 31, pp. 105–22

Liang Sicheng, 'Renmin yingxiong jinianbei sheji de jingguo' [The design process of the Monument to the People's Heroes], in Editorial Committee, *Liang Sicheng xueshu sixiang yanjiu lunwenji* [Research papers on Liang Sicheng's scholarship and ideas] (Beijing, 1996)

——, *Liang Sicheng wenji* [Collected writings of Liang Sicheng], 5 vols (Beijing, 1982–2001)

——, *Zhongguo jianzhu yishu tuji* [Visual materials of the art of Chinese architecture], 2 vols (Tianjin, 1999)

Liang Tieshan, 'Minzhu nüshen yongzai woxinzhong' [The *Goddess of Democracy* will always live in my heart], *Zhongguo zhichun* [China's Spring] (1989), p. 8.

Liu Shanling, *Xiyang faming zai Zhongguo* [Western inventions in China] (Hong Kong, 2001)

Lu Bingjie, *Tiananmen* (Shanghai, 1999)

Lü Peng and Yi Dan, *Zhongguo xiandai yishu shi, 1979–1989* [A history of contemporary Chinese art, 1979–1989] (Changsha, 1992)

Lu Yuan, 'Qingnian fuwubu yu qingnian' [A Youth Service Centre and young people), *Renmin huabao* [People's pictorial], 1/1 (July 1950)

Luo Zhewen, 'Beijing Zhonglou, Gulou' [Beijing's Drum Tower and Bell Tower], in *Jinghua shengdi Shishahai* [Shishahai: a famous spot in Beijing], The Research Association of Shishahai in Beijing (Beijing, 1993), pp. 139–49

Luo Zhufeng *et al*, *Zhongwen dacidian* [A comprehensive dictionary of Chinese], 12 vols (Beijing, 1993)

Mass Photography Editorial Board, *Tiananmen qian* [In front of Tiananmen] (Beijing, 1999)

Museum of Chinese Revolutionary History, *Zhonghua Renmin Gongheguo kaiguo dadian* [The founding ceremony of the People's Republic of China] (Beijing, 1999)

Nie Chongzheng, 'Tan "Kangxi nanxun tu" juan' [On the scrolls of Kangxi's southern expedition], *Gongting yishu de guanghui: Qingdai gongting huihua luncong* [The splendour of court art: Studies on Qing dynasty court painting] (Taipei, 1996), pp. 75–91

Palace Museum, *Gugong Bowuyuan cang Qingdai gongting huihua* [Qing dynasty court painting in the collection of the Palace Museum] (Beijing, 1992).

Peng Zhen, 'Guanyu Beijing de chengshi guihua wenti' [Problems concerning Beijing's urban planning], *Pengzhen wenji* [Collected writings of Peng Zhen] (Beijing, 1991)

Qi Honghao and Yuan Shusen, *Lao Beijing de chuxing* [Transportation in old Beijing] (Beijing, 1999)

Qiu Xiaoyu, 'Xiangzheng' [Symbols], *Beijing wanbao* [Beijing evening newspaper] (19 September 1999), A2

Renmin de daonian [People's mourning] (Beijing, 1979)

Renmin huabao [People's pictorial]

Ruan Yuan, comp., *Shisanjing zhushu* [Annotated Thirteen Classics], 2 vols (Beijing, 1980)

Shi Mingzheng, *Zouxiang jindaihua de Beijing cheng: Chengshi jianshe yu shehui biange* [The city of Bejing moves towards modernization: City construction and social change] (Beijing, 1995)

Shu Jun, *Tiananmen guangchang lishi dang'an* [Historical archives related to Tiananmen] (Beijing, 1998)

Tao Zongzhen, 'Tiananmen Guangchang guihua jianshe de huigu yu qianzhan' [Looking forward and backward at Tiananmen Square's planning and construction], *Nanfang jianzhu* (1999), p. 4

Tiananmen shang kan Zhongguo [Looking at China from Tiananmen's balcony], 2 vols (Chengdu, 1999)

Tong Huaizhou, *Tiananmen geming shiwenxuan* [Selected writings from the April Fifth Movement], 2 vols (Beijing, 1977–8)

Wang Canzhi, *Beijing shidi fengwu shulu* [A bibliographical index of writings on Beijing's history, scenery and customs] (Beijing, 1985)

Wang Jun, *Cheng ji* [The story of a city] (Beijing, 2003)

Wang Tongzhen, *Lao Beijing cheng* [Old city of Beijing] (Beijing, n. d.)

Wen Fu, *Tiananmen jianzheng lu* [History as witnessed by Tiananmen], 3 vols (Beijing, 1998)

Wu Dianyao, *Kaiguo dadian – cong Xibaipo dao Tiananmen* [The founding of the nation: from Xibaipo to Tiananmen], 2 vols (Changsha, 1999)

Wu Liangyong, 'Renmin Yingxiong Jinianbei de chuangzuo chengjiu' [The architectural achievement of the Monument to the People's Heroes], *Jianzhu xuebao* (1978), p. 2

——, 'Tiananmen Guangchang de guihua he sheji' [The plan and design of Tiananmen Square], in *Jianzhushi lunwenji* [Essays on architectural history] (Beijing, 1979)

Wu Muren *et. al.*, *1989 Zhongguo Minyun jishi* [A factual record of the 1989 Chinese democratic movement], 2 vols (New York, 1989) [private publication]

Wu Shizhou, *Zijincheng de liming* [The dawn of the Forbidden City] (Beijing, 1998)

Wu Youru [Wu Jiayou], *Wu Youru huabao* [Pictorial treasures by Wu Youru], 4 vols (Beijing, 1998)

Xia Shangwu and Li Nan, *Bainian Tiananmen* [A hundred years of Tiananmen] (Beijing, 1999)

Xue Fengxuan, *Beijing: You chuantong guodu dao shehuizhuyi shoudu* [Beijing: From an imperial capital to a socialist capital] (Hong Kong, 1996)

Yang Congqing, *Beijing xingshi dalue* [A general description of Beijing] [1737]; reprinted in *Jingjin fentu congshu* [A collection of writings on the local customs in the Beijing and Tianjin region] (Taipei, 1969)

Yang Rong, 'Chongzao youzhuo guoqu jiyi di xinjianzhu' [Creating new architecture with memories of the past], *Jianzhushi* [Architect], 78 (October 1997), pp. 39–45

Yu Jiang, *Kaiguo dadian liuxiaoshi* [The six hours of the grand founding ceremony of the People's Republic of China] (Shenyang, 1999)

Yu Minzhong, *Rixia jiuwen kao* [Examining 'Old stories heard everyday'], (Beijing, 1983)

Yu Xiang, 'Gaoshi xiongdi fangtan lu' [An interview with the Gao brothers], 10–13 July 2003; unpublished manuscript

Yuan Ling, 'Tiananmen qingdian paishe ji' [A record of taking pictures of celebration ceremonies on Tiananmen], in *Tiananmen qian* [In front of Tiananmen] (Beijing, 1999), pp. 19–20

Zhang Bo, 'Renmin Dahuitang xiujian shimo' [An account of the construction of the Great Hall of the People], in *Wo de jianzhu chuangzuo daolu* [The path of my architectural career] (Beijing, 1994)

Zhang Hongtu, *Works by Zhang Hongtu*, exh. cat., HKUST Center for the Arts, Hong Kong (Hong Kong, 1998)

Zhang Jiangcai, *Yanjing fanggu lu* [Searching for ancient sites in Beijing], Jing Jin fengtu congshu [Books on local customs of Beijing and Tianjin] (Taipei, 1969)

Zhang Jinggan, *Beijing guihua jianshe wushinian* [Fifty years of Beijing's urban planning and construction] (Beijing, 2001); slightly revised version of the author's *Beijing guihua jianshe zongheng tan* [A general survey of Beijing's urban planning and construction] (Beijing, 1997)

Zhang Jinggan, Chen Hongzhang and Xu Yixie, eds, *Jianguo yilai de Beijing chengshi jianshe ziliao* [Documents regarding Beijing's urban construction after the establishment of the People's Republic of China], 1: *Chengshi guihua* [Urban planning] (Beijing, 1995)

Zhang Zhaohui, 'Chongxin dingyi jinri xianfeng de jingshen – Gaoshi xiongdi fangtan' [Redefining the spirit of the avant-garde in today's China – an interview with the Gao brothers], www.cl2000.com/modernart/interview/wen010.shtml

Zhao Dongri, 'Tiananmen Guangchang' [Tiananmen Square], *Jianzhu xuebao* (1959), nos 9–10, pp. 18–22

——, 'Cong Renmin Dahuitang de sheji fang'an pingxuan lai tan xin jianzhu fengge de chengzhang' [The development of new architectural style as seen in the selection of the architectural design of the Great Hall of the People], *Jianzhu xuebao* (1960), no. 2

——, 'Lun gudu fengmao yu xiandaihua fazhan' [On the shape and characteristics of ancient Beijing and its modernization], *Jianzhu xuebao* (1990), no. 12

——, 'Beijing Tiananmen Guangchang dongxi diqu guihua yu jianshe' [The design and construction of the eastern and western sections of Beijing's Tiananmen Square], *Jianzhu xuebao* (1993), no. 1

——, 'Huiyi Renmin Dahuitang sheji guocheng' [Remembering the design process of the Great Hall of the People], *Beijing wenshi ciliao*, 49 (1994)

Zhao Luo and Shi Shuqing, *Tiananmen* (Beijing, 1957)

Zheng Lianjie, 'Zheng Lianjie xingdong yishu: *Jiazu suiyue*' [Zheng Jianjie's performance art project: *Family History*]; unpublished manuscript

Zhou Dingfang, 'Renmin Yingxiong Jinianbei' [The Monument to the People's Heroes], *Jinri Beijing* [Beijing Today] (n.p., n.d.)

Zhou Yang, 'Wei chuangzao gengduo de youxiu de wenxue yishu zuopin er fendou' [Struggle to create even more excellent works of literature and art], *Wenyibao* [Journal of literature and art], ser. no. 96 (1953), no. 19, pp. 7–16

Zhu Xizu, *Beijing cheng – yingguo zhi zui* [Beijing: the epitome of capital planning], (Beijing, 1999)

Zhu Yingli and Zeng Yixuan, *Beijing zhonggulou* [Beijing's Drum Tower and Bell Tower] (Beijing, 2003)

Photo Acknowledgements

Much of the illustrative material for this book comes from the collection of the author. The author and publishers wish to express their thanks to the remaining sources of illustrative material and/or permission to reproduce it, as listed below; some locations of artworks are also given.

British Museum, London: 123; Fogg Art Museum, Harvard University (photo © 2005 President and Fellows of Harvard College): 46; National Art Gallery, Beijing: 128; Palace Museum, Beijing: 124; Suzhou Museum, China: 122.

Index